THE DECADENCE OF
THE MODERN WORLD

THE DECADENCE OF
THE MODERN WORLD

I. Robert Sinai

SCHENKMAN PUBLISHING COMPANY, INC.
Cambridge, Massachusetts

Schenkman Publishing Company, Inc.
3 Mt. Auburn Place
Cambridge, Massachusetts 02138

Library of Congress Cataloging in Publication Data

Sinai, I. Robert.
    The decadence of the modern world.

    Includes bibliographical references.
    1. Civilization, Modern—1950-
2. Degeneration.   I. Title.
CB425.S52   909.82   76-30409
ISBN 0-87073-568-3
ISBN 0-87073-569-1 pbk.

Printed in the United States of America

In loving memory of my late parents, Ella and Boris Skikne

CONTENTS

PREFACE

This book continues my exploration of the problems of modernity. In my previous studies on modernization, I analyzed the problems of the underdeveloped societies and discussed the Russian, Chinese and Japanese paths toward the modernization of their societies and the failure of the Mexican and Turkish modernization efforts. In this present study, the discussion concerns the crisis of modernity in all its dimensions. For it ought to be more than obvious by now that our contemporary, industrial, mass civilization confronts not only a whole series of superficial disturbances and dislocations but a structural crisis in its very existence.

This book was written without the support of any foundation or institution. It is the result of long study and personal reflection. Since its completion, I have discussed some of its leading ideas with students and colleagues. Many have received them sympathetically; some, however, have called them too "negative" and "pessimistic."

These are appelations that I completely reject. The present study was not written as an exercise in destructiveness; it does not spring from some cantankerous impulse. It is neither "optimistic" nor "pessimistic"—words alien to my lexicon.

While I certainly reject all the major assumptions about man and society held by Liberalism, Marxism and what passes for modern

Conservatism, I do so not in a spirit of negativeness but out of tough-minded realism. My basic approach, in fact, returns to a profounder view of the human condition and of historical development.

Basing myself upon a tragic view of man and history, I see man as a noble and heroic being who is capable of rising to the most exalted heights of creativity, but who is inevitably, in the end, overwhelmed by the terrors of life becuase of the destructive and ineradicable flaws which are embedded in his very existence. What is true of man, I contend, is also true of all societies or civilizations, without exception. It is our ludicrous modern conceit to believe that, with our science, our industry and our democracy, we have been able to escape from this awesome fate.

Unlike those modern political theorists, philosophers and sociologists who have either forgotten the great wisdom of the past or who have never known it, I do not view the human condition as trivial or base, but as a great drama of always renewed endeavor and failure. That is how, in the broad sweep of human history, it stands revealed in all its splendor and misery.

It only remains for me to thank my friend, Seymour Martin Lipset, for his special efforts in trying to find a publisher for my book and Alfred Schenkman for his great courage and boldness in accepting it for publication.

To my wife, Anne, I must as always express my deep sense of indebtedness for her unfailing support and encouragement. My son, Joshua, helped to prepare the index.

PART I

INTRODUCTION

The last third of the twentieth century ushers the world's developed countries, the United States in particular, into a period of growing dislocation and crisis. Symptoms of disturbance, irregularity and deterioration are to be seen in every sphere of existence. The bonds of partnership of community are everywhere being strained, in some societies to the very breaking point. Cities, the basic building blocks of civilization, are being invaded by the wilderness of the slum and by the terror of insecurity. A menacing population explosion, anarchy in the streets, growing crime rates, riots at universities are accompanied if not caused by the decline of elites. Men unfit for the job of governing are increasingly assuming power. Discord and polarization, excessive contentiousness and malignant neglect induce men to stop acting in concert. Vaulting conceits and utopian pretensions commingle with brash incompetence. The blind impulses of science and technology produce unanticipated ecological dangers. Life is threatened, man disoriented, culture menaced and civilization undermined.

The dramatic events of the last few years—student disaffection, the emergence of a counter-culture which rejects the principal values of modern society, labor unrest, racial outbreaks, insane foreign adventures, spreading political corruption, a corrosive inflation, and brutalizing wars—all point to a crisis in the public order. Everywhere we see outward signs of reduced respect for public symbols and eroded trust in

3

public objects. The appearance of hostilities long suppressed and of aggrieved persons and groups long overlooked reveals the fact that the political system may be no longer capable of governing the national community. Thus a time of crisis is essentially a time when leadership and ideologies have failed. It is a time when customary standards decline and normal proceedings cease to be efficacious. The everyday and the customary produce incalculable consequences and all the normal options hold within them the gravest risks.

This is also a time when the study of man and society is in disarray. The goals and methods, the objectivity and motives of social scientists have been called into question. At a moment when the fullest understanding is demanded, the perspectives presented to us by the principal ideologies of the age are totally inadequate. The beguiling assumptions of the western social sciences, particularly of the structural-functionalist approach of sociology and political science, that human activity functions to assure the continuity and stability of the structures of society have been exposed by the events of the recent past. The notion that democracy, science and technology have proved the triumph of human rationality can now be seen as a pure example of that utopian ideological thinking which its proponents had supposedly abjured. The counter-ideology of Marxism in all its forms has not only become corrupted by the mechanical formulas of an economic determinism belied by its own history but has had its simplistic class analyses and hopes negated by contemporary developments. And the rationalist and scientific modes of thought as applied to man and his social universe have fallen victim to the irrational forces which are so rampant in our world; to the glaring discrepancies that are to be found between knowledge and action, between theory and practice.

Our modern world is not only in disarray and crisis but is also in deterioration and decay. The eighteenth and nineteenth centuries' conception of infinite progress and human perfectability can now be seen as unmitigated illusions. Civilization is no harmonious self-enclosed whole, but is filled with the most violent inner tensions. Civilization is dialectical as well as tragic. All that it creates it continuously threatens to tear apart again with its own hands. Considered in the light of its products, every civilization contains something unsatisfactory and incomplete, something which is profoundly questionable. It is a battleground between good and evil, reason and unreason, life and death, peace and war, and in this struggle between these contending forces the powers hostile to man are most often victorious. Every experienced concrete reality has always contained within itself a negativeness that will ultimately destroy it. It is also by its very nature time-bound. No human creation is infinite or immortal. Every civilization has a history: a beginning, an interlude of growth and expansion and a time of contraction and decline. The spiral of history can go down as well as up. All things in history move toward both fulfillment and dissolution, toward the fuller embodiment of their essential character and toward death. We are now living amidst the ruins of a civilization, with both its mental and material structures crumbling.

Our civilization is not merely dying from its failures but even more from its successes. Progress is not only "a terrible thing" as William James put it, but is also a highly ambiguous notion. It is completely shallow to believe that there is any connection between the purely directional conception of "further" with the assurance of greater and better. It is extremely naive to expect every new discovery or refinement of existing means to contain the promise of higher values and of greater happiness. The uncontrolled and uncoordinated forces released by modern science, technology and politics, each functioning separately with an excess of power, only serve to injure the health and balance of the organism as a whole. The new capitalism of abundance and of innovative technological change has, in the course of the unfoldment of its demonic impulses, destroyed its traditional legitimacy which was based on a system of rewards rooted in a Protestant stratification of work that had once sustained it. The super-abundance of goods produced by our modern industrial society, the hedonism and voluptuousness which it stimulates, promotes apocalyptic moods and irrational methods of behavior, at all levels of society, which are its natural counterparts. The very progress of civilization leads to the release of increasingly destructive forces. Abundance does not bring contentment; where there is more and more of everything they are worth less and less; and prosperity without precedent produces only increased ugliness, boredom and spiritual trouble without precedent. Parts of our society seem mad, and the whole is infected by the madness of its parts. Human existence in this world becomes mere stuff, matter, material which does not have the principle of movement in itself. Growing efficacy involves growing degeneration of the life instincts—the decline of man. Every progressive impulse must sooner or later become fatigued. It is not in the least paradoxical to say that a culture may founder on real and tangible progress.

The American empire, fashioned after the last world war, is now undergoing the agonies of dissolution. This has been the shortest-lived empire in history. Like Spain in its war with Holland, the war in Vietnam plunged America into stupor and impotence. The causes for this lie not only in America's lack of political capacities and experience, in its juvenile illusions and inordinate ambitions but spring from the fact that the tempo of modern time has been drastically speeded up. What took centuries in the slow moving traditional societies of the past is now accomplished in a single volatile generation. Years must now replace centuries as the yardstick of measurement. The world-wide commitments it so rashly undertook, the dream of immoderate greatness it so enthusiastically pursued—one of the basic causes of political decline according to Gibbon—have strained its resources to the very limit. The combination of imperial ambitions with a blind preoccupation with private concerns has eroded the society's foundations. This concatenation of policies and attitudes has robbed the United States of that spirit which transforms a people into a citizenry and converts a physical space into a national polity. Without a sense of public obligation, mesmerized by the pursuit of private pleasures which is its highest aspiration, riven by the conflicts between its warring ethnic clans whose mutual detestation is the chief characteristic of the American way of life, the share of energy devoted to common ends has gradually diminished and the capacity to govern this heterogeneous society has alarmingly weakened.

The United States, then, is now on the way to joining other nations which were once supreme and are now without influence or stature in the world. The burden of being a great power has drained it of strength and confidence. Not the positions it has lost have maimed it but those it has maintained or expanded. Its positions of strength and influence are now thorns in its side. Increasing self-doubt at home will henceforth be accompanied by a purposeless manipulation of power abroad. This does not mean that the United States will fall apart or that it may not even experience brief periods of effervescence and prosperity, but its former position of ascendancy is gone forever and its former claim of proud affluence will be mocked in the future by the realities of discomfort and frustration. Widespread despair, hopelessness and loneliness characterize more and more the life of man in our materially abundant societies and in our regimes of increasingly empty freedoms. Authority has neither the imagination nor the moral capacity to act for the whole community. A strange compound of light and darkness now encompasses everything. The dissolution of the coherence of a civilization is paralleled by the dissolution of the coherence of lives and minds. Like decadent Rome, ours is an amusement society whose standards are set by an establishment of publicity intellectuals. Affluence and poverty, elegance and squalor, culture and savagery live together not only in the same streets but in the same minds. We are not only beset by slums in our cities but by slum minds in our leading institutions and by hollow men at the summits of power.

Although it is difficult to predict the particular forms that our modern movement of decadence will assume it is nevertheless possible to detect all the signs that point to the exhaustion of a style of civilization. Our modern, urban, technological, democratic, bourgeois, mass civilization has exhausted all its potentialities for growth and creativity and has now entered a period (which might continue for generations) of senescence, marked by a lessening of drive and quality, atrophy and stereotyping. It has definitely run its course but there is as yet no successor in view. The barbarian forces are not outside the gate but within it. When a period of supreme strength has ended or when an important or coherent style has passed its zenith there ensues a time of trouble and confusion. Groups and ideologies begin to pull in different directions. Some plunge on ahead, some pull back uphill, others try to stand still or edge sideways. The spread of Oriental cults, the growth in the popularity of astrology, the revival of a nihilistic Anarcho-Marxism, the emergence of a repressive authoritarian backlash, the pathetic fumblings of the Liberal center, the science-fiction predictions of the futurologists, all attest to the extra-ordinary confusion of the interregnum in which we live. The decay of civilization, its descent into a new dark age can be tangibly experienced in the increasing powerlessness of the modern state, the coexistence of perpetual war and perpetual peace, the spread of urban and rural guer-rilla forces, the growing rootlessness and meaninglessness of human existence, the arrogance and impotence of the new meritocracy that has come to the fore, and the presence, side by side, of senility and infantilism.

The decline of the United States is of course nothing new in history. The rise and fall of empires and civilizations, of particular governments and ruling classes within a given civilization, of specific cultural tra-ditions, or of eminent families in a community, or of various types of voluntary associations, or even of more minor historical concretions all illustrate the tragic dialectic of civilization. All societies are ruled by an iron law of decadence. All civilizations or societies decline and fall be-cause they have made mistakes in meeting some new challenge or com-plexity of history. Every civilization makes some fatal mistake in the end and perishes. Sometimes they perish because the pull or push of power has impelled them to extend themselves beyond the limits of human possibilities. Sometimes the ruling class which has been instrumental in organizing a society has become so rigid, unresponsive, greedy and re-pressive that it systematically destroys what it had created. Sometimes the strategies and techniques of yesterday are falsely applied to new situa-tions and problems to which they are not relevant. This mistake reflects that form of intellectual hubris which blindly raises contingent factors in history to the eminence of false absolutes. All these conditions and acts constitute that "nemesis of creativity" which Toynbee has so con-vincingly analyzed and is expressed in that "idolization" of "an ephemeral self" or of an "ephemeral institution" or of an "ephemeral technique" that all civilizations are sooner or later guilty of. Modern technical civilization is declining because it is wrong-headedly worshipping technical advance as a final good and because it is now harnessing its techniques either for the destructive purposes of war or for the preparation for war or because these technological forces are now escaping from human control and appear to us in the form of man's destruction of his environment and technical breakdown.

Civilizations, in short, decline for a whole variety and range of reasons. Civilizations decline as much from the infinity of the will as from the finitude of reason, from demonic irrationality as from mechanical bureaucratic inertia. Some civilizations perish because they rest on their oars, others because they come to suffer from the aberrations of outrageous behavior with its consequent loss of mental and moral balance. Some suffer from the intoxication of victory while others are so intemperate in waging wars of annihilation against their neighbors or in preparing for wars against them, that they deal unintended destruction to themselves. Some civilizations perish from the sins of sensuality while others from the sins of pride. At all times we see man's thoughts translated into acts and these transformed into their opposite; and his dreams when translated into deeds attain that which he least dreamed of. In all cases we are confronted with man, insecure, anxious and restless, swollen with self-love, driven by the will-to-power and by inordinate appetites, corrupted by pride, self-intoxication and self-deception, who sooner or later sins against the laws of proportion and harmony and swept along by blind, headstrong and ungovernable impulses is plunged into decay or self-destruction.

CHAPTER 1

ON THE HUMAN SITUATION

It has been suggested that a time of crisis is essentially a time when ideologies and leaderships have failed. This is as true today as it has been true of the past. Our flounderings and disasters flow as much from inadequate ideologies which have shielded us from the authentic realities of man and the world as they do from incompetent leaderships which are simply incapable of coping with the demands that our social situation presents to them or with the ills that afflict us. Dominated by a shallow positivism, confident in the power of reason as represented by modern science to solve the social problems of our age, possessing a narrow conception of man shaped by the superficialities of behaviorism and rationalism, the philosophies of our time have misunderstood the nature of man, the nature of the social world and the nature of reason itself. Before we can even begin to discuss the failures of ideology and leadership we must present our own conception of man and society.

Man and society can only be understood in terms of dialectical thought and of the dialectical vision. Man and society are basically fields of conflict and contradiction. Freedom and necessity, reason and unreason, good and evil, the individual and society, subject and object, power and prudence, routine and innovation, selfishness and cooperation, passion and calculation, all these dualities are in perpetual tension and conflict and shadowed over by alienation. The dialectical method views the world as in a continual state of flux and the things of the world as in a

9

continual state of transition into other forms of themselves. There are no fixed entities. The structure of reality is a structure of opposition of elements that contradict one another and limit and distort each others' potentialities. Out of this clash of antagonistic tendencies new forms arise that incorporate the antithetical elements albeit in altered form and with their contradictions now temporarily and precariously resolved. Contradictions are not only present in every state of being but are a condition of its very existence and every state of being realizes its potentialities by transcending these limitations and passing on to another phase. But this new phase is also found to generate its own opposition and the resultant world view is one of continual movement, conflict and contradictions.

The dialectic can be applied to the study of changes in the institutional orders of societies and to the course and destiny of civilizations. It can also be applied to the study of the individual life and to man's primary drives. Hegel, Schopenhauer and Freud all made contributions that can enable us to see man in all his multifariousness, in all his heights and depths.

Hegel saw history as the self-realization of the mind and ideas as the ingredients and results of the dialectic. At the same time he understood that the motive force of the process is will and passion. Nothing great in the world has been accomplished without passion. The active element in man's history is man's interests, the impelling drive for power and gain and the impulse toward the fulfillment of his own personal needs. Utilizing the whole energy of will and character, to the neglect of all other actual or possible interests and claims, historical actors devote every fibre of volition and concentrate all their desires and power to the attainment of their self-seeking designs. Although some regarded passion as a thing of sinister aspect, as more or less immoral, Hegel yet argued that without it the World Spirit could not attain its objects. Passion is in the first instance the subjective and therefore the formal side of energy, will and activity. It is the form which natural existence assumes and consists of physical craving, instinct, private interest and also opinion and subjective conception. Hegel viewed the state of nature as predominantly that of injustice and violence, of untamed natural impulses, of inhuman deeds and feelings. Limitation is certainly produced by society and the State but it is a limitation of the mere brute emotions and rude instincts, as also in a more advanced stage of culture, of the premeditated self-will of caprice and passion. The very essence of Spirit, however, is activity, by which it multiplies the material for future endeavors, develops its powers and gratifies its desires in an inexhaustible variety of modes and directions.[1]

Freedom realizes itself in history by external and phenomenal means. Among the aims of men, some may be of a liberal or universal kind such as benevolence or noble patriotism, but such virtues or general views are but insignificant as compared with the World and its doings. It may be possible for us to see the Ideal of Reason actualized in those who adopt such aims and within the sphere of their influence; but they bear only a trifling proportion to the mass of the human race; and the extent of that influence is limited accordingly. Passions, private aims and the satisfaction of selfish desires are on the other hand the most effective springs of action. Their power lies in the fact that they respect none of the limitations which justice and morality would impose upon them and that these natural impulses have a more direct influence upon men than the artificial and tedious disciplines that tend to order and self-restraint, law and morality.

Looking at history we see a display of passions and the consequences of their violence; the Unreason which is not only associated with them but especially with good designs and righteous aims; and the evil, the vice and the ruin that have befallen the most flourishing kingdoms. When we see all this we can only be filled with sorrow at this universal taint of corruption and since this decay is not the work of mere nature but of the Human Will we can only be overtaken by moral embitterment. The combination of miseries that have overwhelmed the noblest of nations and polities and the finest exemplars of private virtue, forms a picture of the most fearful aspect and excites emotions of the profoundest and most hopeless sadness counterbalanced by no consolatory result. Sometimes history witnesses the comprehensive mass of some general interest advancing with slowness and subsequently sacrificed to a complication of trifling circumstances and so dissipated into atoms. Then again, with a vast expenditure of power a trivial result is produced, while from what appears unimportant a tremendous issue proceeds. On every side there is the motliest throng of events drawing us within the circle of its interests and when one combination vanishes another appears in its place. Change, all becoming and passing away, makes kingdoms transitory, decays splendid and highly cultural national entities, imports dissolution into all of them and involves at the same time the rise of new forms of life. History is but a "slaughter bench at which the happiness of peoples, the wisdom of states and the virtue of individuals have been victimized."[2]

More profoundly than any other thinker, Schopenhauer saw Will as the ultimate, irreducible primeval principle of Being, the source of all phenomena, the begetter present and active in every one of them, the impelling force producing the whole visible world and all life—for it was the will to live. Individuals as well as social, political and religious groups are an expression of the blind will to existence and to well-being. The ineradicable reality of all that is alive, of existence altogether is made up of the insatiable desire for well-being and enjoyment, a desire that wells up every time it has been satisfied. The basis of life is an ever-flowing stream of stimuli: unappeasable will. All willing arises from want, therefore from deficiency and therefore from suffering. The satisfaction of a wish ends it; yet for one wish that is satisfied there remain at least ten which are denied. No attained object of desire can give lasting satisfaction, but merely a fleeting gratification. Eternal becoming, endless flux, characterizes the revelation of the will to itself. In fact freedom from all aim, from all limits belongs to the nature of the will, which is an endless striving. Therefore, as long as our consciousness is filled by our will, as long as we are given up to the throng of desires with their constant hopes and fears, we can never have lasting happiness or peace. To pursue, to flee, to fear disaster, to covet pleasure—it is all one: preoccupation with the will's incessant demands fills and animates the consciousness without cease, and thus "the subject of willing is constantly lying on the revolving wheel of Ixion, is always drawing water in the sieve of the Danaids, and is the eternally thirsting Tantalus."[3]

The will then, this "in-itself-ness" of things, existing outside time, space and causality, blind and causeless, greedily and ruthlessly demands life, demands objectivation and this objectivation occurs in such a way that its original unity becomes a multiplicity. The will is avid of life, avid to wreak its desires, to disperse itself into the myriad parts of the phenomenal world existing in time and space; but at the same time it remains in full strength in each single individual and the smallest of those parts. Will at the opposite pole of inactive satisfaction is naturally a fundamental unhappiness; it is perpetual unrest and striving—it is want, craving, avidity, demand, suffering; and a world of will can be nothing but suffering. The will objectivating itself in all existing things imposes on the physical its metaphysical craving for expression and satisfies that craving in the most frightful way. In the process of becoming World the Will forgets its original unity and although in all its divisions it remains essentially one, it becomes divided against itself. Thus it strives against itself, seeking its own well-being at the expense of others and so constantly sets its teeth in its own flesh. At various stages of the objectivation of the will, space, time and matter fall upon each other. Every living thing is moved by an irrational impulse not only to perpetuate itself but even vastly exceeding that to perpetuate the species with many a creature perishing in the very act of procreation. The plant world has to serve as nourishment for the animal, each animal for another as prey and food, thus the will to live gnaws forever at itself in the struggle of all against all. Need and endless striving kindled again and again make up the texture of history and determine man's relationship to Nature.

According to Schopenhauer it was not the intellect that brought forth the will but the converse. It was not intellect, mind or knowledge that were the primary and dominating factors; it was the will and the intellect served it. The development of the intellect rests on that of needs. Hunger, the urge to power and war have been the greatest promoters of knowledge. In the struggle with nature and men, the intellect serves as a weapon by providing rationalizations with which individuals, interests, groups and nations try to accomodate their demands to the moral precepts in force. The intellect is there to do the pleasure of the will, to justify it, to provide it with motivations which are often very shallow and self-deluding, in short to rationalize the instincts. Consciousness is only a small part of the psyche and it is used as its tool. The intellect is a function of the struggle for existence in individuals and in the species; it is inflamed by resistance and disappears with resistance. The will, in other words "is the strong blind man who carries on his shoulders the lame man who can see."[4]

Turning to the human race Schopenhauer views life not as a gift or enjoyment but as a task, as a drudgery to be performed; and in accordance with this we see, in great and small, universal need, ceaseless cares, constant pressure, endless strife, compulsory activity, with extreme exertion of all the powers of body and mind. Many millions united into nations strive for the common good, each individual on account of his own; but many thousands fall as a sacrifice for it. Now senseless delusions, now intriguing politics incite them to wars with each other; the sweat and blood of the great multitude must flow, to carry out the ideas of individuals or of groups, or to expiate their faults. In peace, industry and trade are active, inventions work wonders, seas are navigated, necessities and delicacies are collected from all ends of the world, the waves engulf thousands. But what is the ultimate aim of it all? To sustain the ephemeral and tormented individuals through a short span of time in the most fortunate case with endurable want and comparative freedom from pain, which however is at once attended with ennui; then man is committed once again to the reproduction of this race and its ceaseless strivings.

To fully grasp this evident disproportion between the trouble and the reward it is necessary to understand the "law of motivation" as Schopenhauer defines it. Life is not freely chosen; want and ennui are the whips that keep the top of action and movement spinning. The whole of life and every individual within it bears the stamp of a forced condition; and everyone, in that, inwardly weary, he longs for rest but yet must press forward, is like his planet, which does not fall into the sun because the force driving it forward guards it from that catastrophe. Everything therefore is in continual strain and forced movement. Men are only apparently drawn from in front, really they are pushed from behind; it is not life that tempts them on but necessity that drives them forward. The will to live is thus not a consequence of the knowledge of life and is in no way a conclusive *ex praemissis* and in general is nothing secondary. Rather it is that which is first and unconditioned, the premise of all premises. For the will to live does not appear in consequence of the world but the world in consequence of the will to live.

Schopenhauer's approach to the realm of morals too is worth considering. He finds three basic springs or pervasive motives of conduct: *egoism* or self-love, which is the impulse to one's own weal or good; *malice* or the impulse to others' woe or hurt; and *compassion* or the impulse to others' weal and well-being. Now each of these is a distinct and basic motive and not one which—like the love of gain, for instance —is derivative from something more fundamental. Egoism, the most pervasive driving force within man, is the impulse to one's own good as an end in itself, rather than as a means to something ulterior to it. It is the most reliable and ubiquitous of the motives that shape human conduct. Malice, which exists only in human nature and is quite foreign to all other creatures, is disinterested nastiness; that is, the impulse to hurt others without any hope of actual benefit to oneself. This impulse to cruelty cannot be regarded as an artificial product of social life and culture; it is in the strictest sense an original sin which an advanced civilization might endeavor to combat but never by itself implants. And pure compassion—which like all noble things is above all rare—is loving kindness and sympathy without ulterior motive; that is, the impulse to the weal or joy of other creatures without any hope of gain to oneself thereby. Egoism augmented by malice forms the basis for civilized existence while compassion is the basis of genuinely moral conduct.[5]

This human world in general, however, is the "kingdom of chance and error," which "rules without mercy in great things and small," and along with which "folly and wickedness also wield the scourge."[6] Hence it arises that everything better only struggles through with difficulty; what is noble and wise seldom attains to expression, becomes effective and claims attention, but the absurd and the perverse in the sphere of thought, the dull and tasteless in the sphere of art, the wicked and the deceitful in the sphere of action really assert a supremacy, only disturbed by short interruptions. On the other hand everything that is excellent is always a mere exception, one case in millions, and therefore if it presents itself in a lasting work, this, when it has outlived the enmity of its contemporaries, exists in isolation, is preserved like a meteoric stone, sprung from an order of things different from that which prevails here. Everyone who has awakened from the first dream of youth, who has considered his own experience and that of others, who has studied himself in life, in the history of the past and of his own time, and finally in the works of the great poets, will if his judgment is not paralyzed by some indelibly imprinted prejudice actually arrive at these conclusions.

Of all the great dialectical thinkers Freud was the most concerned with opposition and dissonance in human affairs. Freud consistently sought out processes of conflict and contradiction; where others looked for structure in personality Freud sought perpetual restlessness of self-realization and becoming, the efforts of the psyche to realize its potentialities by overcoming its built-in limitations. Where others dealt with duality as a mechanical process that produced entities that stood in a structural relationship to one another Freud's dualisms are inherent in life and are immanent in the fundamental contradictions of a mind that is rooted in an organism, the body, but which has at the same time become alienated from it. The mind's differentiations are precarious formations that clash with each other and then pass into something else. They struggle for unity yet another dialectic, that between the self and others, forces them apart. The development of a more or less autonomous ego passes through a destructive process wherein the tendency to drift back into the depths of one's organism is counteracted by the tendency to lose oneself by immersement in others.

Conflict, in fact, is the key notion throughout all Freud's thinking. In all of Freud's most far-reaching theories one basic human experience is pitted against another; love is set against hate; civilization opposes and represses the individual; the instincts of self-preservation conflict with the explosive sexual drives; solidarity and repulsion, the binding and dissolving forces are in destructive antagonism; the pleasure principle, although often supposed to be served by the managing reality principle, basically clashes with it; positive and negative features of a personality always live side by side in uneasy juxtaposition; child, mother and father are in conflict in the Oedipal situation; the two basic instincts of life and death, Eros and Thanatos, are in a state of deadly war with each other; the thrust of life clashes with the tendency toward inertness and dissolution. However, Freud does not only postulate the idea of conflict, he also complements it with the notion of ambivalence. Ambivalence is the psychological expression of the struggle in the form of contradictory attachments to the same objects. It is not a choice between one or the other. The opposing elements are, on the contrary, always present because they define each other. The opposites are in an active relationship of mutual contradiction. They negate each other through moving into each other; they are the opposite sides of the same coin, and their clash and fusion produce ever new forms and combinations. The human personality is thus characterized by incompleteness and inconsistency and the human situation is always precarious and ambiguous.

Freud, furthermore, conceived of the self not as an abstract entity, uniting experience and cognition, but as the subject of a struggle between two objective forces—unregenerate instincts and overpowering culture. In Freud's definition, instinct is desiring, intention, drive, containing within it an implication not only of imperious will but of active resistance. Human relations are therefore seen in terms of clashing intentions which culture at best can attempt to regulate but can never finally suppress. Since the individual can neither destroy his instincts nor wholly reject the demands of culture, his character expresses the way in which he organizes and appeases the conflicts between the two. Nature and culture, individual and society, are forever fixed into a painful trap of contradictions.

One of Freud's great discoveries was the "unconscious". According to Freud's theory of man, parts of the ego, as well as the super-ego, are submerged in the subterranean world of the unconscious, where they mingle with the unruly forces of the id. He designated as unconscious any mental process the existence of which we are compelled to assume— because of its effects upon us—but of which we are not directly aware. It is primitive chaos. The unconscious is fertile nature, it is everything that is left of the responses of the amoeba and of the impulses of the ape, of the blind spasms of our intra-uterine existence, the identity in which every distinction disappears and all things reunite. It is everything which would make us mere creatures and is indestructible. Freud thought of the unconscious as somewhat like a hidden God—indifferent, impersonal, unconcerned about the life of its creation. This notion of the unconscious is similar to Schopenhauer's concept of the Unconscious Will as the source of all that happens—of character, of the whole of life, of all that we repudiate and like our nightmares do not (consciously) will. It can only strive blindly to gratify its instincts in complete disregard of the superior strength of outside forces. Instincts fill the unconscious with energy but it has no organization, no unified will. The laws of logic —above all the laws of contradiction—do not apply to it; it knows no values, no good and evil, no morality. Yet it is something upon which civilization must draw for the sake of its life, something which contains "the true psychic reality."[7]

Freud's idea of conflict is central to the various schemes he elaborated for describing the psychic apparatus. His earliest conception of mental conflict is the opposition between a conscious and an unconscious mind. This dichotomy he never discarded. But he later outlined a new anatomy of the psyche which is even of greater breadth and complexity. In this conception mind is seen as consisting of three parts in conflict and balance: an id, an ego and a super-ego.

The great profundity of this conception is that it goes beyond the relatively simple division of the mind into rational and irrational elements and the conflict between them. It does not merely proclaim the supremacy of the irrational, nor does it give everything to passion and disease but creates a mediator between reason and unreason. This mediator can take the side of either and moreover has some of the energy which in a two-part division is handed over entirely to the irrational. This tripartite division of the mind is very similar to Plato's final formulation in the *Republic* in which the mediator which holds the balance of power, the volitional agency that acts on behalf of either reason or the appetites is spirit or the "personal emotions." Freud proceeded in a similar fashion, depicting the psyche in three "parts" or "agencies" each of which has its special function. The id is the agency of bodily appetite, the ego performs the mediating function and the super-ego is the guardian of moral prohibitions. Freud saw the mind as no peacefully self-contained entity but rather compared it "to a modern state in which a mob eager for enjoyment and destruction had to be held down forcibly by a prudent superior class."[8]

What is significant about Freud's division is that he separates reason from moral judgment. Freud locates reason in the ego in the middle position separating appetite (id) from conscience (super-ego). Reason in this image is like a man on horseback who has to hold in check the superior strength of the horse (the id) but is now disengaged from any moral commitments. The ego was separated from the observing, critical punishing agency of the super-ego. Conscience like id is also irrational and the social personality which it represents is alien from the genuine self which is the ego. The mind is thus in a state of civil war, goaded on by the chaotic id, hemmed in by the rigid super-ego, rebuffed by reality[9] and with the ego needing all the flexibility and craft it can muster in order to resolve all the discordant impulses, unappeased conflicts and unsolved doubts to which it is subject.

The Oedipal situation provides another good example of Freud's antagonistic model of the psyche. It was not by accident that Freud found its genesis in a mythic parricide, for he saw the Oedipal phase, whether in history or ontogeny, as the means by which man breaks away from the undifferentiated state of nature into a higher stage of development. The attachment of the child to the mother which is initially expressed in total unity and later in complete possessiveness comes into conflict with social reality in the form of paternal authority. The father effectively blocks the desires of the son, appearing to him as a threatening and forbidding figure. The interposition of the father between the mother and the son, full of the intensity of love and hate and guilt, of yearning and jealousy, of fury and fear, is not only emasculating in itself but specifically emasculating through the threat that sexual expression of any kind will draw the punishment of castration. The son's sensual current is thus inhibited by deference to the father's authority and in this way becomes a precondition of culture. By identifying with the father, by repressing his incestuous urges and by incorporating the rules and values of society he transcends his former state of dependency, breaks out of his enclosure within the family and develops a semi-autonomous ego. The resolution of these contradictions teaches the child how to play the reality game by suppressing the truth; imparts a gnawing sense of guilt; and the erotic dualism which is contained in the Oedipus Complex accounts for the characteristic tension between order and rebelliousness present in every culture.

Culture, according to Freud, is a product of three independent variables: 1) necessity (Ananke) imposed by nature; 2) the instinctual polarity in man: Eros and Thanatos, love and death ultimately fused in the "seething cauldron" of the id; and 3) the institutions and ideals developed by society. The tragic dialectic of civilization is produced by the interaction of these three variables. Culture, like the individual, is a precarious unstable compound because the process of reconciling and synthesizing these components is never complete, final or successful. If as it has been suggested, civilization is a series of institutions evoked for the sake of security and order, then this security system is constantly menaced by the explosive and destructive tendencies in the three partners. Nature imposes harsh necessities which are never completely mastered. The instincts will always break out in overt or subversive revolt against the repressions imposed by society. Man is not the oversocialized creature that sociologists and political scientists have described him to be and the controls built-in during the socialization process are only partially effective. The temporary compromise with reality that the ego achieves is accomplished through evasion, subterfuge, deception of both self and others and rationalization and projection as well as by conformity. And the ideological superstructure may crush man because it becomes unbearable and unworkable.

More specifically, Freud envisaged the dialectical struggle as "a battle between the Titans," Eros and Thanatos, or as a result of the insoluble quest to press these two "heavenly forces" into service on behalf of a satisfactory and lasting adaptation to a neutral or hostile environment. This quest, however, is never completed. Eros, defined as the great unifying force that preserves all life, which aims at binding together single individuals through families, tribes, races, nations, into the one great unity of mankind is forever opposed by the natural instinct of aggressiveness in man, the hostility of each against all and of all against each and thereby opposes this program of civilization. This instinct of aggression is the derivative and main representation of the death instinct (Thanatos) that exists alongside of Eros and shares with it the rule over the earth. The meaning of the evolution of culture is now no longer a riddle to Freud. It is the struggle between Eros and death, between the instincts of life and the instincts of destruction as it works itself out in the human species. This struggle is what all life essentially consists of and so the evolution of civilization may be simply described as the struggle of the human species for existence.[10]

The truth is, as Freud describes it, that men are not gentle, friendly creatures wishing for love, who simply defend themselves when they are attacked but that a powerful measure of desire for aggression has to be reckoned as part of their instinctual endowment. The result is that their neighbor is to them not only a possible helper or sexual object but also a temptation to them to gratify their aggressiveness on him, to use him sexually without his consent, to humiliate him, to cause him pain, to torture and kill him. The existence of this tendency to aggression which we can detect in ourselves and rightly presume to be present in others is the factor that disturbs our relations with our neighbors and makes it necessary for culture to institute its high demands. Civilized society, Freud argues, is perpetually menaced with disintegration through this primary hostility of men toward one another. Their interests in their common work do not hold them together; the passions of instinct are stronger than the reasoned interests. Culture has to call up every possible reinforcement in order to erect barriers against the aggressive instincts of men and hold their expressions in check by reaction-formations in men's minds. Hence its system of methods by which mankind is to be driven to identifications and aim-inhibited love-relationships; hence the restrictions on sexual life; and hence too "its ideal command to love one's neighbors as oneself, which is really justified by the fact that nothing is so completely at variance with original human nature as this."[11]

The price that man pays for battling with these two forces, for trying to transform and to domesticate both the instincts (by displacement and sublimation) to achieve both a greater mastery over nature and a more secure gratification of the instincts in interpersonal relations is the feeling of discontent that torments him and the feeling of unhappiness that oppresses him. All men are ill and neurotic in varying degrees and all are subject to pain and malfunction. Man is ill at ease within civilization and the price of progress is paid through the heightening of the sense of guilt.

This sense of guilt is the most important problem in the evolution of culture. Its origins stem from the perennial revolt against the mythical father and in the establishment of the first taboos in the primordial society of the brother horde. This mythical prototype of the origins of civilization led Freud to assert that that which began in relation to the Father is then extended to all the socio-political relations within the community. All cultural systems thus reflect the conflict of ambivalence, the eternal struggle between Eros and the destructive instinct originally felt toward the mythical father image. Culture has however found a precarious resolution of this ambivalence. It checks the destructive impulse by turning it inward where it is then discharged as a sense of guilt or moral anxiety against the individual himself. As the libidinal ties were extended from the group of the family to the group of humanity a cycle of repression, guilt and anxiety was repeated through countless generations. Each successive resolution of the original conflict or each successive response to the growing need to internalize aggressive and destructive tendencies in the form of a vigilant and punishing conscience reinforces the feelings of guilt. In this way the super-ego is progressively strengthened in the course of history and the destructive elements, in man and society, gain at the expense of Eros.

Freud's philosophic view of man and his body of speculative insights is essentially gloomy, stoic and tragic. In this universe proud man is locked in mortal struggle with the inner force of evil. Man, unlike the animals, does not allow himself simply to be absorbed by the naturally given order. He tears himself loose from it, places himself in opposition to it, makes demands of it, tries to dominate it and is himself dominated by it. Freudian man is an imperfectible animal and, as biological punishment for having risen in the scale beyond the micro-organism, a dying animal. Man's animal nature can only be controlled and channeled in the least harmful direction possible not changed or abolished, and the cure lies not in destroying animality but in facing it and living with it. Libido, the blind energy of sexual impulses is equivalent to the ancient Greek "wild Ate", the daughter of Zeus and strife, the wrath or madness that possesses the hero and impels him to senseless violence, destruction or self-destruction. Sublimation is the small moment, the reintroduction of possibility, the birth of arts and all human culture out of muck and strife. Through the great tragic rhythm of pride and fall we may achieve that limited self-knowledge which is the only partial victory we can achieve in this bitter struggle which is life.

Civilization, thus, is both a blessing and a curse, and it has been both throughout history. Human history is the record of this ambiguity: a repetitive cycle of progress and suffering, order and anarchy, achievement and failure, stability and upheaval, security and insecurity, liberation and enslavement, freedom and unhappiness. Being both a blessing and a curse it is ineluctably embroiled in a fatal and destructive dialectic: the perpetual restrictions on Eros ultimately weaken the life instincts and thus strengthen and release the very forces against which they were called up—those of destruction. Men have in fact now brought their powers of subduing the forces of nature to such a pitch that, as Freud predicted in 1929, by using them they could now very easily destroy one another to the last man.[12]

Man is then a strange mixture of the most conflicting and contradictory impulses. Emerging as all other natural phenomena out of primeval chaos and pervasive flux he becomes human through blind will and the lust for power. Driven by the unappeasible will to live with all its antagonistic attributes he is a creature of wants, cravings, appetites, passions and strivings. Avarice, ambition, hatred and love are let loose upon the world. Unstable in his psyche he is forever restless and filled with the most extravagant visions and dreams and his imagination extends his appetites beyond the requirements of mere subsistence. Human passions are always characterized by unlimited and demonic potencies of which animal life is innocent. Agitated by an ever-flowing stream of stimuli, stirred by a throng of desires, subject to all the vitalities and fatalities of human existence, he is condemned by his own nature and by circumstances to eternal limitation, unhappiness, dissatisfaction and frustration. Life, as the Buddhists well know, is a progress from want to want, not from happiness to happiness. Men who desire life are as men athirst and drinking of the sea. Life is an overwhelming and insatiable thirst; it is not satisfaction or attainment. The tragedies and comedies in which man is involved develop inevitably from the impetus of his cravings for things to which he becomes attached but these things are all transitory and perishable. Attachment and the satisfaction of desire only cause disappointment, disillusionment and other forms of suffering. All these cravings are rooted in man's life which is a pathological blend of unfulfilled cravings, vexing longings, fears, regrets and pains. Impelled by the heedless energies and intentions of the id toward pleasure, resisted and repressed by super-ego and ego and yet permeating both its antagonists and partners with some of its destructive force man is a sick and unbalanced creature. Nature plays with him like a cat with a mouse. Man is compacted of innumerable invisible tensions, arrested impulses and unstable equilibriums and his enacted wills are often comically cheated by his innermost desires. He perpetually swings over into opposites, from dark into light and light into dark, making him a slave of action and reaction. The law of nature at bottom as Santayana has written, "would seem to be that the object should disappear when attained, devoured or forgotten, and that the avid chase should recur forever, only to keep the ball rolling."[13]

Man is also egocentric and dominated and driven by self-love. Man regards himself as more important than any one else and views all common problems from the standpoint of his own interest. Man's ambitions, desires, fears and hopes both set him at variance with his neighbor and implicate him in his neighbor's destiny. No moral or rational arguments have ever sufficed to restrain one person from taking advantage of another. Man pursues power, wealth, eminence, honor, respect and prestige with all the vital resources which his will may control. And these most valuable resources will always remain in short supply and set men in perpetual competition and contention for their precarious possession. This vital freedom of the self, its capacity for both good and evil, has defied any rational or natural system into which men have contrived to coordinate it. This powerful force of self-love, this tendency of the self to make itself the center of whatever community it inhabits, to make itself its own end has sown confusion, contention and corruption into every human community.

Self-love is both creative and destructive. Through self-love man seeks to live truly, to attain freedom to act and realize himself, to surpass himself, to strive for excellence and to outdo and overpower his neighbor. Self-love, however, also breeds the sins of pride and self-righteousness. Assuming his own self-sufficiency and self-mastery, believing himself to be the master of his own existence and destiny, man arrogates to himself powers and pretensions which can only end in that excessive pride which produces nemesis. To give free reign to his vital liberty is only to invite grief and failure. Self-righteousness on the other hand presumes that his highly conditional virtue is the final righteousness and that his very relative moral standards are absolute. For Niebuhr, self-righteousness is our greatest guilt and has been responsible for "our most serious cruelties, injustices and defamations against our fellowmen."[14] The whole history of racial, national, religious and other social struggles is in his view a commentary on the objective wickedness and social miseries which result from self-righteousness. Trying to live truly and yet forced to live only through power, man is perennially at variance and at war with himself.

According to Sartrean existentialism relations between human beings can only be those of conflict—of one freedom pitted against another. Every person's situation includes the existence of other persons and naturally the inescapable consequence of the juxtaposition of free human beings is conflict. According to this argument it is impossible for anyone to treat another person as other than an object with the result that the very existence of other people produces guilt. Love is as much an illusion as is sincerity: what the lover is really interested in is to subjugate his partner. The power struggle takes place even in the accidental look of one man at another. It is thus absolutely impossible for people—regardless of their intentions—to treat others according to the Kantian dictum. People cannot be treated as ends; they are for others always objects and this means that they are inevitably treated as means. Far from greeting each other with mutual respect human beings cast baleful glances at one another which strips them of their comfortable disguises and makes them feel naked and ashamed. Shame in fact is the token and measure of human inadequacy; it suggests the impossibility of living at peace with one's fellow men and in the enjoyment of a good conscience. Living in a world of scarcity, society becomes a web of different organizational efforts characterized by the desire of some people to produce effects on others and by the desire of others to escape the intended effects.[15]

Man is furthermore according to Heidegger, the Violent One. Using and gathering power, he departs from his customary and familiar limits, disturbs the tranquility of the existent and becomes an historical being, a creator, and a man of action. The violent one is he who breaks out and breaks, who breaks open the earth with his plows and drives the effortless earth into his restless endeavor; he who captures and subjugates. Man in his view is always thrown back on the paths he himself has laid out; he becomes mired in his paths, caught in the beaten track; and thus caught he compasses the circle of his world, entangles himself in appearance and so excludes himself from being. The violent one, the creative man, is he who sets forth into the un-said, who breaks into the un-thought, compels the un-happened to happen and makes the unseen appear. He always stands in venture and in venturing seeks to master being, to use power against the overpowering but at the same time he must risk the assault of the nonessent, he must risk dispersion, instability, disorder, mischief and disaster. The higher the summit of historical being—there, the deeper will be the abyss, the more abrupt the fall into the unhistorical which merely thrashes around in issueless and placeless confusion.[16]

Man however is not only will, aggressiveness, power, the unconscious, egoism and violence. He is also a creature capable of reason, cooperation, creativity and freedom. Living in groups, interacting with one another, man creates a social order based on superiority and subordination, competition, division of labor, inner solidarity coupled with exclusiveness toward the outside. Utilizing his creative capacities for social organization man builds political systems to manage and control, for limited periods of time, the turbulent and competitive forces by which he is beset, to moderate the pretensions of every group to unlimited power and by the weight of competing power in balancing power to restrain those groups and classes which might become inordinate and oppressive without ever fully succeeding in this goal. Faced with the divisions and conflicts of social life man devises precarious systems of justice that attempt to provide that "reasonable" degree of concord and cooperation for all its competing components without which government is merely a "band of robbers". Though like the animals man too submits to the rules of society he is additionally capable of bringing about and changing the forms of social life. Developing his rational capacities he has elaborated those forces of science and industry which enable him to impose himself upon his natural environment and to exploit for human betterment those natural resources which confront him as both promise and eternal threat. As symbolmaker man overcomes his own natural inertia and endows himself with a new ability, the ability to constantly reshape his human universe. Through language, religion, art and science, he in fact creates his own world—a symbolic world that makes it possible for him to understand and interpret, to articulate and organize, to synthesize and universalize his bewildering human experience. Inventing utopias he makes room for new and novel possibilities as opposed to a mere passive acquiescence in the present actual state of affairs. Art, in all its forms, above and beyond all its excellences, provides vision, spreads wide the world beyond the deliverances of material sense and intensifies and illuminates the seemingly infinite potentialities of life. Philosophy searches for wisdom without ever finding it and without ever relinquishing its quest. Through the study of history, at its best, man is capable of revivifying the past and of imparting an eloquence and meaning to all the fragments and remnants of his political, religious and cultural life. Impelled by the will to power and egoism he is yet capable of sacrificing himself for an ideal, of giving his life to save his child, friend or even a stranger. Love between man and woman lifts both, if only for brief moments, above the cruelties and absurdities of human existence. And on supreme occasions man would rather die as a rebel than live as a slave.

Man's capacity for reason, cooperation, creativity and freedom, however, never exists in a pure or untarnished form. The precarious oases reason are always surrounded by a perpetual fringe of irrationality and crime. Self interest and class interest taint and distort all human knowledge. Knowledge has advanced human freedom but it has also caused the wound in the existence of man, his crime and guilt. The majority of our opinions are wish-fulfillments like dreams in the Freudian lexicon.

The mind of the most rational among us may be compared, as Bertrand Russel has said, to a stormy ocean of passionate convictions based upon desire, upon which float perilously a few tiny boats carrying a cargo of scientifically tested beliefs.[17]   Power, greed, ambition and selfishness corrupt the most noble of endeavors. Most of our learned cultural behavior operates exactly like instinct and the rigidity of cultural habits, the powerful conservative force of habit, are just as invulnerable to change as any instinct. All civilizations do not only finally decay but decay is intermingled with the forces of creativity in the very act of their unfoldment. Every culture may be defined as a crisis constantly held back, until overcome by the fatal crises and evils which it ineluctably generates. The habits of virtue which man acquires have always stamped upon them a terrifying mask of vice. Ignorance, stupidity, pious frauds and mass hysteria are always an integral part of the human scene. Man can never help sinning when he acts in relation to his fellow men and though he may be able to minimize that sinfulness of social action he can never escape it. The lust for power always blinds the political actor to the limits of power and always impels him to overstep the boundaries of both prudence and morality. Despite all his achievements man is both imperfect and imperfectible, an eternal battleground between conflicting urges and impulses, host alike to seeds of nobility and ignominy.

CHAPTER 2

THE WILL TO POWER

The blind and irrational will which drives man finds its political expression as the will to power. Political science is thus concerned with the whole problem of power in society, its nature, basis, scope and results. In politics the basic struggle is not to gain or retain wealth or ownership of production but to gain or retain power, to exercise power over others or to resist that exercise. Through power the objective world of willing beings can be changed; control and influence over the minds and actions of other men achieved, domination and authority established and one's will executed. We can therefore say with Thucydides that "of the gods we believe, and of men we know, that by a necessary law of their nature they rule wherever they can," and with Hobbes that "I put for a general inclination of all mankind a perpetual and restless desire for power after power that ceaseth only in death."

The struggle for power is universal in time and space and the most dramatic fact of human existence. The drive to dominate is on a par with the drive to live and to propagate. It is one of the elemental bio-psychological drives by which society is created. The drive to power is the dynamic self-affirmation of life. It is the drive of everything living to realize itself with increasing intensity and extensity. Most men would like to be like God, and rule a host of worshipful followers. The history of states, regardless of social, economic and political conditions is the story of their power struggles. The desire for domination is a factor of all human

0492176

associations and individuals, families and states exist in a ceaseless condition of tension and struggle. In the family there is a constant struggle between parent and parent, parents and children and between the children themselves. Social clubs, voluntary organizations, religious groups, faculties and business organizations are arenas of continuous struggle for power between individuals and groups that either want to preserve whatever power they already possess or seek to attain greater power. Classes, status groups and individual business and labor organizations are involved in a perpetual struggle for the acquisition, retention or expansion of power and the influence it brings. The political life of every nation, democratic or dictatorial is marked by the struggles between different elites, interest groups and factions for power and position. In all the outward manifestations of political activities—elections, voting in legislative assemblies, administrative and executive decisions—men try to maintain or to impose their power over other men. Power struggles envelop all human activities, enter into all modes of human intercourse and corrupt and derange all human relations. The dialectic of power generates domination and resistance, excess and extravagance, sin and crime and makes every society a precarious arrangement rather than a balanced, self-regulating entity.

What, then, are the impulses, rooted in human nature, that propel men toward power? For Thucydides the life of nations is distinguished first by the struggle for existence and then the struggle for supremacy, with fear and greed as their motive forces and the honor of the state as the great monument to their individual greed and fear. Man in his vision is chained by necessity, driven by these compulsive forces, momentarily transcending them by building states greater than himself which are worthy of his sacrifice and then again because of his inherent flaws, dissolving these states into an association of men fearful and greedy.[1] According to Plato, the state at fever heat, which is what the power state is, is brought about by the emancipation of the desire for unnecessary things, that is, for things which are not necessary for the well being of the body. This luxurious state is characterized by striving for unlimited acquisition of wealth; is marked by dissatisfaction and conflicts; and leads to war, expansion and all the evils in states, private as well as public.[2]

For Saint Augustine the City of Man is built on self-love, on pride and the "diverse lusts" of men. This single principle of *cupiditas* (the love that builds the earthly city)[3] sustains and moves all things. In addition to sexual appetite and economic greed it includes also the lust for political rule and for knowledge. Although men are held together by the bonds of a common human nature mankind the world over is divided against itself, and although men might desire peace their passions and appetites prompt them to pursue these ends in such a way that the satisfaction of one person often, if not always, involves the frustration of another. The power of self-love sows confusion into every society and generates social factions, tensions and competition of interest in every human community. Conflicts occur between individuals, groups and states; the strong overcome the weak; brutalities and crimes are committed; and mankind is plunged into immeasurable evil and suffering. The earthly city is constantly subject to an uneasy compromise between contending forces with the danger that factional disputes may result in "bloody insurrection" at any time. Commonwealths are bound together by a common love, or collective interest, rather than by a sense of justice; and they could not maintain themselves without the imposition of power. Without recourse to injustice neither republics nor imperial cities could subsist. The earthly city is thus also the diabolical city.

The brutal facts of power rule not only the relations between states but also the realities of national states. In every state a small dominant group or oligarchy holds the dominant form of social power and this group is often required to commit lies, betrayals of pacts, crimes and low deceptions in order to realize its public policies and aims. Not one iota of man's self-destructive force can ever really be purged from him. All political regimes therefore are able to maintain a semblance of peace and order in the world by using coercive force, veiled or naked, to restrain coercive force. And when this more dominant group fails to hold on to the power concentrated in its hands and neglects to use it effectively it will inevitably fall into the hands of the multitude. The multitude, giving expression to all their passions and appetites, to all their private aims and selfish desires, will soon enough be reduced to such a condition of complete unrestraint and greed that only the emergence of a new dominant group will be able to save it from self-destruction. Then the strong will again prevail over the weak, power will again be concentrated perhaps more tightly than before in the hands of the few, and man will again come to understand what really holds the city of man together.

Machiavelli saw man as naturally egoistic and moved by a lust for domination and power. Men are driven by ambition which is so powerful in their minds that even when they arrive at the height of good fortune they might attain, they are "never contented but are still laboring for more." All this happens because "we are naturally capable of desiring many things, which we are unable to compass, and therefore our desire being greater than our power to acquire, our minds are never at rest with what we enjoy. And this is the occasion of all our varieties of fortune."[4]

Human history was thus perceived as a great arena of strife and dissention involving violence, deceit and treachery, redeemed only now and again by individual and collective acts of heroism and self-denial. Through action, violent as it usually is, man realizes his humanity, founds or reinvigorates states and religions, and prevents tyranny by securing and strengthening the citizens' liberties. Through action, man can purposely make history instead of becoming the victim of mere circumstance. Politics for Machiavelli is similar to warfare and the style of the accomplished political leader is comparable to the art of war as practiced by the skilled military commander.

According to Hobbes, man's desire for power sprang from appetite, from the particularities of natural appetite, the passions, and from the competitive war of all against all. Man as distinct from the animal strives after honor and positions of honor, after precedence over others and recognition of this precedence by others and is ruled by ambition, pride, envy, fear, anxiety, vanity and the passion for fame. Never at ease and never satisfied, continually provoked to fresh responses by changes in the world, afraid that he might fall behind in the race for eminence, man has "no other goal, no other garland but being foremost." The natural striving after power and thus man's natural appetite is described by Hobbes as follows: "Men from their very birth and naturally, scramble for everything they covet, and would have all the world if they could, to fear and obey them."[5]

To Hobbes, then, men are by nature egoistic and since the selfish ego is never contented in a society marked by a scarcity of goods they are always entangled in a perpetual condition of warfare among themselves. Men and states are consequently always poised between pride and fear. Pride, which is an expression of our sense of omnipotence and immortality, which makes us restless and is a manifestation of our vitality, leads to a state of war. Fear, which is an expression of dread and the longing for security, leads men into a state of civil society. Thus man lives forever in a state of tension between these two impulses. Even society most often merely provides an arena wherein his passions are ever clamoring for release and for the most part merely provides an occasion for him to get what he wants, to invade others, and to diminish others to his own advantage. The thoughts and fantasies of men recognize no limits. In our imaginations at least we pillage, we murder, we rape. Propelled by this inner clamour, by the extravagant passions of our state of nature men breed a society of rivalry, fraud and remorselessness. Each of us conceals within him an untamed man raging for sensual license, bursting to express his thoughts into words and to put these thoughts into action. These are the wild and extravagant passions that always threaten to tear societies and the relations between states to pieces. Stubbornly quarrelsome and irrascible, naturally inclined to competition, suspicion and the pursuit of glory, men invade others for gain or for personal safety or for reputation. For Hobbes the state of nature is always within us, always threatening to burst out of the terrifying darkness of the soul or to escape from the laws, customs and institutions which we have created to contain them into the light of day and engulf us all.

For Spinoza too, man is essentially a creature of desire, passion, selfishness, ambition, avarice, love, hatred, anger, envy and pity and suffers from other "perturbations of the mind." Men are led more by blind desire and fear than by reason. Everyone seeks with the utmost passion his own advantage and would rather rule than be ruled. The end of every act is the self-preservation of the actor. Liable by necessity to passions men are so constituted as to pity those who are ill and envy those who are well off, are more prone to vengeance than to mercy; and wish the rest to live after his own mind, to approve what he approves and reject what he rejects. Men are most eager to be first and so they fall to strife and do their utmost to oppress one another. He who comes out conqueror is more proud of the harm he has done to the other than the good he has done to himself. States are therefore natural enemies and as such must be constantly on guard one against the other. Although religion teaches every man to love his neighbor as himself, that is to defend another's right just as much as his own, yet this persuasion has had too little power over the passions. The passions in fact obscure the best interests of men and states. In so far as men are tormented by anger, envy or any passion implying hatred, they are drawn asunder, made contrary to one another, become naturally enemies and therefore are so much the more to be feared as they are more powerful, crafty and cunning than other animals. All those who rule grow haughty, cause fear if they do not feel it, and transgress against the truth. Although reason can indeed do much to restrain and moderate the passions, the road to reason, which reason itself points out, is very steep. Those who succeed in persuading themselves that the multitude of men distracted by politics "can ever be induced to live according to the dictates of reason must be dreaming of the poetic golden age or of a stage play."[6]

Although there are few open statements in de Maistre's work on man's psychological makeup he nevertheless incidentally points to two characteristics which he seems to consider natural to men—their lust for power and their tendency to move into society. Man has both a good and evil nature, a theomorphic and a theomachic nature. This dualism arises as the inevitable consequence of his creation in the image of God and his fall from grace. His lust for power is the child of pride, the over-weening satanic pride endemic in the human soul; the result of the original sin he suffers from "which explains everything and without which nothing can be explained" and derives from his free will. Born a rebel he is yet an impotent one. As long as he worships his own free will he is doomed to perpetual frustration. Animals are happy in the place they occupy. All are degraded but are ignorant of it; man alone senses it and this feeling is the proof at once of his grandeur and his misery, of his sublime pre-rogatives and his incredible degradation. Evil has stained everything and man in his entirety is nothing but a malady. The dialectic of sin makes man lose his grip, makes him fumble and stumble and sink down, en-snared and maddened. Happiness is not his right, his reason not his infallible guide and his will not the final sanction. Man is thus "an incredible combination of two different and incompatible powers, a monstrous Centaur. He feels that he is the result of some unknown crime, some detestable mixture that has corrupted him even in his deepest nature."[7]

Moved by his lust for power man is capable of committing the most monstrous follies and crimes. His lust for power, and especially for the power beyond his possession, is insatiable, he is infinite in his desires and always discontented with what he has, he loves only what he has not. Moreover, there is no man who will not abuse the power he wields, who will not use other men as far as he is able for his own ends, finding plea-sure in the very acts of tyranny. Every human being is a potential despot, from the most absolute Asian monarch to a child smothering a bird in his hand to enjoy the pleasure of seeing that there exists in the world a being weaker than himself. There is not a man who does not abuse power and experience shows that the most abominable despots, if they manage to seize the sceptre, are precisely those who rant against despotism. But power also steadfastly ignores the means of conserving itself. The "author of nature" has set bounds to the abuse of power; He has willed it that it destroy itself once it goes beyond its natural limits. This law is written in both the physical and the moral world. Produce a gun beyond its limits and its effectiveness will be reduced; perfect a telescope beyond its limits and invincible nature will turn all your efforts to perfect that in-strument against it. To conserve itself, power must restrict itself, and it must always keep away from that point at which its most extreme efforts lead to its own death.

The law of the world is not harmony but inequity, injustice, violence and murder. The universe is not susceptible to the criteria of mathema-tical logic and rational consistency. It is irrational at its core. The hap-penings in it stem from some dark and powerful obsessions and per-

versions, the baffling incoherences are due to some unfathomable
ambivalences and the heart rending frustrations are caused by dumb,
intractable obtuseness. Man, furthermore, "lives under the hand of an
angry power and . . . this power can be appeased only by sacrifices."
Murder on the one hand and sacrifice on the other—these are the two
laws of the universe; and two institutions symbolize this order in the
most striking and uncanny manner: the hangman and war. Of all the
instruments of divine wrath, war he believes is the most crushing and
effective. He rejects totally the charge that wars spring from the evil
designs of rulers: they originate rather in some blind instinct that grips
men and pushes them into conflict. Violence and violent death are inescapable laws of existence. From the lowest to the highest the stronger
kill the weaker, and every creature lives on the blood and the fat of the
lower. All animals have their beasts of prey, and man, to satisfy his needs
and instincts, must kill, must subdue the animal world. It is in the grip of
the same law that man, seized by a "divine fury" seeks to kill his fellows.
He undertakes with enthusiasm that which he holds in horror. The
divinity of its origins justifies, even sanctifies, this instinct; in the act of
slaughter the soldier like the executioner is only "an innocent murderer,
a passive instrument in a formidable hand." As a penalty for its sins
mankind is condemned to flounder in this welter of bloodshed and terror,
mysterious in its causes and unforseeable in its results. "The whole earth
continually steeped in blood, is nothing but an immense altar on which
every little thing must be sacrificed, without end, without restraint, without respite, until consummation of the world, the extinction of evil,
the death of death." Men are inextricably trapped in this tragic dilemma
of inevitable crime and necessary punishment, of certain pride and its
certain and terrible consequences.[8]

Nietzsche's philosophy posits the will to power as a universal drive
found in all men. It prompts the slave who dreams of a heaven from
which he hopes to behold his master in hell no less than it prompts the
master. Both resentment and brutality, both sadism and asceticism are
expressions of it. The will to power is evidence of man's ruthlessness
and a source of evil to him, but it is also the essence of life and of the
world. Life is merely an individual instance of the will to power. It
springs from fullness of life and its overflow. The extent of our feeling for
life and power provides us with a measure of Being, that is, of willing,
acting and becoming. The will to power is inseparable from the existence
of conflict. It is a struggle with others and within the self; in either case
it develops out of the will to grow and to increase. To have and to want
to have more—growth—is life itself. The will to accumulate force is
special to the phenomena of life, to nourishment, procreation, inheritance

—to society, state, custom, authority. The only reality is the will to grow stronger of every center of force—"not self-preservation but the will to appropriate, dominate, increase, grow stronger."[9] Striving is nothing other than striving for power. All change is the result of the encroachment of one power upon another power. Life is thus always lived at the expense of other lives and is as a result always appropriation, overpowering the foreign and the weak, and at the very least, exploitation. In the performance of its basic functions life employs injury, oppression, annihilation and cannot be conceived without these characteristics. It is a struggle between ruler and ruled and resistance in the relation of the obedient to his commander. Life is not merely lived at the expense of others; it is also lived at one's own expense. It is that which must always overcome itself and wherever life appears it appears as pain and contradiction. Life requires enmity and death and the cross of the martyr; and to live at all is to be in danger.

But power is ambiguous. Power and value are not simply identified by Nietzsche. The drive to power may either ennoble the mind or degrade whole peoples. It is as much to be found in the attempts of Alexander and Napoleon to conquer the world with armed might as it is to be discovered in Aristotle's and Hegel's attempts to subdue the entire cosmos, without cavalry and cannon, by sheer force of mind. The Greeks' will to outdo, excel and overpower each other was responsible for their philosophic discourses, the ancient tragedies and comedies, the Platonic dialogues and the sculptures of the Periclean age. On the other hand, others pay dearly for coming to power, for power can make one tedious and stupid. Political dominance without genuine human superiority is the greatest possible desecration. The political defeat of Greece was the worst possible misfortune for it gave rise to the theory that the cultivation of culture is possible only when men are armed to the teeth. The victory of the Roman empire was the triumph of brute force over aristocratic genius. When the state abandons its creative ground it becomes the force that destroys the true being of man through a process of levelling. When this form of state, the most unfeeling of all monsters, is glorified, he sees it as the enemy of all that the genuine state should make possible or bring forth: the people, culture, and man as the creative individual. Human destiny involves no greater misfortune than for the most powerful men to be less than first rate. When that happens everything becomes false, distorted and monstrous. In the present age everything is determined only by the coarsest and most evil forces; by the egoism of those engaged in acquisitive pursuits and by military despotisms. The *Existenz* of modern man, in possession of immense forces and powers, reveals an unspeakable poverty and exhaustion; the greatest mediocrity; and in his inner self grey impotence, gnawing dissatisfaction, busiest boredom and dishonest misery prevail.

Of the infinite desires of man, the chief, according to Bertrand Russell, are the desires for power and glory, which for most practical purposes may be regarded as one. Imagination is the goad that forces human beings into restless exertion after their primary needs have been met. While animals are content with mere existence and reproduction, men desire in addition to expand and their desires in this respect are limited only by what the imagination suggests as possible. Every man would like to be God and some few find it difficult to admit the impossibility. These are the "Satanic" types who combine nobility with impiety (in the sense of refusing to admit the limitations of human power). This Titanic combination of nobility with impiety is most pronounced in the great conquerors but some element of it is to be found in all men. The presence of this combination of qualities makes social cooperation difficult, produces competition, the need of compromise and government, the impulse to rebellion and with it instability and periodic violence. The need for morality arises from the necessity to restrain this anarchic self-assertion.

Russell disagrees with the orthodox economists, as well as with Marx, that economic self-interest could be taken as the fundamental motive in the social sciences. The desire for commodities, when separated from power and glory, is finite, and can be fully satisfied by a moderate competence. The really expansive desires are not dictated by a love of material comfort. When a moderate degree of comfort has been obtained both individuals and communities will pursue power rather than wealth; they may seek wealth as a means to power or they may relinquish an increase of wealth in order to increase their power, but in both cases their fundamental motive is not economic. It is only by realizing "that love of power is the cause of the activities that are important in social affairs that history, whether ancient or modern, can be rightly interpreted."[10] Though the love of power is unevenly distributed it is the chief motive producing those changes which social science has to study.

The fundamental concept in social science, for him, is Power, in the same sense in which Energy is the fundamental concept in physics. Like energy, power has many forms—wealth, armaments, civil authority, influence on opinion. He argues that no one of these forms can be regarded as subordinate to any other and there is no one form to which the others are derivative. No form of power can be treated in isolation and all the forms of power must be taken into account. The laws of social dynamics are laws which can only be stated in terms of power, not in terms of this or that form of power. Power like energy must be regarded as continually passing from any one of its forms into any other form which power assumes.

Power is defined by Russell "as the production of intended effects".[11] It is thus a quantitative concept and if one person achieves more intended effects than another it is possible to say that he has more power than the other. Power over human beings may be classified by the manner of influencing individuals, or by the type of organization involved. An individual may be influenced by direct physical power over his body, e.g., when he is imprisoned or killed; by rewards and punishment as inducements, e.g., in giving or withholding employment; by influence on opinion, i.e., by propaganda in its broadest sense through schools, churches and political parties. Different societies, moreover, differ in many ways in relation to power. They differ in the degree of power possessed by individuals or organizations; it is more than obvious that the modern state has much more power today than in former times. They differ again, as regards the kind of organization that is more influential; a military despotism, a theocracy, a plutocracy, a single party regime, are very dissimilar types. They also differ in the diverse ways through which they acquire power: hereditary kinship produces one kind of personality type, the qualities required of an ecclesiastic produce another type, democracy a third type, a revolutionary regime a fourth kind and war a fifth. An age thus appears in history through its prominent individuals and derives its apparent character from these men. As the qualities required for achieving prominence change so the prominent men change.

For Reinhold Niebuhr man's lust for power springs from evils inherent in the human situation and from original sin, which is a composite term for man's innate tendencies toward self-regard, self-deception, aggression and domination. Man is insecure and involved in natural contingency; he seeks to overcome his insecurity by a will to power which overreaches the limits of human creatureliness. Man is ignorant and involved in the limitations of a finite mind; but he pretends that he is not limited. He assumes that he can gradually transcend finite limitations until his mind becomes identical with the universal mind. All of his intellectual and cultural pursuits as a consequence become infected with the sin of pride. Man's pride and will to power disrupt the harmony of creation. The ego which falsely makes itself the center of existence in its pride and will to power inevitably subordinates other egos to its will and does injustice to them. Man, moreover, tries to ignore the presence in life of death. Life will always continue to be fragmentary and will always continue to be challenged by death no matter how powerful men become. The fear of death prompts men to complete life falsely and to express their frustrations in lust for power, envy of one another and a sense of false security in material comfort and power.

Bound and free, limited and limitless, weak and strong, blind and far-seeing, a dwarf who thinks himself a giant, man is riddled with anxiety. Anxiety is the inevitable concomitant of the paradox of freedom and finiteness in which man is involved. At the mercy of an anxious and contingent world and of his own freedom, man attempts either to deny the contingent character of existence in pride and self-love or to escape from his freedom in sensuality. Anxiety as a permanent accompaniment of freedom is thus both the source of creativity and a temptation to sin. It is the condition of the sailor climbing to the mast with the abyss of the waves beneath him and the "crow's nest" above him. He is anxious about both the end toward which he strives and the abyss of nothingness into which he may plunge. Man's ambitions are always partly prompted by this fear of meaninglessness which always threatens him. Man is thus "tempted by the basic insecurity of human existence to make himself doubly secure and by the insignificance of his place in the total scheme of things to prove his significance." The will to power is, in short, "both a direct form and an indirect instrument of the pride which Christianity regards as sin in its quintessential form."[12]

Man's sense of insecurity has prompted another form of the pride of power. This is the sin of those who knowing themselves to be insecure, seek sufficient power to guarantee their security, inevitably of course at the expense of others. It is particularly the sin of the advancing forces of human society in oppostion to the established forces. Among those who are obviously less secure either in terms of social status and recognition or economic strength the temptation arises to overcome or hide insecurity by trying to arrogate a greater degree of power to the self. Sometimes this lust for power expresses itself in the form of man's conquest of nature, in which man's legitimate attempt to master nature for his own good is corrupted into his brutal exploitation of it. Man's sense of arrogant independence of nature and his greedy efforts to overcome the insecurity of nature's rhythms and seasons by attacking it with excessive zeal and beyond natural requirements is an expression of man's inordinate ambitions to hide his insecurity in nature. Greed as a form of the will to power has been a particularly flagrant sin in the modern world because modern science and technology have tempted contemporary man to overestimate the possibility and value of eliminating his insecurity in nature. Greed is thus the besetting sin of a bourgeois culture. This culture is continuously tempted to regard material comfort and security as life's highest good and goal and to hope for its attainment beyond human possibilities. Its commitment to these shallow goals has made it forget that nature intends to kill man and will probably succeed in the end.[13]

Though the will to power is rooted in a feeling of human insecurity, authentic security is never to be attained. The more man establishes himself in power and glory the greater is the fear of falling from his eminence, or losing his wealth, or being exposed in his pretensions. Wealth is always, even when most secure, full of itch and fear. Poverty is a threat to the wealthy, not to the poor. Obscurity is feared, not by those who have lived in its twilight but by those who have become accustomed to public applause. The tyrant fears not only the loss of his power but the possible loss of his life. Even the most successful man possesses no sense of moral security, no happy freedom, no mastery over anything. The powerful nation, seemingly secure against its individual enemies and rivals, lives constantly in the fear that its power may provoke its enemies and rivals to organize themselves against it. The will to power is thus an expression of insecurity and anxiety even when it has achieved a position which would seem to guarantee relative security. The fact that human ambitions know no limits must therefore be attributed not merely to the infinite capacities of the human imagination and self-deception but to a gnawing recognition of man's finiteness, weakness and dependence, which become the more apparent the more we seek to conceal them and which generate ultimate perils the more the immediate insecurities seem to be eliminated. "Thus man seeks to make himself God because he is betrayed by both his greatness and his weakness; and there is no level of greatness and power in which the lash of fear is not at least one strand in the whip of ambition."[14]

Man, contrary to the superficial dogmas of liberalism, is according to Niebuhr not interested only in survival. Man desires to fulfill the potentialities of life and not merely to maintain its existence. The will to live is thus transmuted into the will to self-realization; into the will to power or into the desire "for power and glory." Man being more than a natural creature is not interested merely in physical survival but in prestige and social approval. He is a source of vitality and energy. Having the intelligence to anticipate the dangers in which he is placed in nature and history he invariably seeks to gain security against those dangers by enhancing his power, individually and collectively. The conflicts between men are thus never simple conflicts between competing survival impulses. They are conflicts in which each man or group seeks to guard its power and prestige against the peril of competing expressions of power and pride. Since the very possession of power and prestige always involves some encroachment upon the power and prestige of others this conflict is by its very nature a more difficult and stubborn one than the mere competition between various survival impulses in nature. Human ambitions, lusts and desires are more inordinate, human creativity and evil reach greater heights and depths, and conflicts in the community between competing expressions of vitality are of more tragic proportions than was ever anticipated in the basic philosophy which underlies democratic civilization.[15] History for Niebuhr is filled with tragedy because there is no final solution to the conflicts between the individual and the community and between classes, races and nations.

The same forces and vitalities that shape relations between individuals also mold relations between groups and states. All inter-group relations are marked by self-interest and collective egoism and the behavior of all human collectivities is distorted by brutality and hypocricy. The limitations of the human imagination, the easy subservience of reason to prejudice and passion and the consequent persistence of irrational egoism, particularly in group behavior, make social conflict an inevitability in human history. Society is perennially harassed not only by the fact that the corrosive forces in social life create injustice in the process of establishing peace; but also by the tendency of the same factors which make for an unstable peace within a social group to exacerbate inter-group conflict. Power sacrifices justice to peace within the community and destroys peace between communities. It is not true that only kings, ruling groups or capitalist corporations make war. No personal whim which a human being might indulge is excluded from the motives which have prompted these individuals and groups to shed the blood of their unhappy subjects. Pride, jealousy, hurt vanity, greed for greater treasures, lust for power over larger domains, petty animosities between individuals, momentary passions and childish tantrums, these have all been not the occasional but the pervasively recurring causes and occasions of intergroup conflict. The common members of any community, however, while sentimentally desiring peace, nevertheless also indulge impulses of envy, jealousy, pride, bigotry and greed which make for conflict between communities. It is thus always possible for the dominant groups within any society to engage in social conflict for the satisfaction of their self-interest, their pride and their vanity, provided only that they can compound their personal ambitions with, and hallow them by, the ambitions of their group and the pathetic passions, vanities and fantasies of the individuals who comprise the group.

Yet the ambitions and greed of the dominant groups within each nation are not the only causes of international conflict. Every social group without exception tends to develop imperial ambitions which are aggravated, but not caused, solely by the lusts of its leaders and privileged groups. Every group, every individual, has expansive desires which are rooted in the instinct of survival and soon extend way beyond it. The will to live becomes the will to power. Man fights for his social eminence and increased significance with the same fervor and the same justification with which he fights for his life. Only rarely does nature provide armors of defense which cannot be transferred into instruments of aggression. The frustrations and discontents of the average man who can never realize the power and glory which he dreams of, make him the more willing tool and victim of the imperial ambitions of his group. His frustrated individual ambitions gain a measure of satisfaction in the power and the expansion of his nation. The will to power of competing national groups is the cause of the international anarchy which the moral sense of mankind has thus far vainly striven to overcome. Since some nations are more powerful than others they will at times contain anarchy by establishing a system of effective imperialism. But the peace thus gained is based on force and must always be an uneasy and unjust one. As powerful classes organize a nation so do powerful nations organize a primitive society of nations. In each case the peace so established has to be a tentative one because it is based on injustice and force. It has only partially been achieved by a mutual accomodation of conflicting interests and only rarely by a rational and moral adjustment of the rights in contention. It will therefore last only until those who feel themselves too weak to challenge the existing power constellation become, or feel themselves, powerful enough to do so. Every social order, democratic or dictatorial, is thus a precarious arrangement and the same power which prompts the fear that prevents action also creates the mounting hatred which guarantees ultimate defiance and rebellion. All through history, one can therefore observe the tendency of power to destroy its own raison d'être.[16]

According to Hans Morgenthau, the root of the lust for power is man's loneliness. Of all creatures only man is capable of loneliness because only he feels the need not to be alone, without being able, in the end, to escape from being alone. It is that striving to escape his loneliness which provides the impetus to the lust for power and it is the failure to escape that loneliness, either at all or for more than a moment, that creates the tension between aspiration and lack of achievement, which is the ultimate tragedy of power. Man's loneliness moreover reveals his insufficiency. He cannot fulfill himself, he cannot become what he is destined to be, by his own effort, in isolation from other beings. The awareness of that insufficiency drives him on in his search for power. "It drives him on to seek the extension of his self in his offspring—the work of his body; in the manufacture of material things—the work of his hands; in philosophy and scholarship—the work of his mind; in art and literature—the work of his imagination; in religion—the work of his pure longing toward transcendence."[17]

Man's lust for power is, for Morgenthau, the complement to man's longing for love. For love and power both try to overcome loneliness and the sense of man's insufficiency stemming from this loneliness; through duplication of his individuality. Through love, man seeks another human being like himself, the Platonic other half of his soul, to form a union which will make him whole. Through power, man seeks to impose his will upon another man, "so that the will of the object of his power mirrors his own." What love seeks to discover in another man as a gift of nature, power must create through the artifice of psychological manipulation. Love is reunion through spontaneous mutuality, power seeks to create a union through unilateral imposition. However, love in its purest form is the rarest of experiences and in its most typical form is tantamount to what could be called a relationship of power with "A" trying to submit "B" to his will. Frustrated in love, incapable of achieving that reunion of two human beings which is love, for any length of time, man is driven to let power accomplish what love is unable to accomplish by itself. Man's longing for love is thus corrupted and the lust for power is as it were, the twin of despairing love. Power becomes in fact a substitute for love. What love can at least approximate and in a fleeting moment actually achieve, power can only give the illusion of doing.

Power is a psychological relationship in which one man controls certain actions of another man through the influence he exerts over the latter's will. It is thus in the very nature of the power relationship that the position of the two actors within it is ambivalent. "A" seeks to exert power over "B"; "B" tries to resist that power and seeks to exert power over "A", which "A" resists. The actor on the political stage is therefore always at the same time "a prospective master over others and a prospective object of the power of others." While he seeks power over others, others seek power over him. Victory comes to him who marshalls the stronger weapons of influence with greater skill.

However, political victory won with the weapons of threats and promises is likely to be precarious; for the power relationships established in this way depend upon the continuing submissiveness of a recalcitrant will and are dependent on the master's continuing influence. Although political masters, actual and potential, and on all levels of social interaction, from the family to the state, have sought to meet this issue by trying to base their power upon the spontaneous consent of their subjects and have tried to found their power not upon threats and promises but upon the subject's love for his master this has been more an ideal than an attainable goal.

Denied love, aware of the love that is beyond their reach, the great political masters have sought to compensate for the love they must miss with ever greater accumulations of power. From the subjection of ever more men to their will they seem to expect the achievement of that communion which the lack of love withholds from them. Yet the acquisition of power only begets the desire for more; for the more men they hold the more they are aware of their loneliness. There is thus in the great political masters a demoniac and frantic striving for ever more power which will be satisfied only when the last living man has been subjected to the master's will. "More! More!" in the words of William Blake, "is the cry of a mistaken soul; less than all cannot satisfy man." The heights of the master's power therefore reveal the depths of his despair. For the world conqueror can subject all inhabitants of the earth to his will, but he cannot compel a single human being to love him. His power cannot cure his loneliness and the fruitless search for love through power "leads in the most passionate seekers after power from a despair, impotent in the fullness of power, to a hate, destructive of the objects of their successful power and frustrated love."

The loneliness of man is, then, impervious to both love and power. Power can only unite through the unilateral imposition of subjection which leaves the master's isolation intact. Behold the master, who can compel millions to obey him and yet cannot find a single being with which to unite his own. And love can only unite in the fleeting moments when two souls unite in spontaneous mutuality; they see the promised land in their longing and imagination and enter it only to be expelled from it. Thus in the end, "his wings seared, his heart-blood spent, his projects come to nought—despairing of power and thirsting for, and forsaken by, love—man peoples the heavens with gods and mothers and virgins and saints who love him and whom he can love and to whose power he can subject himself spontaneously because their power is the power of love. Yet, whatever he expects of the other world, he must leave this world as he entered it: alone."[18]

A few other significant explanations for man's lust for power have also been advanced. For Alfred Adler, man's inferiority complex guides and spurs on his longing for supremacy and he declared it to be his most general supposition that "the psyche has as its objective the goal of superiority."[19] Karen Horney's premise is that in our culture the individual develops an urgent need to "lift himself above others". Disappointed with his real self he creates an idealized image of himself which he endows with unlimited powers and with extraordinary faculties: he becomes a hero, a genius, a supreme lover, a saint, a god. Neuroticism develops when the qualities of the idealized image triumph over the real self. Since the idealized image regularly provides for self-glorification the search for glory becomes the comprehensive and dominant drive. This search involves a drive toward perfection, toward external success, and toward vindictive triumph. The chief aim of the drive toward vindictive triumph is "to put others to shame or defeat them through one's very success; or to attain the power, by rising to prominence, to inflict suffering upon them—mostly of a humiliating kind." This vindictive drive stems from impulses to take revenge for humiliations suffered in childhood and which are then reinforced during later neurotic development.[20] According to Erich Fromm all men feel a necessity to belong, to avoid isolation and moral aloneness, to avoid powerlessness and insignificance. He argues that the development of Protestantism and Capitalism, though enhancing freedom from regimentation, has produced the very things men want to avoid. Alone, insignificant and powerless in modern society, many groups of men cannot go on bearing the burden of freedom and seek to escape from freedom altogether. Two among the many mechanisms of escape are masochistic and sadistic strivings. Masochism aims at "dissolving oneself in an overwhelming strong power and participating in its strength and glory": sadism aims "at unrestricted power over another person more or less mixed with destructiveness." The sado-masochistic personality is both ready to submit to power, that is, to domination by the strong, and at the same time ready to impose power, to attack, to dominate and to humiliate the weak.[21] Harold Lasswell's key hypothesis about the power seeker is that he pursues power as a means of compensation against deprivation. An individual, for all kinds of reasons, feels deprived; he does not command the values which for some reason he thinks he should command. He might be suffering from a disturbed childhood, a physical handicap, a lack of well-being or from a low income. Or perhaps while thinking that he deserves deference he feels that he does not actually obtain it—that others hold him in low esteem. Alternatively, if the individual does not feel currently deprived, he may fear the loss of values in the future, while in some circumstances the individual accepts the actual or threatened deprivation without struggle, in other circumstances he seeks to compensate for deprivation or to safeguard himself against the future deprivation which he fears by striving for power. Power is thus "expected to overcome the low estimates of the self, by changing either the traits of the self or the environment in which it functions."[22] The same factors that lead individuals to desire power also operate on groups and collectivities.

The river of the will to power is fed, as can be deduced from the preceding analysis, by a myriad of streams. Stemming from the blind, irrational will with its avid craving for life, for wreaking its desires;

emerging from the primitive chaos of the unconscious with all its seething instincts seeking gratification; man's will to power finds its expression in all the multiform passions and drives which impel him to attain his self-seeking designs. Alone and insignificant in the world, man tries with all the force and desperation at his command to achieve some coherence, significance and mastery through the power that he so precariously attains. Insecure, afraid of death, filled with anxiety, man seeks to arrogate a greater degree of power to himself, to compensate for the meaninglessness, emptiness and absurdity which always threaten him. Goaded by the imagination, puffed up with self-love and hubris, man desires to expand, to accumulate force, to break limits, to transcend his finite existence and in the process over-reaches his human creatureliness.

Frustrated and thwarted, he vents his frustration in aggression against others. Master and bondsman do not only represent two forms of opposed consciousness but each aims at the death and destruction of the other. Seeking power and glory for himself, man humiliates, injures and oppresses his fellow men. Wanting to have and to grow he diminishes the life chances of others and blindly eats into his own substance. Estranged within himself and from himself, in conflict with his fellow men, his craving for power beyond his possession is insatiable. Disturbed by a secret unrest and perplexity, stirred by his lust for power, he soars to the greatest creative heights and then plunges into crime and folly, into corruption and imbecility, into injustice and insanity. Power elevates individuals, classes and nations and then as systematically does it degrade them. Trying through power to impose form upon that chaos, which is at the bottom of everything, chaos revenges itself and proves its fundamental dominance by besieging that form with all sorts of violence and cunning diseases until that form dissolves and the flux of existence reverts to its anonymous continuity. In all the wars which the struggle for power engenders, every cause is ultimately lost and every nation destroyed. Man can as little escape the compulsions and conflicts of power as he can disengage himself from the vitalities and fatalities of life itself.

The lust for power tends to corrupt and stain with evil all those who are caught in its toils. Give a finger of power to a bedraggled clerk and he becomes devious and mean in its use. Permit a reformer to succeed and he too in turn will abuse the power that he has attained. Grant a liberated slave power and he will outdo his former master in oppression and cruelty. Lure a "respected" academic with the prospects of serving the masters of power and he becomes even more ferocious, dogmatic and bloodthirsty than the "princes" he comes to serve. Provide a so-called "independent" academic with the largesse of the state's immense resources and he will compete for it with all the venom that is within him, become a partner in crime and folly and feed at the trough with the appetite of the starved. Challenge men in positions of authority, in all walks of life, with a man of integrity and excellence and they turn rigid and vindictive. Place a new and inexperienced ruler in office and the first thing he learns are its vices and not its limited virtues. Raise your head too high and you will have it cut off by the fear of those above you and the envy of those below you. Power distorts the image of self held by those in its grip and breeds a kind of tumor that ends by killing the victim's sympathies and reason. It turns worthy men into wicked men and wicked men into worse. It is a kind of diseased appetite like a passion for drink or perverted tastes. Move incompetent men, with all their insecurities and appetites into posts of power and institutions are jeopardized and states threatened. Institutionalize power in organizations—parties, governments, bureaucracies, corporations, universities and the like—and a kind of obtuse conservatism slowly stultifies them. Power is always surrounded by flunkeydom and prostitution, by self-servers and sycophants. Even thought itself which in former times had, at its best, been contemptuous of princes and their brawls, has now eagerly joined this game and devotes itself to proclaiming their virtues. Wherever power relations prevail there all the vices and evils, all the crazy and morbid ambitions that men are capable of are exhibited in their purest and most repulsive form.

The struggle to magnify itself, moreover, is of power's essence. To the extent that power is a species of egoism it tends naturally to grow. Power is authority and makes for more authority. It is force and makes for more force. Ambitious wills, drawn by the attractions of power, unceasingly expend their energies in its behalf so that they may bind society in an ever tighter grip and extract from it more and more of its resources. Man, according to Rousseau, is a limited creature, "his life is short, his pleasures know bounds, his capacity for enjoyment is always static," but the state on the contrary, "being an artifical body, knows no fixed bounds; the greatness which belongs to it is unlimited, and can always be increased by itself."[23] The egoisms which shape the life of the state and give it life expand its conquests. The instinct of growth is proper to power; it is part of its essence and does not change with its changing political form. The struggle to expand is as much a motive of monarchies as of republics, of democratic as of totalitarian states. For power is command, with the passions proper to command, of which the first is to expand the area under its rule. It is possible for this passion to lie dormant for decades but its inevitable awakening is in the very nature of things. For like attracts like; authority attracts the authoritarian, and empire the imperious. It is only necessary to look at the map of the world, not in its static form, but rather as the moving picture which has been showing down the centuries. We then observe how one state has expanded at the expense of one or more of the others, and how states have contracted under the compression of the alliances organized against them. Now a tentacle has been put out to sea, now campaigns have been launched for the conquest of continents, or a strategic piece of territory has been taken in its stride, or a foreign body or bodies has been engulfed and absorbed. At long last the particular octopus has lost its vitality and a day appears when it becomes the prey of another's appetite and disappears. The picture evoked by these shifting power struggles is that of the amoebas observed under the microscope. This is, for all those who have eyes to see and minds to comprehend, the history of states.

Imperialism is hence an inherent component of all inter-state relations. Originating in blind desire, and human freedom and vitality, imperialism is an expression of the fact that human desire, freedom and vitality have no simple, definable limits. Man, unlike the animals, is not merely interested in self-preservation but is a center of inordinate ambitions and lusts. Man is not an essentially tame, cool and calculating creature but is driven by expansive desires and vitalities. Human vitalities, moreover, express themselves from both individual and collective centers in many directions and both are capable of unpredictable creative and destructive consequences. Driven by these vitalities of human existence, possessed of self-consciousness, man and collectivities have the urge to preserve and to extend life. In man the impulses of self-preservation are very easily transmuted into desires for aggrandizement. Recognizing his finiteness within infinity man protests against this finiteness by trying to universalize himself and to give his life a significance beyond himself. This attempt at universalization leads to expansion and imperialism. Man fights for his social eminence and increased significance with the same fervor and with the same sense of justification that he fights for his life. The will to live is thus transformed into the will to power and in the field of inter-state relations into imperial purposes and policies.

Human collectivities or states strive unceasingly for power or glory. Proud of their independence, jealous of their capacities to make decisions of their own, they are all rivals by the very fact of their autonomy. All seek to impose their wills upon each other. Although all seek to be strong in order to survive in the war of all against all, they do not only seek to be strong in order to discourage aggression and enjoy peace. They seek to be powerful—that is, capable of imposing their wills upon their neighbors and rivals in order to influence the fate of humanity and the future of civilization. The sheer intoxication of ruling more often than not transcends every other consideration. In addition to dominion and authority states also desire glory. This struggle for glory is expressed in the desire for absolute victory, that is, for a peace dictated without appeal to the victor; for the honor of leading all their competitors; for the fame that spreads across the world; for the indefinite accumulation of force not only for the sake of security and power but for the satisfaction of that amour-propre that animates men once they measure themselves against each other.

Human collectivities are driven to imperialism as we have noted by a multiplicity of objectives. One of the original stakes in the rivalry among peoples was the possession of space. Another objective has been the acquisition of wealth and manpower. The armed prophet is sometimes less anxious to conquer than to convert; seemingly indifferent to wealth and manpower, he seeks to spread the true faith and he wants the world so organized that it will correspond to his interpretation of life and history. Another impulse has been the missionary one to mould other societies in one's image so as to assure the validity of one's own institutions by imposing them upon others. Wars of expansion have been waged for military or strategic advantages, for economic profit, for revenge and for prestige. Wars have been caused by military machines that were first created by military conflicts that required it and then the machines created the wars that it required. Under these circumstances we have had a will for broad conquest without tangible limits; for the capture of positions that were manifestly untenable. Imperialism is thus a compound made up of utilitarian and irrational elements, of objective goals and human delusions.

According to Schumpeter, the true reasons for imperialism do not lie in the aims which are temporarily being pursued but spring from an aggressiveness that is only kindled anew by each success. It is an aggressiveness conducted for its own sake and is reflected in such terms as "hegemony", "world domination", and so forth. History in his argument shows us nations and classes "that seek expansion for the sake of expanding, war for the sake of fighting, victory for the sake of winning, domination for the sake of ruling."[24] This determination cannot be explained by any of the pretexts that bring it into action or by any of the aims for which it seems to be fighting at the time. It confronts us, independent of all concrete occasions and purposes, as an enduring disposition, seizing upon one opportunity as avidly as the next. Imperialism thus values conquest not so much on account of its immediate benefits—benefits that more often than not are more than dubious and that are later heedlessly cast away with the same frequency—as because it is "conquest, success, action." Expansion in fact is in a sense its own object, and it has no adequate object beyond itself. The tendency of such expansion is to transcend all bounds and tangible limits, to the point of utter exhaustion.

He, as a consequence, defines imperialism as "the objectless disposition on the part of a state to unlimited forcible expansion."[25]

The military and diplomatic struggles of the post-second world war period amply illustrate some of the theoretical assumptions that have been advanced. Entering the immediate post-war world in 1945 with exaggerated self-confidence, stemming mainly from its possession of the nuclear monopoly, and morbid fears, the United States believed that it could, in the first instance, prevent by economic and diplomatic pressure the establishment of communist regimes in Eastern Europe—made inevitable by Russia's military victories in that area. Rebuffed by the Russians, seeing capital after capital engulfed by Russian power and local communist regimes in that area, the United States and other countries of the West not only began to organize the necessary and justified measures of counter defense—the Marshall Plan and NATO— but also almost simultaneously saw itself as engaged in a struggle to prevent the realization of what they perceived to be the communist design for the conquest of the world—which in fact has been shown never to have existed. Beginning with necessary limited economic, political and military programs of self-defense, mixed though they were from the start with extravagant notions of its own capacity to affect the course of world history, the United States in particular was soon enough embarked on a vast and ambitious buildup of its military and political strength. The policy of political containment was as a consequence over-militarized; American power began to spread throughout the world through the establishment of military bases and the dispatch of fleets to all the oceans; and its limited aims were universalized and overextended into a struggle for the imposition of a world-wide American order congenial to its economic interests and to its basic values and beliefs. Swiftly accumulating military and political power; creating overblown military, intelligence and diplomatic establishments; pouring investments into every part of the globe; engaging the academic community to rationalize its aims and policies; the United States began to exert its will upon allies and neutrals on all the continents. Politicians, generals and diplomats, C.I.A. agents and academics, began to thrill to the exhilarations of authority and power and became arrogant with their ability to advise and command other countries as to the best policies they should follow. The United States did not only seek to be a Great Power but a Global Power with all its attendant authority and splendors.

Accompanying this whole process of power building, an anti-communist ideology was elaborated that lumped all communist regimes indiscriminately into one "world camp" or "world conspiracy" without distinguishing the specific conditions, purposes and ambitions of each particular communist regime. This anti-communist ideology which became for most a blind faith liberated its votaries from the requirements of empirical thinking, from the necessity of observing and evaluating the actual behavior of the states and leaders the United States was in contention with. It became a species of medieval scholarship which explained everything in advance and everything that did not fit the theology could be readily dismissed as a fraud, a lie or an illusion. Reality was simplified and distorted. Partial truths became holy writ, and objective scholarship was sacrificed to national ambitions and pre-set diplomatic considerations. The American image of the world therefore replaced reality, wishful thinking was substituted for the pressure of facts, and self-deception and messianic delusion became the driving forces of American policy.

Building up the sinews of power the United States was thus launched on a career of imperialism. It was not the compulsions of capitalism that drove it but the compulsions of power itself which prompted its policy of intervention and expansion. Power, all forms of power, once accumulated in sufficient quantity, cry out to be used. And used it was in overt and covert forms. Unfriendly regimes were overthrown in Guatemala and Iran; military interventions were launched against Cuba and the Dominican Republic; foreign aid was utilized to buy and corrupt allies and to attempt, albeit incompetently and with no genuine commitment or comprehension to "reform" and "modernize" and "build" modern societies on the American model. Secret armies financed by the C.I.A. were organized to fight insurgent and guerrilla forces; regimes friendly to the United States were either installed or subsidized in dozens of countries; the American military drew up contingency plans to wage two nuclear wars and a number of minor wars simultaneously around the globe; and a determination evolved to prevent any further revolutionary or communist regimes from coming to power. Intoxicated by the power it had accumulated, filled with an aroused sense of national and imperial mission and purpose, pressed by the military to be permitted to use its sinews of war and to be allowed to practice its skills so as to earn promotion and glory, convinced that the American example and in consequence American influence might become irrelevant if additional revolutionary regimes were to arise, led by an upstart and vainglorious Irish-American politician from Boston and a dizzy cowboy from Texas, the United States plunged into the disaster of Vietnam. Vietnam was not the product merely of liberal anti-communist illusions, of American innocence and moralism, it was the inevitable outcome of the imperatives of power which sooner or later drive all nations to overreach themselves, to violate all sense of proportion and balance and in the process destroy the very raison d'être of their own power.

Filled with an extravagant sense of power and frustrated and mocked by the intractable realities that faced it, the United States went on a spree of violence. It tried to over-ride the disorderly diversity of the world by the application of an indiscriminately uniform type of violence. Mobilizing and deploying an immense conventional military force of planes, tanks, warships and manpower it began to assault North and South Vietnam and Laos and Cambodia. More tons of explosives were dropped on these countries from the air, to no avail, than were dropped during the entire Second World War. In revolt against the complexity of things the United States relied on and used force to attempt to bring order out of disorder. In the process it committed atrocity after atrocity and in the course of saving villages and towns it destroyed them. Trying to bomb the enemy to its knees or to the conference table it had to kill its own allies and ravage the country it was supposed to save. Dazed and deafened by its own gunfire, it forgot who it was, who the enemy was and who its allies were, and indeed what its original objectives had been. The enormity of American power drove America's leaders to neglect all the arts of politics. Policy went blind and turned pathological. The United States continued to use force to protect the integrity of its own delusions. And then the delusions and the methods used to cope with its problems in Vietnam spread to the United States itself. A police riot thus made a shambles of the Democratic Convention in 1968; unarmed students were killed by National Guardsmen who could think of no other response than firing at point blank range; ghetto riots were met with indiscriminate gunfire; hostages in a prison riot were shot by the authorities who were trying to save them; a cancer of violence spread across the country; and the fabric of the society has been rent and its very future called into question. Having entered this private, self-enclosed fictional world of its own devising, America still remains trapped in this fictitious world born of its fears and violent power impulses.

This brief analysis of American policy during the last twenty-seven years demonstrates the aberrations and corruptions of power. It shows the natural tendency of power to grow and expand; it reveals the sheer intoxication that power brings; and it points to the obstinacy with which positions of power are defended even when their actual utility has disappeared. Unleash the machine of power and it begins to move on its own momentum and mangle those who are ostensibly in control of it. The machine's normal state then becomes one of ceaseless dynamic agitation and aggrandizement. The difficulty is not in setting it in motion but in stopping it. Faithful always to its internal laws of growth, attentive always only to its own propaganda, oblivious of reality and complexity, the machine moves with ever greater violence and uncontrollability until it either destroys society itself or is destroyed in its turn.

Russia emerged from the Second World War motivated by two contradictory impulses. On the one hand it too was filled with a new sense of national and imperial mission and purpose as a result of the victories it had gained against the German invader. On the other hand the behavior of the Russian leaders was shaped by deep-rooted fears, suspicions and mistrust of the outside world. The effort to achieve security by expanding Russian space into Eastern Europe so as to constantly push back the menacing pressure of the foreigners across the Russian borders was, they felt, met by what they considered to be Western hostility and provocation. Contrary to what was believed at that time, Russian policy in the early post-war period was more defensive than aggressive, more cautious than expansionist. Ferociously consolidating its empire in Eastern Europe, frantically rebuilding and then expanding its military, economic and political power at home by sacrificing the living standards of its people and by a vandalistic reparations policy in its conquered lands, Russia slowly began to pursue a more aggressive foreign policy. To counter the spread of American power it began to seek allies or gain the support of neutrals in one area of the world after the other by the wholesale supply of arms and limited financial aid. Accumulating military resources it too began to plan to become a global power and not merely a great power. Attaining a position of near military parity with the United States, worried both by Chinese potential strength and by the consciousness of its own potential weakness, the Soviet Union became involved in regions whose problems and conditions were beyond its comprehension. Its engagement in these areas did not serve any rational Russian national interest but merely reflected its extravagant and objectless power drives and ambitions.

Like the United States, the Soviet Union has also become enmeshed in the power machine it has constructed and which is now taking control of its builders. Determined to protect its hegemony in Eastern Europe it brutally crushed the Hungarian uprising for independence and invaded a reforming Czechoslovakia. Reacting to the global American naval force it has now constructed a naval force of global dimensions. Entrapped in the desperate intricacies of the Middle East it not only became the victim of the nihilistic and impotent Arab camp it was supporting but seemed to relish, beyond all reason, the dubious influence and power which it had acquired. The Russian ambassador in Egypt began to behave like the former British Pro-Consul; and the Russian fleet began to show the flag in strict imitation of nineteenth century British practice, which is now irrelevant. Gripped by a neurotic fear of China it became involved in the religious and communal conflicts of the Indian sub-continent and became the ally and instigator of an India whose only future is to be sucked dry and disintegrated by the "vampire of geography"—the Indian sub-continent itself. To spite and harass the United States it has assumed the burden of financial support for the erratic and economically incompetent Cuban regime. Systematically and heedlessly devoting the major part of its resources to feed and expand its massive military machine; blinded by the blinkers of its own ideology, establishing an over-inflated military, diplomatic and intelligence establishment to support its over-ambitious foreign policy objectives; it is beginning to impose great strains upon the structure of its dictatorial political system at home. Exhilarated by the power it has now accumulated, intoxicated by the world role it is now beginning to play (though it still continues like the last, decadent Czars, to send sane dissidents to the insane asylum or to forced labor) it has now started to over-reach itself. The Soviet Union, like all imperial powers before it, is now seized by the demon of power and is being driven by its imperious and destructive imperatives.

The post-war period is replete with other examples of nations driven by the will to power and expansion. Japan has poured all its concentrated and highly disciplined energy into economic expansion and has in the process not only over-reached itself by its stunning successes but has frightened both its former enemies and its present allies. Fortified and made slightly dizzy by its economic power, Japan has perhaps already begun to dream political and nationalist dreams of a less than pacific or moderate content. A still very poor, backward but modernizing and regenerated China entering with pride the game of international power rivalries extends financial aid which it can ill afford to a Tanzania with whom it has no common interests whatsoever; meddles with impotent revolutionary guerrilla groups in the Middle East; and while thinking of itself, not without arrogance, as the Mecca of do-it-yourself revolutions, pursues at the same time a policy of cautious realpolitik. Great Britain during this whole period, persisted, against all the evidence, in believing itself to be a great power, the center of a meaningless, multiracial commonwealth, retained bases all over the world which served no rational purpose except to bolster British pride, stubbornly continued to maintain London as the center of the sterling area not for the sake of its own economic advantage but for empty prestige, is now engaged in a brutal campaign of violence to shore up its indefensible position in northern Ireland and has by pursuing these immoderate policies, severely injured its position and prospects at home. The fires of nationalism continue to burn in France and Germany and any untoward event could rekindle their ambitions in all kinds of unexpected ways. Pacific and spiritual Hindu India did not hesitate to use its military forces to revenge itself on its Muslim Pakistani enemies by invading East Pakistan, now glories in its "stupendous" military victory despite the Himalayan problems, iniquities and decadence which press it to the ground, and even continues to dream of establishing its hegemony over the entire sub-continent and beyond. Impoverished, pathetic and effete Egypt still continues to be mesmerized by the glories of the Arab past and has been squandering its limited resources in a futile attempt to become the leader of the Arab world and to defeat its Israeli enemy. It has pursued all these policies not only for the sake of victory but to achieve that self-respect and pride which have so far cruelly eluded it. And Israel, which has won a piece of land for itself in order to establish a home for displaced and persecuted Jews, has in the course of so doing inflicted injustice and oppression on others; has had to construct an ever-expanding military machine and live in a garrison state in order to survive; and through its partial victories in four military battles, has expanded its territory and become an occupying power, however moderate. These victories have furthermore made its policies toward its enemies rigid and unyielding and have infected the Israelis with a mixture of hubris and fear. Overconfident and overanxious, overemphasizing the power of force to solve its problems, fixated on nineteenth century conceptions of geographical security, Israel lives suspended between dreams of blinding splendor and the fear of being plunged into bottomless misery.

The power factor in politics is thus not the benign force that many social scientists imagine it to be. Power is rarely served by knowledge and wisdom. It is not mere bargaining and negotiations between interest groups and collectivities, though it is that too. At its core it is profoundly irrational. Through the struggle for power societies are precariously held together but in the final analysis power always overturns the very foundations of its own existence. In its march toward the mastery of nature and men it turns against man, his freedom and his life. Man strives for power but power then uses and manipulates man. Born to seek power and yet made a slave to the power of others, he is entangled in contention and frustration. Power in fact is the most protean of forces. It drives man to rise above mere nature and himself and yet it also corrupts, hypnotizes, intoxicates, deranges and exhausts him. It breeds megalomania. Once set in motion, it grows and expands against all reason, limit and utility. It is the most dangerous potion that man can drink and sooner or later, even with those most experienced in its use, it brings out the greatest evil in him. It breeds deception, betrayal and crime. It lures and ensnares, it leads to contention, confusion, dissatisfaction, impotence, stupidity, despair and hate. It never fully satisfies. And in the end it drives men and states, lacerated, bloodstained and maddened, to self-destruction.

CHAPTER 3

ON ELITES

The struggle for power manifests itself in the life and history of societies as the struggle between elites for rule and pre-eminence. The history of all hitherto existing society is not only the history of class and group struggles but it is also the history of the rise and fall of elites. Political development in every historical epoch—indeed all politics—is essentially a process of elite formation. The goal of politics is to enable effective elites to emerge and to provide them with the cohesion and experience of mutual interaction that will give them the feel for and the capacity to govern. It enables them to achieve that minimum of group consciousness, coherence and unity without which they simply would not be able to maintain their position of rule in relation to the ruled groups in society. The art of governing is thus not merely one of the problems of politics but the primary one. This art has made history what it is. It has raised tiny nations to the summit of decision and power and has destroyed larger ones. In a decisive way the ruling elite is the mirror of a nation, its most delicate indicator. When a nation has a superior ruling elite that nation is undoubtedly great. The decline of that ruling elite, its failure to renovate itself in a way conforming to the historical demands of the time clearly signifies that the nation itself is declining. Having failed to renew itself, supported only by its privileges and naked force, a revolutionary situation is produced which can lead either to the emergence and triumph of a new ruling elite or to the further decay and disintegration of the society. The absolute extent of aptitude for leadership in a given nation, or the qualities on which it is based, determine the creativeness of its endeavors and the level of its accomplishments.

All societies are governed by a ruling elite or class of one kind or another and all societies are divided into a ruling minority and a majority that is ruled. Through the ruling elites amorphous, inchoate masses are formed into coherent societies. A multitude of men is nothing but dust. It is only when leaders create the forms and channels that this human dust is turned into a functioning social order, a nation, and a political community. Elites provide the ideologies, the "political formulas," the "myths" and organize the institutions—social and economic, political and military—that make it possible for men to live a life in common, to build communities, to maintain a genuine independence, to organize a state with a long stability, to pursue great projects in common and to compete with other human collectivities in the perpetual struggle for power that takes place between them. An elite at the top of its form can lift the society it is governing to new levels of historical existence and can liberate those energies required to break out from the confines of the every day, the traditional and bureaucratic and thereby dig out new channels for the otherwise sluggish flow of social life. The coming to power of creative minorities can awaken moribund nations grown sterile, can give form, style, direction and dynamism to young peoples and can purge older civilizations of decadence and weakness and infuse them with strength and vitality. However, these periods of creativity do not usually last for too long. Periods of creativity are usually followed by periods of routinization and crystalization and then by periods of decline. All creative elites sooner or later lose the very qualities of excellence that raised them to the role of leaders in the first place. With the slow loss of these creative qualities a period of breakdown and decadence sets in.

The history of any society is thus the history of its ruling elite. A nation's strength or weakness, its culture, its power of endurance, its prosperity, its decadence, depend in the first instance upon the character of its ruling elite. In order to be able to study a nation, to predict what will happen to it, we must first of all and primarily study the nature of its ruling elite. Political history and political science should be predominantly the history and "science" of ruling elites, their origin, development, composition, structure and changes. The greatest historical movements only attain historical significance when they alter major institutions and result in shifts in the character and composition of the ruling elite. The theory of the ruling elite in this way provides a principle with the help of which the innumerable and otherwise amorphous and chaotic facts of political life can be systematically assembled and made more intelligible.

According to Mosca a primary and universal fact of social existence is the existence of what he calls two "political classes", a ruling class—always a minority—and the ruled. This is among the constant facts and tendencies to be found in all political organisms. In all societies two classes of people appear, a class that rules and a class that is ruled. "The first class, always the less numerous, performs all political functions, monopolizes power and enjoys the advantages that power brings, whereas the second, the more numerous class, is directed and controlled by the first, in a manner that is now more or less legal, now more or less arbitrary and violent, and supplies the first, in appearance at least, with material means of subsistence and with the instrumentalities that are essential to the vitality of the political organism."[1] The existence of this minority ruling class holds no matter what social and political forms prevail—whether the society is feudal or capitalist, slave or collectivist, monarchical or oligarchical or democratic, no matter what the constitutions and laws, no matter what the professions and beliefs.

The ferment that goes on within the body of every society is produced by the struggles for pre-eminence within it. In every society there is a competition between individuals of every social unit for its higher positions, wealth and authority and for control of the means and instruments that enable a person to direct as many human activities and as many human wills as fall within the range of his operations. To rise in the social scale certain qualities are useful and required. Deep wisdom, altruism, readiness for self-sacrifice, goodness and extreme sensitiveness are not among these qualities, but on the contrary, are usually hindrances. The prime requisite for success is hard work; the requisite next in importance is ambition, a firm resolve to get on in the world, to outstrip one's fellows without any moral compunction or restraint. If one is to govern men, more useful than a sense of justice—and much more useful than altruism, or even than extent of knowledge or broadness of view— are "perspicacity, a ready intuition of individual and mass psychology, strength of will and especially confidence in oneself".[2] Another means for entering the ruling class is to be born into it; and a little of what is commonly called luck does not come amiss either. Thus a capacity for hard work, ambition and a certain callousness, luck in birth and circumstances, all help toward membership in any ruling class at all times in history.

In addition to the qualities that have been mentioned, there is another group of qualities that are variable and dependent upon the particular society in question. "Members of a ruling minority regularly have some attribute, real or apparent, which is highly esteemed and very influential in the society in which they live."[3] To give simple examples: in a society which lives primarily by fishing, the expert fisherman has an advantage;

the skilled warrior in a predominantly military society; the able priest in a religious group—and so on. Considered as keys to ruling, such qualities as these are variable; if the conditions of life change, they change. For when religion declines the priest is no longer so important, or when a military society gives way to an industrial society, the warrior drops in the social scale. Thus changes in the general conditions of life are correlated with far-reaching changes in the components of the ruling class.

The various sections of the ruling class, moreover, express or represent or control or lead what Mosca calls "social forces" which are continually varying in number and importance. By "social force" Mosca means any human activity which has significant social and political influence. In primitive societies the chief forces are ordinarily war and religion. "As civilization grows, the number of the moral and material influences which are capable of becoming social forces increases. For example, property in money, as the fruit of industry and commerce, comes into being alongside of real property. Education progresses. Occupations based on scientific knowledge gain in importance."[4] All of these—war, religion, land, labor, education, science, technological skill—can function as social forces if society is organized in terms of them. Thus a given ruling class rules over a given society precisely because it is able to control the major social forces that are active within that society. If a social force—war, let us say—declines in importance, then the section of the ruling class whose position was based upon its military prowess likewise, over a period of time, declines. If the entire ruling class had been based primarily upon war then the entire ruling class would either adapt itself to the new conditions and change its character or if it could not adapt, it would be overthrown. Similarly, if a new major social force develops—commerce for example, in a previously agricultural society, or applied science—then either the existing ruling class proves itself flexible enough to gain leadership over this new force by absorbing in part new members into its ranks or if it does not, the leadership of the new force grows up outside of the old ruling class and begins to challenge it for supreme social and political power. Hence, the growth of new social forces and the decline of old forces is in general correlated with the constant process of change, dislocation and dissolution in the ruling class.

What we see during such a period is that when there is a shift in the balance of political and social forces, then the manner in which the ruling class itself is constituted changes also. A need is then felt that new capacities different from the old should assert themselves in the management of the state. It is indeed possible to say that the whole history of civilized mankind comes down to a conflict between the tendency of dominant elements to monopolize political power and transmit possession of it by inheritance, and a tendency toward a dislocation of old forces and an insurgence of new forces; and "this conflict produces an unending ferment of endosmosis and exosmosis between the upper class and certain portions of the lower."[5] Ruling classes decline inevitably when they cease to find scope for the capacities through which they rose to power, when they can no longer render the services they once rendered, or when the talents and the services they render lose in importance in the social environment in which they live. When this occurs there comes a period of renovation or revolution during which individual energies have free play and certain individuals "more passionate, more energetic, more intrepid or merely shrewder than others"[6] force their way from the bottom of the social ladder to the topmost rungs.

In Pareto's analysis individuals are not intellectually, morally or physically equal and society is not homogeneous. On the contrary it is composed of a host of numerous social groups, mixing in innumerable ways. In any particular grouping, however, some people are more capable than the others. Those who are most capable in their particular branch of activity, whether it be playing chess or playing the prostitute, stealing or defending criminals in court, writing, philosophy or governing the country, are the "select" persons of their particular group: the elite. Society is therefore divided into elite and non-elite, into a superior stratum and a lower stratum. The elite in turn can be divided into two groups; those who "directly and indirectly" play some considerable part in governing and who are referred to as the "governing elite" or "governing class" and the rest of the elite not in government: the non-governing elite. In terms of this division, there are a few at the top, considerably more in the middle, and the overwhelming majority grouped at the bottom. The elite is thus always a minority, and an oligarchy even where universal suffrage prevails always governs.

The elite in any society is never static. Its structure, its composition and the way in which it is connected with the rest of the society is always changing. An elite changes through the death of its members, though this is of no great significance. What influences social development is not the mere replacement or shift of individuals but change in the types of individuals who are recruited. If in the selection of members of the elite there existed a kind of condition of perfect competition, so that each individual could, without any obstacle, rise just as high in the social scale as his talents and ambitions permitted, the elite could be presumed to include, at every moment and in the right order, just those persons best fitted for membership. Under such circumstances, which Pareto seemed to view after the analogy of the theoretical market of free competition or the biological arena of the struggle for survival, society would remain dynamic, creative and strong, automatically correcting its own weaknesses.

However, this kind of equilibrium is never found in reality. There are always obstacles or "ties" that interfere with what Pareto calls the free "circulation of elites" or of individuals up and down the social scale. Special principles of selection, different in different societies, affect the compostion of the elite so that it no longer includes all those persons best fitted for social rule. Weakness and degeneration set in. The "aristocratic principle" helps to place the children of the members of the elite in positions within the elite for which they are not suited. If this principle is carried far enough the elite becomes "closed" or almost so and degeneration encroaches. The percentage of weak and infirm persons within the elite increases, while at the same time superior persons accumulate among the non-elite. When all these weaknesses are not compensated, a point is sooner or later reached where the elite will be overthrown and destroyed. A healthy society thus requires a relatively free circulation of the elites. Conversely, it follows that when in a society the elite becomes closed or nearly closed, the society is threatened either with internal revolution or with destruction from the outside. The revolution then, merely supplants the old governing class by a new one. Thereafter this new class is slowly transformed. "The governing elite . . . flows like a river. Every so often . . . the river floods and breaks its banks. Then, afterwards, the new governing elite resumes again the slow process of transformation. The river returns to its bed and once more flows evenly on."[7] This cycle of rise and decay is ineluctable and necessary. It is one of the uniformities of human history.

Elites, according to Pareto, are formed by what he calls residues, that is, by instincts or sentiments or states of mind which are constant throughout history and condition their social behavior and action. Pareto discerned a number of important residues, most of which he finally subsumed under two classes which afford the key to the explanation of society including elite domination and elite replacement. Individuals marked by Class I residues—"the instinct of combinations"—are the Foxes of Machiavelli. They live in the present and take little thought of the future. They are always ready for change, novelty and adventure. They live by their wits; and put their reliance on fraud and deceit, shrewdness and compromise. In economic affairs they incline toward speculation, promotion, innovation. They are not adept as a rule, in the use of force. They are innovative and chance taking. The individual comes markedly to prevail over the family, the community and the nation. Individuals marked by Class II residues—those of "the persistence of aggregates"— are Machiavelli's Lions. They are able and ready to use force, relying on it rather than on brains to solve their problems. They resist innovation and seek to preserve old forms and traditions. They are aggressive and authoritarian and contemptuous of maneuver, pursuasion and compromise. In economic affairs they are cautious, frugal and orthodox. They give rise to ideals which are embodied in religions, whether supernatural or secular, among the last being such religions as nationalism, socialism and imperialism. Their goals are set for a distant future. They are concerned for posterity and the future and are ready to subordinate the individual's interests to both of these.

What is crucially important in every society is the distribution of the residues of their corresponding instincts. Elites are predominantly either Foxes or Lions and the two sets of qualities are mutually exclusive. Politics, however, requires both the Lion and the Fox—it is partly a matter of force and partly one of persuasion, meaning in Pareto's view, gaining the consent of the governed by cunning. The style of governing at any time will depend on whether the elite is composed predominantly of those with Class I or those with Class II residues. The non-elite are overwhelmingly Class II in character—stolid, unimaginative, lacking in individuality but also with strong attachments to political ideals which satisfy their need for stable commitments. Hence the appeal of religion, from Christianity to nationalism, imperialism and socialism.

Foxes govern by attempting to gain consent. They devise ideologies to attract the masses, construct policies to meet immediate crises and satisfy the demand of the moment. They increase the wealth and prosperity of the society. The ideal politician is the political fixer or "wheeler-dealer:" If the exercise of government consisted solely of astuteness, cunning and artful devices then the foxes would be very long enduring and would come to an end only if that group destroyed itself through senile degeneration of the breed. But the foxes are not however ready to use force to solve political problems. A misplaced humanitarianism leads to compromise and pacifism which fatally weakens the regime when the ultimate manoeuver has failed to deceive the elite's more tough minded opponents. This produces an unstable equilibrium and revolutions ensue like that of Protestantism against the governing class of the Renaissance and of the French people against its rulers in 1789.

The Lions' manner of governing represents the opposite pole in political styles. The pursuit of consensus is abandoned in favor of the use of force. Opposition may be ruthlessly suppressed. Public order rather than private satisfaction becomes a chief end of government. Such elites are, however, far from lacking in ideals. Violence, including the overthrow of a previous "Class I elite" may be employed to defend religion and morality against "materialism", "atheism" or corruption. Yet this elite too ultimately loses its power. There seem to be two reasons for this. The first is external pressure. States which are governed by the Class II residue type of governing class, after a brief burst of energy and prosperity due to the replacement of an effete elite by a new upthrusting and bustling one, become petrified. That is to say they become hidebound, bureaucratic and unadaptable,[8] like Sparta or Byzantium. Other things being equal, a state of this kind is no match for a state in which the masses, rich in their Class II residues are yet led by the imaginative, unscrupulous and highly adaptable Class I residue type of governing class. This to Pareto's mind was why the Thebans were able to beat the Spartans and why the Entente Powers were able to defeat the hidebound and overweening Germans and Austrians in the 1914-18 war. The other reason is internal. Class II governing classes do not possess the talent and moneymaking skills which societies require. Thus, very often, they readily accept those who are well endowed with these skills and devote themselves to economic and financial pursuits because usually these persons are great producers of wealth and so increase the wealth of the governing class. The immediate consequence of their accession to power is therefore advantageous to many people and they strengthen the governing class. Then, little by little, they act like the woodworm, impoverishing the governing class of those elements in it who are well endowed with Class II residues and are capable of using force. So the "speculators" in France fast brought about the triumph of the absolute monarchy and then its ruin. So too nowadays in certain countries they have helped on the victory of the so-called democratic (better described as demagogic plutocratic) regime and are now preparing its ruin.[9]

Failing to achieve a balance of the ideal of lion and fox—which was also Machiavelli's ideal—the balance swings in history from one elite type to another and all governing classes are sooner or later condemned to decay and degeneration.

Guido Dorso, a follower of Mosca, sees society as divided into three groups: the ruling class, the political class and the ruled class. The ruling class in its widest connotation means the organized power structure which enjoys the political, intellectual and material leadership of the society. The concept also includes the class that is narrowly termed the "political class." The political class is that segment of the ruling class strictly dedicated to political tasks. This segment constitutes a sort of board of directors of the ruling class. In an agrarian society, for example, the great landlord belongs to the ruling class but as long as he remains on his property he does not belong to the political class. Yet a popular representative in any public office belongs to the ruling and political class at the same time. The ruling and subject classes too are connected by many relationships and linkages. A continuous process of exchanges takes place between them in the modern world. Access to the ruling class takes place by cooption, by the rise of the most active elements from below into the ruling class and it is always rejuvenated when new elites have joined it and when old elites of the ruling class "are peeled off and plunged into the masses."

The ruling class then is the mirror of the nation, it contains in germ all the characteristics of the race. The continued exchange of social cells secures in the least imperfect manner possible a certain correspondence between the nation and the ruling class. It is thus the veritable duty of the ruling class to direct the collective welfare and not just its "personal and particular affairs and interests."[10]

Although oligarchies, because of the flaws of human nature, constitute the skeleton of the entire social structure, rule politics, the economy and even humanistic culture, they can only be supported as long as they "express the interests of the community, contribute to the collective welfare and fulfill a social function."[11]   Naturally, membership in these oligarchies confers material and moral benefits that are often envied by the masses. But these benefits Dorso believes are the reward for burdensome and difficult functions which the masses are not capable of exercising directly and which must therefore be delegated to the men at the pinnacle of society. This condition engenders inevitable conflicts and when these appear in an acute form it is an indication that the ruling class has become involved with its own private interests, is jeopardizing the interests of the country and obstructing its free development. Then, privilege, always the basis of the social status of the ruling class, shows its true colors and its lack of justification. The disequilibrium resulting from meaningless privilege can only be overcome by destroying the privilege itself and demoting the ruling class.

Revolutions, in general, have as a consequence resulted when an energetic populace is subjected to domination by a privileged oligarchy which fails to open its ranks to able elements in the masses. A decadent ruling class is one which has failed to renew itself by coopting the "free formations of the ruled class" and which has fallen into a "legalism that is slowly transformed into a tissue of privileges." This results in the formation of an alienated counter-elite outside the system which awaits the opportunity to seize political power and in this way renovate the society.

The relations between the ruling and political classes is of the same nature as the relations between the ruling and ruled classes. In fact "the political class is recruited from within the ruling class and constitutes one of its specialized subdivisions."[12]   A continual and delicate process of exchange takes place between them. The selection of the political class involves the selection of people who are to influence most directly and intensely the progress of the community by means of state action. The selection of the political class is therefore of primary importance to the ruling class. Through its actions and policies the interests of the ruling class are either advanced or harmed; crises involving the very existence of the ruling class are either resolved or provoked; and the very process of selecting the ruling class is either facilitated or dangerously damaged. When a political class begins to harm the collectivity it is the responsibility of the ruling class to intervene quickly and change the political class. If the ruling class does not respond in the appropriate manner then this means that the corruption of the political class extends to the the ruling class as a whole and what is demanded for the health of the body politic is a change in the entire ruling class. If, despite the normal functioning of the circulation of elites from the masses to the ruling and political class, a defective political class still continues to remain in power, then the "entire society is obviously sick and has entered a period of decadence."[13] Another sign of decadence is when the ruling class begins to aspire to nonpartisanship and political quietism, when much of it wearily dreams of an impossible end to the eternal struggle. When this happens its composition begins to grow defective and its ideas no longer suit the circumstances. Emphasizing the autonomy of the political sphere he contends that a serious crisis usually begins in the strictly political stratum, spreading from there into the society and finally infecting the entire social structure. The decadence of a society is thus intimately linked to the decadence of the ruling class and only a great and vigorous people can produce a great and vigorous ruling class.

In Collingwood's analysis, political life is the characteristic of a body politic. This body politic is a non-social community which by a dialectic process also present in the family, changes into a society. At a relatively early stage in this process the body politic is a mixed community consisting of a social nucleus and a non-social circumnuclear body. The first are called the rulers and the second the ruled. This first class is called a society and rules itself. The first class consists of "persons" or "agents" possessed of free will. It also rules the second class which is a community only because it is ruled and whose members are devoid of free will. The first class is the council of the body politic and the second its nursery. The body politic as consisting of council and nursery has to provide for the recruitment of each. It therefore recruits the council by promoting from the nursery and it recruits the nursery by breeding babies.

The political society is thus a permanent society. The council or "state" or "sovereign" is a permanent society because its work is never done. In a body politic new babies are always being born, the nursery is always being replenished and the work of imposing order upon it is never concluded. Equally, the work of establishing relations between it and the council is never concluded, nor the work of ordering the council itself, for that too is being constantly recruited. These three problems—the problem of determining a way of life for the council, of determining a way of life for the nursery, and of determining the relation between the two—all have to be resolved by the council, the ruling class, and are the main part of what is called the constitutional problem. And because the composition of a body politic is always changing the constitutional problem can never be solved once and for all; there must always be a "state" ready to solve it. "The state therefore is a permanent society."[14] The simplest analysis of a body politic, then, rests on the fact that any body politic consists in part of rulers and in part of ruled. This again rests on the fact that it includes some members who, having reached the necessary point in mental development, have a will; and others who, not having reached that point, have none. Will however depends on freedom and freedom is a matter of degree. Those who are capable of free action are the rulers, are fit to rule, and those who have not are the ruled. Where the strains are greater, greater strength of will is needed to resist them and to make a free decision. The ruling class may therefore be subdivided into a multiplicity of graded subclasses demanding as their qualification for membership strength of will in different degrees. The highest subclass will consist of those members who are able to resist the severest emotional strains and make a free decision about the hardest political problems in the hardest political circumstances. Lower subclasses will find places for persons who can only solve easier problems or solve them in easier circumstances. Thus "the ruling class as a whole becomes a hierarchy of ruling subclasses, differently endowed with strength of will."[15]

Collingwood then arrives at what he calls the Three Laws of Politics. The First Law of Politics is that a body politic is divided into a ruling class and a ruled class. The second is that the barrier between the two classes is permeable in an upward sense. That is, members of the ruled class must be susceptible of promotion into the ruling class. For the ruling class must not be allowed to die out; it always has work to do and must always be fit to do it; for it constitutes a permanent society. All rulers must therefore have some quality which makes them fit to be rulers. They must possess the quality of rule-worthiness and this quality will differ with circumstance and the characteristics of the ruled. The Third Rule of Politics states that there is a correspondence between the ruler and the ruled, whereby the former becomes adapted to ruling these as distinct from other persons and the latter to being ruled by these as distinct from other persons. Working directly, or from the ruling class downwards, the ruler sets the fashion and the ruled fall in with his lead. But it also works inversely, from the ruled class upwards and determines that whosoever is to rule a certain people must rule them in a way in which they let themselves be ruled. Thus vigorous rulers teach the ruled to cooperate with them and to develop under their tuition a vigorous political life, a similarity in political enterprise and resource like their own. In this way that portion of the ruled class which is more closely in contact with the ruling class receive a training for political action which enables them, in time, to succeed their rulers. Let the rulers, however, be of a slavish sort and "what will percolate is slavishness"[16] and the mere blind unpolitical stupidity of the ruled will impose limits on what their rulers can do with them.

Although Collingwood stressed that politics contains an indispensable element of force and fraud he also emphasized that it should be "dialectical." A distinctive political process is one based on discussion and one which aims at agreement rather than victory. It tries to achieve harmonious. cooperation between contradictory principles, theoretical and practical at once (democracy and aristocracy for example). The dialectic of internal politics "is the conversion of a ruled class into collaboration in the act of ruling: the percolation of freedom throughout the body politic."[17] And the dialectic of external politics is the process whereby problems arising out of relations between different bodies politic, about which they do not agree at first, "are converted from matters of non-agreement into matters of agreement."[18] The process leading to agreement begins not from disagreement but from non-agreement. However, in the event that non-agreement hardens into disagreement the stage is set for an *eristic* in which each party tries to vanquish the other.

According to C. Wright Mills the "power elite" is composed of men whose positions enable them to transcend the ordinary environments of ordinary men and women. They are in a position "to make decisions having major consequences . . . in command of the major hierarchies and organizations of major society."[19] The elite is thus defined more in terms of its potential power than the actual exercise of power. The power attached to elite positions may not in fact be used by their occupants. They may, instead, allow events to take their own course, let matters drift and history be made "behind men's backs."[20] But at the core of his analysis is his belief that within the dominant positions of modern American society the means for exercising power are more narrowly concentrated into a few hands than at any previous time in history. This power enables the elite "to make history"—it enables one person or one group to change the course of large numbers of persons' activities in a significant way. The major policy decisions of the American government in the last generation—the bombing of Hiroshima and the commitment to the Korean War are instances of this power of decision—illustrate the enormous centralization of the means of decision-making in the hands of a very few institutional office holders. The history-making power of this elite is thus sufficient to overturn the status quo, call into question the existing social relationships and establish new structures. The inner core of the elite is able, potentially, to determine the role both it and others will play in society.

Major power in American society, as Mills sees it, now resides in the economic, the political and the military domains. Within each of the big three, the typical institutional unit has become enlarged, has become administrative and "in the power of its decisions, has become centralized."[21] The economy—once a great scatter of small productive units in autonomous balance—has become dominated by two or three hundred giant corporations, administratively and politically interrelated, which together hold the key to economic decisions. The political order, once a decentralized set of several dozen states has become a centralized, executive establishment which has taken unto itself many powers previously dispersed and now enters into every cranny of the social structure. The military, once a slim establishment in a context of distrust fed by state militia, has become the largest and most expensive feature of government. Not only have all these domains become enlarged and centralized but there is "an ever-increasing interlocking of economic, military and political structures."[22] The decisions of the military establishment rest upon and affect political as well as economic activity. The decisions made within the political domain determine economic activities and military programs. The political economy is linked, in myriad ways, with military institutions and decisions and while the government intervenes in the corporate economy the corporate economy intervenes in the governmental process. In the structural sense, "this triangle of power is the source of the interlocking directorate that is most important for the historical structure of the present."[23]

The power elite for Mills is thus composed of the men who hold the leading positions in the strategic structures. It consists of those "higher circles" which operate at the pinnacle of each of these three enlarged and centralized domains. At the top of the economy, among the corporate rich, there are the chief executives; at the top of the political order, the members of the political directorate; at the top of the military establishment the elite soldier-statesmen clustered in and around the Joint Chiefs of Staff and the upper echelons. The higher circles in and around the command posts have the most of what there is to have—money, power and prestige—not because of their personal or class attributes but because of their positions in the great institutions. Power in modern society has become institutionalized. Institutions are the necessary bases of power, wealth and prestige. The men of power are powerful because they have command of major institutions. Although not all power is anchored in and exercised by means of such institutions it is only "within and through them" that power "can be more or less continuous and important."[24]

The cohesiveness of this power elite is in large part determined, in this analysis, by the closeness of the many interconnections and point of coinciding interest and tend "to form a coherent kind of grouping."[25] There is contact between the leaders of the different hierarchies. Such contact may range from conscious conspiracy to a mere consensus amongst the leaders as to policies and values. This "institutional proximity" is at its strongest where individuals "interchange commanding roles at the top of one institutional order with those in another."[26] Thus presidents and directors of large business corporations have taken up major posts in the government and have then returned to business or the great foundations. Thus too, one man might move between the military and industrial circles, another might move between the military and political domains, while a third might move between the worlds of politics and of opinion-making. The inner core of the elite also includes men of the higher legal and financial types from the great law factories and industrial firms who are almost professional go-betweens of economic, political and military affairs who act to unify the power elite and who, by the nature of their work, are able to transcend the narrower milieu of any one industry and can speak and act for the corporate world as a whole. The corporation lawyer who serves as a key link between the economic, military and political areas, the executive who becomes a general, the general who becomes a statesman, the statesman who becomes a banker all lace the various milieux together and are the "core members of the power elite."[27]

The people of the higher circles are also members of a top social stratum, a set of groups whose members know one another, see one another socially and at business and so in making decisions take one another into account. The elite feel themselves to be, and are felt by others to be, the "inner circle of the upper social classes."[28] They therefore form a more or less compact social and psychological entity and have become self-conscious members of a social class. They are more or less aware of themselves as a social class and they behave toward one another differently from the way they behave toward members of other classes. They accept one another, understand one another, marry one another, tend to work and think if not together at least alike. They are involved in a set of overlapping "crowds" and intricately connected "cliques" and are mutually attracted to one another. Their members tend to have similar social origins and they maintain a network of informal connections and to some degree there is "an interchangeability of position between the various positions of money and power and celebrity."[29] The emergence of this power elite, Mills argues, has had far-reaching effects on the society. It has exposed the liberal myth that freedom and democratic values are safeguarded in the U.S.A. by the existence of a plurality of elites competing for public support. At the middle levels of power there now prevails a semi-organized stalemate and at the bottom level there has come into being a mass-like society which has little resemblance to the image of society in which voluntary associations and classic publics hold the keys to power. The top of the American system of power is now much more unified and much more powerful, the bottom is much more fragmented and in truth, impotent, than is generally supposed by those who are distracted by the middling units of power which neither express such will as exists at the bottom nor determine the decisions at the top.

The elitist theorists whom we have discussed have made some of the most important contributions to modern political theory. They have shown that all societies are characterized by a struggle for social power in all its diverse, open and concealed forms. By discovering—or rediscovering (Plato, Aristotle and Machiavelli had been aware of the vital importance of elites, even if they did not use the precise term)—the crucial importance of elites in any body politic, by emphasizing that every society is ruled by an elite of one kind or another, by stressing that the primary object of every ruling elite or ruling class is to maintain its own power and privileges, they have focused attention on the real character of politics and political regimes and not on their mere formal attributes. Different regimes are to be distinguished by the mode in which elites are selected and replenished, by their quality and social composition, and by the openness to permeation from below of the various ruled and subordinate classes. Not constitutional forms but the men who make them work are the key considerations for a critical political science.

Another important contribution that this school of theorists has made has been its emphasis on the vital importance of leadership for every society. The quality of the society is determined by the quality of its leadership, that is, of its elite. To lead and to rule requires special attributes. It means to decide, to command, to prevail, to advance. The art of politics is therefore the art of ruling. An elite driven by an inordinate greed for money-making will provide a different style of leadership from one that is motivated by a sense of honor and public service, or by ideals of excellence. The charismatic ruler, in Weber's sense of that much abused term, will differ from the traditional or bureaucratic ruler. Although every form of rule is marked by the struggle for power, by ambition, by force, cunning and fraud, it must, to be effective, also be shaped by an overriding concern for the society it is ruling. A creative and effective ruling elite will know how to serve the public interest, how to integrate and conciliate the diverse and antagonistic groups into which every society is divided into a coherent community and how to teach a whole manner of life to that community. To rule is to command but it is also to persuade, to impose one's will but also to arouse respect and trust, to exercise power but also to teach.

The ruling elite is not a conspiratorial group. It never constitutes a common will to action. Every ruling elite is divided into a number of sub-elites and can never attain either complete unity of thought or action. All sorts of interest conflicts will divide the different sub-elites—political, economic, military and intellectual—and set one group in contention with another. The different sub-elites will view the common interests of the ruling elite in a different light and from a different angle of vision and interest. Every ruling elite, even what has been called the totalitarian ruling class, is thus split, in one form or another, into diverse groupings. In a democracy the political elite is divided between the governing party and opposition party or parties. What is crucial, however, is that despite these differences and divisions a ruling elite with common interests and common bonds does exist and it exists precisely because it is capable, as against the ruled, of transcending these differences and cleavages when its vital interests as a ruling elite are challenged. When a ruling elite can no longer function as a more or less united, coherent and self-conscious grouping in the event of a practical collision in which the elite itself is endangered, or when it begins to split into irreconcilable factions, or when irreparable divisions appear within its ranks, then one of the elements of a revolutionary situation is already present, as Lenin well understood.

The history of all societies is the history of the rise, decay and fall of elites. A new historical epoch is inaugurated when a new elite with new ambitions, energies, skills and capacities assumes the leadership of society. This new elite has in the first place to possess "extraordinary qualities" that provide it with unique powers. A charismatic elite is thus capable of attracting and dominating its followers because it breaks with the rules of everyday thought and action which have lost their validity and legitimacy.[30] In its pure and authentic form charisma is a kind of spiritual energy, a creative eruption, which is capable of struggling against the entrenched and decayed conditions of the traditional and bureaucratic order and which supplies the measure of faith and energy requisite to break out from the confines of the everyday world and to impart a new direction to its otherwise exhausted flow. Charismatic elites break precedents and create new ones. From them come the impulsions that decide the fate and nature of a social order. In the second place, a new elite, contrary to Pareto's analysis, is capable for a time of uniting within itself the qualities of the Fox and the Lion. It is an elite which is innovative and chance-taking, knows how to obtain consent and at the same time is ready to use force when necessary and to establish new traditions and myths. And in the third place it must be an elite which, according to Mosca, is capable of utilizing the new social forces that society has unleashed and controlling and exploiting them in its members' interests.

The key element in every ruling elite is, however, the political class. Politics as the "master science" has the supreme task of managing the social conflicts and tensions that are inherent in every society. The qualities and skills of the political class therefore determine the manner in which a society's resources are utilized and allocated, and the way the ruling elite determines its relations to the mass of the people. The political class is the business manager for the ruling elite. It is the governor of the country. In its role as manager for the ruling class as a whole it has the responsibility for advancing the general welfare. An effective political class will listen to the non-elite groups so as to conciliate them as far as possible, give them a legal position and a sense of security, provide them with some clear, and reasonably safe means for articulating their interests and needs, and maintain order. Responsive and elastic it will adjust and adapt itself to all the continuous changes which every society is always subject to. Adopting a flexible posture it will open its ranks to the most active elements from the masses and coopt those most suitable for governing. By means of this continuous process of exchange of social cells it will keep itself fit and vital for the tasks of ruling and make possible in the least imperfect manner a certain correspondence between the nation and the ruling elite. Practicing a form of dialectical politics it will aim to achieve harmonious cooperation between contradictory principles and interests and convert the ruled class into a collaborator of the ruling elite. The political class is thus the mirror of the society; it contains in germ all the characteristics of that society. A mediocre ruling class cannot therefore produce a great political class and the character and qualities of the political elite reflect the character and qualities of the ruling elite as a whole.

However, all these "ideal" qualities are by their very nature ephemeral and transitory. They are all subject to change and decay. No social or political structure is permanent and no static Utopia is possible. All ruling elites sooner or later, and in no fixed or sequential order, begin to lose the superior qualities that brought them to power in the first place. Power corrupts, deranges and exhausts them. With mastery comes narrowness. Charisma is routinized and the blight of bureaucratic conservatism and stupidity spreads. The ruling elite ceases to serve and lead the society and substitutes its own narrow private privileges and interests for the interests of the community. It is incapable of renewing itself. Blinded by passion and ideology it loses contact with social realities and conditions and no longer controls or comprehends the major social forces at work in the society. Become hidebound, bureaucratic and unadaptable, it recruits degenerate and corrupt elements into its ranks and simply loses the will and ability for governing. The forces of integration give way to the forces of disintegration, great inequalities of power and wealth appear, and the majority of the people begin to lose confidence and trust in their rulers. The elite itself is fractured and disoriented. The bonds of consensus and legitimacy begin to fray. Naked force replaces consensus and attraction. When all these conditions coalesce there occurs a very rapid shift in the composition and structure of the elite: that is, a social revolution; or, if no counter-elite arises to power, the society slides into a process of decay and degeneration. Neither revolution nor social decay is therefore an unfortunate accident that can be readily avoided. This cycle of rise, decay and fall is inevitable and necessary in every social and historical formation.

CHAPTER 4

ON IDEOLOGY

Another important factor that disfigures social existence is ideology. It is our contention that all human knowledge and all political and social thought is tinged with an ideological taint. It all pretends to be more true than it is. All social, political and philosophical knowledge is finite knowledge, conditioned by social circumstances, gained from a particular perspective and stained by self-interest and class-interest. The intellect is a weapon in the struggle for existence and power and is not a manifestation of "pure" reason. Human selfishness and passions use ideas for their own ends. The human mind is a very weak instrument and is easily enslaved and prostituted by material interests and the affections. Even the more objective social and philosophical speculations and insights are only approximations of the truth and can only be arrived at by the solitary thinker, removed from the passions and conflicts of the outside world. All social research, whether pure or applied, of necessity rests on certain value assumptions and can neither be value-free nor neutral. It is of course true that every ideology has a starting point and foothold in reality but at the same time it carries with it a baggage of falsehoods and mystifications. Ideological thinking may contain real concepts, scientific insights, yet it must always be inextricably mixed up with rationalizations, apologetics, lies, deceptive representation and self-deception. Emergent truth is always coupled with illusion and error. And because all knowledge is tainted by ideology, error, illusion and falsity never stand off in sharp and obvious contrast from knowledge, truth and certainty. Every social order shaped by its own specific ideology, can thus only perceive the world through its distorted lenses, can never totally escape from the bondage of its basic assumptions, can only have a fragmentary and partial conception of reality, and is to a greater or lesser extent immersed in inauthenticity and contradiction.

The inevitability of ideological thinking stems from a number of causes rooted in the human condition. Contrary to the superstitions of rationalism human reason does not hold dominion over all human affairs. Plato anticipated this modern contention when he argued in the *Symposium* that philosophy originates in erotic passion. Aristotle declared in the *Nicomachean Ethics*: "Intellect itself, however, moves nothing." Roger Bacon saw the sources of human error in the "idols", "phantoms" or "preconceptions" of the tribe, of the cave, of the market and of the theater. The unapt formation of words constitutes a wondeful obstruction to the mind and society and tradition are obstacles in the path to true knowledge. "The human understanding," he wrote, "resembles not a dry light but admits a tincture of the will and passions, which generate their own system accordingly, for man believes more readily that which he prefers." For Hume, in sharp opposition to the illusions of rationalism; "Reason is, and ought only to be the slave of the passions, and can never pretend to any other office than to serve and obey them." From this conception he concluded: "And as reasoning is not the source, whence either disputant derives his tenets, it is in vain to expect that any logic which speaks not to the affections will ever engage him to embrace sounder principles." Accepting the notion that self-interest always rules judgment, Helvetius said: "What man . . . if with a scrupulous attention he searches all the recesses of the soul, will not perceive that his virtues and vices are wholly owing to different modifications of personal interest? . . . For after all interest is always obeyed; hence the injustice of all judgments." And William James put Hume's thought in a negative way: "Reason is one of the feeblest of nature's forces, if you take it at only one spot and moment. . . . Appealing to reason as we do, we are in a sort of forlorn-hope situation, like a small sandbank in the midst of a hungry sea ready to wash it out of existence."

Reason far from pursuing its own inherent impulses is, following from this analysis, rather driven toward its goal by the irrational forces the ends of which it serves. Insofar as reason rules it only does so owing to the irrational forces which push for this extension of its rule. Reason is like a light which by its own inner course can move nowhere. It must be pushed in order to move. It is propelled by the irrational forces of will, passion and interest to where these forces want it to move, in disregard of what the inner logic of abstract reason would demand. To trust in pure and simple reason is to leave the field wide open to the stronger, irrational forces which reason serves. Although man is driven by will, passion and emotional impulses and dominated by interests, as well as motivated by reason, he likes to see himself primarily in the light of the latter, more appealing human quality. It is because of this that he gives his irrational qualities the earmarks of reason. Ideology is the result of this process of rationalization. But the triumph of reason, or what passes for it, is in truth, the triumph of the irrational forces which succeed in using the processes of reason to satisfy themselves. All experience teaches us that it is never for the lack of the right reason or doctrine that men hate and fight, deceive and subjugate one another.

Human reason, then, plays only a small part in human affairs. It is man's will, passions and struggle for power that principally affect the course of events. The will and the affections are ascendant over man's capacity for reason. According to Schopenhauer, man's intellect is a function of his will; the intellect is above all an instrument in the struggle for existence; the prejudices of estates, classes, nations and religions determine and falsify our judgments; and in the struggle with men and nature the intellect rationalizes man's instincts and interests. For Nietzsche all thought is ideological; history is a masquerade in which men drape their real biological drives and goals in idealist costume; the unconscious function of thought is to serve the life-process and the will to power; and the real Being of the world remains irreducible to discursive reasoning. Even for Max Weber: "Not ideas, but material and ideal interests directly govern men's conduct," and passion, material striving and ideation are basic features of the human condition. One of Freud's most important contributions was his understanding that man was not the master in the home of his own mind; that he was motivated by unconscious drives beyond his comprehension and control; and that one of the defense mechanisms that man employs in the conflict between the variety of mental forces that beset him is that of rationalization. By means of defense mechanisms man can either accept reality or escape from reality, postpone the gratification of instincts or avoid human relations entirely. It is these defenses which keep us ignorant of our motives and feelings. And through rationalization man provides false explanations that have a plausible ring of rationality for his behavior, and dresses in the cloak of a more acceptable motive those impulses which he unconsciously finds unacceptable to his self-image.[1]

Mannheim's *Sociology of Knowledge* is based upon the premise that all the social sciences and metaphysics are ideologies and can only be understood by referring them to the "social context," to the "historical reality," of which they are expressions. Each group occupying a definite historical situation, has its own manner of conceiving the world. There are consequently as many perspectives as there are points of view, as many partial truths as there are classes. Sentiments and desire guide and distort the work of the social scientist and these psychological factors are often the expression of a social situation, that is, of a social class. All human interest groups, particularly political parties, hide their real interests by more or less conscious deceptions and disguises and the task of the study of ideologies is to unmask them. These deceptions "range all the way from conscious lies to half-conscious and unwitting disguises, from calculated attempts to dupe others to self-deception."[2] In his view, opinions, statements, propositions and systems should not be taken at face value but should be interpreted in the light of the life-situation of the one who expresses them. The specific character and life-situation of the subject influence his opinions, perceptions and interpretations. Ideas, therefore, are a function of the one who holds them and of his position and his social milieu.

Reinhold Niebuhr locates the ideological taint in all culture to the intellectual pride of man. Exactly analogous to the more brutal and obvious pride of power, the pride of intellect is derived on the one hand from ignorance of the finiteness of the human mind and on the other hand from an attempt to obscure the known, conditioned character of human knowledge and the taint of self-interest in human truth. Philosophers who imagine that they have stated final truths are clearly the victims of the ignorance of their ignorance. All pretentions of final knowledge and ultimate truth are partly prompted by the uneasy feeling that the truth is not final and also by an uneasy conscience which realizes that the interests of the ego are compounded with this truth. The will to power uses reason as kings use courtiers and chaplains, to add grace to their enterprise. The insinuation of the interests of the self into even the most ideal of enterprises and most universal objectives, envisaged in the moments of the highest rationality, makes hypocrisy an inevitable product of all virtuous endeavor. Man's reason is thus corrupt and is corrupted by his interests.[3]

According to Pareto, most human conduct is non-logical. Human beings simply do things without any purpose at all; it is natural for them to be active, whether or not there is any consciously understood point in the activity. Man acts first from his attitude or impulse and cogitates afterwards. The theory he elaborates as to why he is performing the action is ex post facto a logical veneer, or justification of the urge to act. It is a "rationalization" of the prior impulse or attitude. Most conduct which has a bearing on the social and political structure, on what he calls "the social equilibrium," is above all the arena of the non-logical. What happens to society is only to a very slight degree influenced by the deliberate, rational purposes held by human beings. Men are influenced in every culture and at every period by taboos, magic, superstition, personified abstractions, myths, gods, empty verbalisms and vague, ambiguous or meaningless goals. The forms may change but the fundamentals remain. The entities with which they work, such as "liberty," or "equality", or "progress," are fictitious and imaginary and the reasoning with which the theories are elaborated are often shown to violate the rules of logic. Thus gods and goddesses like Athena or Janus or Ammon are replaced by new divinities such as Progress, Democracy, Socialism and even Science; hymns to Jupiter give way to invocations to the People; the magic of votes and electoral manipulations replaces the magic of spells and wands; and faith in the Historical Process supersedes the faith in the God of our Fathers. Rational, deliberate, conscious belief does not in fact determine what is going to happen to society; and social man is not as he has been defined for so many centuries a primarily "rational man". Men's socially decisive actions spring not from logical but from non-logical roots.

The various means of a verbal nature, the fictions and illusions by which individuals and groups lend an appearance of logic to what at bottom has none, Pareto called "derivations". A derivation, as he conceived it, is a theory or at least a closely related set of beliefs, that people accept regardless of its truth, because it serves to justify and to some extent even to direct their activities. It represents a group ideology and guides the actions of groups. This group ideology always contains a large measure of the false and the absurd. The actions which the ideology helps to guide spring from "instincts," "impulses," or "sentiments" that correspond to what he calls "residues". The actions that proceed from these instincts are for the most part non-logical. People who are sustained by these derivations do not share consistent and realistic purposes and do not come together to try to achieve them. Pareto rather thought of them as drawn to one another by their need to give effect to "instincts" of which they are unaware. Although he also admitted that from some instincts there arise rational activities—for example, science, from what he called the "instinct for combinations"—this did not in any way invalidate his basic belief that human behavior is more often than not non-logical. In the field of politics in particular men are persuaded, swayed, seduced and corrupted by words which have no precise meaning, and which exercise a kind of magical influence over individuals and crowds. The instinct for combinations also impels men to "system making"—that is, to elaborate logical or rather pseudo-logical combinations of ideas and mental elements in general, to theologies and metaphysics and ideologies of all sorts. It is that class of residue that chiefly accounts for derivations expressing man's need to make his own beliefs seem rational. All these "are manifestations of the human being's hunger for thinking . . . This is satisfied in a number of ways: by pseudo-logical arguments, by words which stir the emotions, by fatuous and inconsequential chatter."[4]

Pareto furthermore argues as we have noted that all societies are ruled by a governing class or rather a set of "elites" who among them make all the important decisions that the masses accept. Derivations, in this connection serve, among other things, to justify the established order in the eyes of the elite and the masses. That order is presented to the elite and the masses in the least precise of terms, or as promoting ends vaguely conceived, or as having aims that are not publicly admitted, or that are incompatible or unrealizable. It is presented differently to different elites and masses. There are moreover derivations that subvert the established order. There is the circulation of elites, some giving way to others or ruling elites being forced to give way through revolution to counter-elites. Some instincts are more active in some elites and even some masses than in others. Derivations vary not only with the instincts of the groups that accept them; they also vary with social and cultural conditions. Since derivations serve to maintain or subvert the established order rather than to promote the vague and largely unattainable aims they profess, the groups and classes that accept them always labor under illusion. They imagine that they are seriously engaged in pursuing those aims when in fact they are merely pursuing their own instincts and impulses, their own selfish goals and ambitions.[5]

Although Marxism has claimed that it is a science and not an ideology, a pretence which its subsequent history has completely destroyed, it has   nonetheless made an important contribution toward an understanding of the nature of ideologies. According to Marx men are the producers of their conceptions, ideas, moralities, metaphysics, etc. Yet these men are not representatives of some Hegelian World Spirit but "are real, active men, as they are conditioned by a definite development of their productive forces and of the intercourse corresponding to these, up to its furthest forms." Embedded in concrete "relations of production," involved in class division and class conflicts, different groups of men develop different ways of looking at the world. The different modes of thought which men articulate are the expressions of discrete social conditions. It is not consciousness that determines life but life that determines consciousness. However, the social consciousness generated by a given praxis faithfully reflects it only in specific circumstances: namely, when the praxis is not shrouded in mystical veils, when interhuman relations are direct and natural, without "opaque" intermediaries. Under the system of commodity production, in particular, commodities, representations of reality, appearances, are enveloped in a fog. While in analytical reflection the commodity is a pure and transparent form, in practical everyday experience the commodity is opaque and the cause of opaqueness; its very existence is strange, the more so because men are not aware of its strangeness; it is a social thing whose qualities are at the same time perceptible and imperceptible by the senses; and it is a very peculiar thing abounding in "metaphysical subtleties and theological whimsies."[6] The world of commodity production is characterized by alienation, mystification and reification.

Ideology in this approach is part of that general process of alienation by which the products of human activities assume a life of their own and rule over the men who produce them. The life which man has given to the objects sets itself against him as an alien and hostile force. Men are frustrated and estranged by the social order of their own making which they do not understand or control, and are the victims of their own illusions about that order and themselves. In other words, alienation is the process by which man forgets that the world he lives in has been produced by himself. The insistence on the autonomy of the state in German political theory was for Marx a case of mystification—similar, precisely, to the thought processes of religion. Mystification therefore occurs when imaginary entities obscure the real relationships of human activity and this has its roots in turn in reification. The idea of reification is a generalization which finds concrete application in the more familiar notion of the fetishism of commodities. The world of things produced by men not only dominates them in an external fashion. It actually shapes their conscious and unconscious spiritual activity. Men regard themselves and the relationships in which they are immersed as things. Human activity produces a world of things and nothing can be conceived of as real that does not have the character of a thing.

Ideology is then an inverted, mutilated, distorted reflection of reality. In ideologies men and their conditions appear upside down like images on the lens of a camera. This is similar to the physical process which accounts for the way images are reversed on the retina. In the representations to which various types of social praxis give rise individuals similarly grasp the reality "upside down" and this fact is part of reality. Consciousness is no more or less than individual consciousness, yet one law of consciousness orders that it must be perceived as a thing apart from the self. Human beings do not perceive themselves as they really are but instead as projected upon a screen. Man's relations with nature and with other men are marked by illusion. Ideologies by this account are reduced to false representations of history or to abstractions from history. Every ideology is consequently a collection of errors, illusions, mystifications, which can be accounted for by reference to the historical reality it distorts and transposes.

The starting point of all ideologies for Marx is reality, but a fragmentary, partial reality. The totality of reality always escapes the ideological consciousness because the conditions of this consciousness are limited and limiting and the actual historical process eludes the human will under such conditions of intervention. Ideologies refract rather than reflect reality via pre-existing representations, selected by the dominant group and acceptable to it. Ideologies though distorted and distorting, tend however, to constitute a self-sufficient whole and advance the claim to be such. Yet this whole is praxis and it is precisely this that ideologies pervert by constructing an abstract, unreal, fictitious theory of the whole. Though the degree of reality and unreality varies with the historical era, the class relations and other conditions which obtain at any given moment, ideologies operate essentially by extrapolating the reality they interpret and transpose. The theoretical, philosophical, political and juridical systems they create are all characterized by the fact that they lag behind the actual movement of history. At the same time, ideologies strive to achieve universality and make an effort at a certain breadth and rationality. This effort to achieve universality is only partially successful when the ideology serves as the instrument of the historical interests and goals of a rising class. For a time the ideology represents and advances the interests of society, but sooner or later the fatal gap between ideology and reality begins to appear and to widen and to impede and threaten the society it is supposed to serve.

Following from this analysis Marx argues that "the ideas of the ruling class are in every epoch the ruling ideas."[7] The class which is the dominant material force in society is at the same time "its dominant intellectual force". The class which has the means of material production at its disposal has control at the same time over its means of mental production. The dominant ideas are nothing more than the "ideal" expressions of the dominant material relationships, the dominant material relationships grasped as ideas, and thus the relationships which make one class the ruling class. Insofar as they rule as a class and determine and color the whole extent of an epoch, "they do this in their whole range and therefore among other things, they also rule as thinkers, as producers of ideas, and regulate the production and distribution of the ideas of their age." However, even in this regard, the division of labor manifests itself in the ruling class as the division of mental and material labor so that within this class one group appears as the thinkers of the class—its active conceptualizing ideologists, who make it their chief source of livelihood to develop and perfect the illusions of the class about itself—while the others have a more passive and receptive attitude to these ideas and illusions because they are in reality the active members of this class and have less time to make up ideas and illusions about themselves. This cleavage within the ruling class may even develop into a certain opposition and hostility between the two parts, but in the event of a practical collision in which the class itself is endangered, it disappears of its own accord and with it also the illusion that the ruling ideas were not the ideas of the ruling class and had a power distinct from the power of this class.

Ideologies consequently have two aspects. On the one hand they are general, speculative, abstract. On the other they are representative of determinate, limited special interests. On one level they set out to answer all questions, all problems; they create a comprehensive view of the world. On another level they reinforce the specific ways of life, behavior patterns and values of the society in which they function. Ideologies are thus ignorant of the exact nature of their relations with praxis. They do not really understand their own conditions and presuppositions, nor the actual consequences they are producing. They are ignorant of the implications of their own theories, they comprehend neither the causes of which they are effects nor the effects which they are actually causing. The real why and how escapes them. Involved in practice, at once the starting points and results of actions in the world, ideological representations invariably serve as instruments in the struggles between nations and classes. But their intervention in such struggles takes the form of masking the true interests and aspirations of the groups involved, universalizing the particular and mistaking the part for the whole.

Yet ideologies according to Marx are not altogether false. They contain illusions and lies on the one hand and myths and utopias on the other. They are rooted in reality and generate deception and self-deception. Sometimes the ideologies have served as the vehicle of sound thinking, sometimes as agents of its distortion or suppression. Class ideologies exalt the image of a class that they seek to uphold and defend and devalue the image of the classes they seek to drag down, defeat and despoil. Ideologies are instruments of persuasion, guide the individual and give him a sense of purpose. Viewed from the outside ideologies are self-contained rational systems; viewed from the inside they imply faith, conviction, adherence. Ideology seeks to obtain the consensus of the majority, if not a totality of the society's members; it seeks the assent even of the dominated. However, no historical situation can be stabilized once and for all though this is what ideologies aim at. All ideologies eventually ossify and produce counter-ideologies. Although an individual might seek fulfillment in ideology, in actual fact he cannot fulfill himself but can only lose himself and alienate himself. Including as it does interpretations of reality it yet acts as a brake on creation and progress. It is at once illusory and efficacious, fictitious and real. Linked to reality, ideology imposes rules and limitations on actual living men. Part of actual experience, it sooner or later becomes unreal and formal and reflects only a portion of human reality. Mediating between praxis and consciousness, ideology serves as a screen, as a barrier, as a break in consciousness. Ideology thus distorts reality, introduces error, illusion and mystification into all its mental creations and envelops every social group and every historical epoch with a "false consciousness."[8]

Even scientific thought which is not directly involved in and tainted by social struggles, passions and prejudices is not a consistent and tidy march of the mind. The growth of science has not been, according to Thomas Kuhn, a smooth and continuous process without abrupt jumps. It has on the contrary developed through a succession of phases each of which is separated by a radical break from the phase before and the phase after. Instead of scientific thought evolving in a smooth, gradual and continuous fashion it develops through a sequence of scientific revolutions. Though the passage of time and interaction between individual scientists impose some element of continuity on scientific thought it is in its most important respect not continuous at all. One need only look at the content of theory, at the fundamental principles and concepts dominating the thought of a given period—contrasting the styles and explanations in vogue, for example, among physicists during the second half of the eighteenth century and a hundred years later—to end up with a very different picture of the scientific enterprise. From this point of view, Kuhn claims, the history of physics as of other branches of science, is a series of intellectual revolutions. Aristotelean patterns of thought are displaced by Cartesian patterns, Cartesian patterns by Newtonian ones. Newtonian patterns are transformed almost out of recognition by Maxwell, only to be dismantled and replaced by the consequent theories of Einstein. At each transition point an intellectual convulsion transforms the whole landscape of the science in question, sweeping away the intellectual landmarks of the previous phase and imposing a new configuration on the whole field.

These scientific revolutions are made necessary by the fact that most scientific work is carried on within a framework of what he calls "normal science." This activity in which most scientists inevitably spend most of their time is predicated on the assumption that the scientific world knows what the world is like. Its research is a strenuous and devoted attempt to force nature into the conceptual boxes supplied by professional education. Normal science means research based upon one or more past scientific achievements, achievements that some particular scientific community acknowledges for a time as supplying the foundation for its further practice. These achievements are then recounted though seldom in their original form by science textbooks, elementary and advanced. It is thus no part of normal science to call forth new sorts of phenomena; indeed those that will not fit the box are often not seen at all. Nor do scientists normally aim to invent new theories and they are often intolerant of those invented by others. Normal research which is cumulative owes its success to the ability of scientists regularly to select problems that can be solved with conceptual and instrumental techniques close to those already in existence. The cumulative acquisition of unanticipated novelties proves to be an almost nonexistent exception to the rules of scientific development.

Scientific work is furthermore carried on on the basis of what Kuhn calls "shared paradigms". Closely related to normal science it implies that accepted examples of actual scientific practice laid down by a great master of science—examples which include law, theory, application, instrumentalities, textbooks, lectures and laboratory exercises—provide models from which spring particular coherent traditions of scientific research.[9] It is the study of paradigms that mainly prepares the student for membership in the particular scientific community with which he will later practice. Joining there men who have already learnt the bases of their field from the same concrete models, his subsequent practice will seldom produce overt disagreement over fundamentals. Men whose research is based on shared paradigms are committed to the same rules and standards of scientific practice. Paradigms thus set a style, a fashion or mode in a particular scientific field—not just an intellectual model but a vogue. Men argue the way they do, not merely because the set of concepts and axioms which they hold match their experiences; they do so also because that was the thing to do, in terms of the particular paradigm they followed. The whole of their thought and vision is shaped by it and as a result they become rigid, dogmatic, orthodox and blind to new phenomena.

However, because these paradigms are sooner or later found inadequate they usually lead to anomalies and crises. Something goes wrong with normal research. The rules of normal science no longer define a playable game and some scientists, usually younger men, begin to conceive another set that can replace them. Like political revolutions, scientific revolutions are inaugurated by a growing sense, experienced at first by a narrow subdivision of the scientific community, that an existing paradigm has ceased to function adequately in the exploration of an aspect of nature to which that paradigm had previously led the way. There is a growing sense of malfunction that leads to a crisis. It is this feeling of malfunction and crisis that makes it possible for a new scientific revolutionary to arise and to lay down a new table of laws and a new set of paradigms. When this happens the transition from one paradigm to another is not accomplished by logical and neutral experience but is effected by a life and death struggle between the two competitors. In this period of transition there is no real conversation between supporters of the old orthodoxy and the advocates of the new. The new theory does not and cannot refute the old; its business is rather to bury it, to outlive it and so to be in at its funeral. Max Planck, surveying his own career in his scientific autobiography, sadly summed up the situation by stating that "a new scientific truth does not triumph by convincing its opponents and making them see the light, but rather because its opponents eventually die, and a new generation grows up that is familiar with it."[10]

This brief discussion of the nature of ideology should make it clear that most social thought is characterized by illusion, rationalization and mystification. Reason plays only a marginal role in human affairs and is subordinate to that of the blind and irrational emotions. Even the highest form of reason always borders on unreason. Liberal philosophy has overestimated the power of the intellect and has revealed a pronounced lack of insight into the asocial, selfish and regressive trends in man. Man's conduct is not governed by reason but by will, passion, myth and material interest. Man's intellect is above all an instrument in the struggle for existence; the function of thought is to serve the life process and the will to power; and all social thought is socially determined and tainted by class and personal interests. Rational, deliberate conscious belief does not determine what is going to happen to society and men's socially decisive actions spring not from logical but from non-logical roots. Ideologies are thus ignorant of the exact nature of their relations with praxis. They do not really understand their own conditions and presuppositions, nor the actual consequences they are producing. They are ignorant of the implications of their own theories and they comprehend neither the causes of which they are effects nor the effects which they are actually causing. Involved in practice, serving as instruments in the struggle between classes and nations, they mask the true interests and aspirations of the groups involved. All social thought is enveloped in a fog of deception and self-deception, is rooted in intellectual pride and is the victim of the ignorance of its ignorance.

The role of ideology is particularly dominant in politics. The basic manifestations of politics do not appear to be what they actually are. The struggle for power, as the immediate goal of policy, is always explained away and justified in ethical, legal or biological terms. The true nature of policy is always concealed by ideological justification and rationalization. Vast collective actions are made acceptable to their participants by the considerations and justifications invented by those who organize and lead them. The actor on the political scene cannot help but "play an act", and must conceal the true nature of his political actions behind the mask of an ideology. Politicians therefore have an ineradicable tendency to deceive themselves about what they are doing. The ultimate goals of political action—the lust for power—are always concealed behind false fronts and pretexts. It is the very nature of politics to compel the actor on the political scene to use ideologies in order to disguise the immediate goal of his action. The political actor will thus consider his own desire for power just and will condemn the desire of others to achieve power over him as unjust; he will regard his nation's struggle for existence as morally justified and will regard the same struggle of his adversaries as reprehensible. John Adams summed it up well when he said: "Power always thinks it has a great soul and vast views beyond the comprehension of the weak and that it is doing God's service when it is violating all His laws. Our passions, ambitions, avarice, love and resentment, etc., possess so much metaphysical subtlety and so much overpowering eloquence that they insinuate themselves into the understanding and the conscience and convert both to their party."

Every social order, all political, social and philosophical thought, all political action are thus distorted by ideology. Even the physical sciences are not free from preconceptions and the rigidities of paradigmatic thought. It is not reason, the pragmatic or experimental temper or objective science that rule the social world. All societies develop an ideology, that is, a certain perception of the world, a certain system of values and beliefs that serve to reinforce and rationalize the dominant political, economic and social interests of that society. Although this ideology and the system of interests it serves has some basis in empirical reality and manifests some forms of pragmatic behavior and although it can bend and twist in response to changing circumstances and pressures it can never become so flexible and experimental as to be able to transcend itself without a revolutionary upheaval. "All dogmatic situations in life," as Henry Adams put it, "have the effect of fixing a certain stiffness of attitude forever as though they mesmerized the subject."[11] The world of ideology is supple, adaptable and closed. It bends to the interests of the times but without being able to supersede them. Ideology changes but only imperceptibly and without ever losing its ideological character. It moves but with an immobile motion which basically maintains it where it is in its place and in its ideological role. All ideologies— capitalism, democracy, liberalism, conservatism, and so on—screen out certain elements of reality from their consciousness, creating a brake in their perception of reality. The ideologies that ruling elites develop and hold can thus never fully comprehend the social environment they operate in. They must all lag behind social reality, they must all be in conflict with that social reality to a greater or lesser extent, they must all be driven by a frenzy of self-conceit, and they must all finally become so mired in their own illusions, prejudices and mystifications that they must first weaken and then ultimately help to wreck the social system it is their purpose to sustain.

CHAPTER 5

ON POLITICS

Our analysis of power, the role and character of elites and ideology has, we hope, revealed some of the powerful forces that shape and determine the social world in general and the world of politics in particular. Driven by the will to power, blinded by the illusions, mystifications and irrationalities of ideology, all elites fight their battles enveloped in fog and uncertainty. Although this analysis has focussed attention on some of the principal forces at work it has still not sufficiently emphasized a few other crucial elements of political life—its Centaur-like quality, its militancy and its essential corruption, immorality and evil.

Machiavelli was one of the first among the "moderns" to perceive the duality of political man. In his theory man was a creature of "insatiable appetites" yet was never capable of fully satisfying them. While man's ambitions were limitless his means of realizing them were always restricted. Politics was always plagued by the dilemma of limited goods and limitless ambitions. Within any state conflict takes place between the many who wish to be free from domination and the few who desire to dominate the many. The peace and leisure so necessary for human improvement and welfare rest upon the violence both potential and actual which the state can apply. Violence in fact is the dynamic of the universal chaos of intramural and interstate contention. One half of our lives is determined by the contingent and fortuitous while the other half is within our power to command. Although man could acquire political wisdom it was extremely difficult to apply it. On the one hand man was egoistic, shortsighted and imitative and once his character had been formed, inflexible. On the other he was capable of acting with energy, decisiveness, courage and foresight, carefully preparing for the future. Machiavelli portrayed life as a continuous contest between *Virtù* and *Fortuna*, the former representing the principle of freedom, consciousness, self-directed energy and movement and the latter symbolizing the unforseeable and uncontrollable. The dual nature of politics was best summarized in this famous passage:

> . . . there are two methods of fighting, the one by law, the other by force: the first method is that of men, the second of beasts; but as the first method is often insufficient, one must have recourse to the second. It is therefore necessary for a prince to know well how to use both the beast and the man. This was covertly taught to rulers by ancient writers, who relate how Achilles and many others of those ancient princes were given to Chiron the centaur to be brought up and educated, under his discipline. The parable of this semi-animal, semi-human teacher is meant to indicate that a prince must know how to use both natures, and that the one without the other is not durable.
>
> A prince being thus obliged to know well how to act as a beast must imitate the fox and the lion, for the lion cannot protect himself from traps, and the fox cannot defend himself from wolves. One must therefore be a fox to recognize traps, and a lion to frighten wolves.[1]

This passage is highly characteristic and illustrative of Machiavelli's approach to politics. Although he does not say that the teacher of princes should be a brute he yet makes it very clear that in approaching politics and the art of ruling he has to deal with brutal things and must not recoil from seeing them eye to eye and from calling them by the right names. For humanity alone will never do in politics. Politics is full of crimes, treacheries and felonies. The quantity of evil will always remain firmly constant in the world and it is the peculiar nature of political action that it cannot be dissociated from evil consequences. Evil is implicated in the very nature of political activity and creativity. All princes must partially dwell outside the realm of what is usually considered goodness. Ethical norms had to be subordinated to the necessities of politics regarded as an autonomous sphere of activity. To maintain his rule

> . . . a new prince cannot observe all those things which are considered good in men, being often obliged, in order to maintain the state, to act against faith, against charity, against humanity, and against religion. And, therefore, he must have a mind disposed to

adapt itself according to the wind, and as the variations of fortune dictate, and, as I said before, not deviate from what is good, if possible, but be able to do evil if constrained.[2]

In political life thus one cannot draw a sharp line between "virtue" and "vice". The two things often change places. If everything is considered we shall find that some things that seem to be very virtuous, if they are turned into actions, will be ruinous to the prince, whereas others that are regarded as vicious are beneficial. In politics all things change their place; fair is foul and foul is fair. Even at its best politics still remains an intermediary between humanity and bestiality. The teacher of politics must therefore understand both things; he must be half man, half beast.

Although Machiavelli is regarded by some as the first "political scientist" he in fact well understood that there could be no science of politics. In politics we can to some degree anticipate the future but we cannot foretell it. Our expectations and hopes are more often than not frustrated; our actions, even the best planned actions more often than not fail to have their effect. The best political advice is often ineffective, even when it is accepted, which is rare. Things will go their own way and they will thwart all our wishes and purposes. Even the most artful and cunning schemes are liable to defeat; they may suddenly and unexpectedly be crossed by unanticipated events, by mere chance. The world of politics is an inconstant, irregular, capricious world that defies all our efforts of calculation and prediction. In this world men are not governed by reason and they cannot be described in terms of reason. To solve all these tensions and irrationalities Machiavelli had recourse to another power—that of *Fortuna* or Fortune—as the seeming ruler of all things.

Fortune in his hands becomes an element in his philosophy of history. Whimsical and capricious, defying all attempts to reduce it to certain rules it plays a leading part in all human things. It is the power of Fortune that brings to the fore now one nation, then another nation and gives it the dominion of the world. At all times, says Machiavelli in the preface to the Second Book of the *Discourses*, the world has always been pretty much the same. There has at all times been nearly the same portion of good and evil in it; but this good and evil have sometimes changed their stations and passes from one empire to another. Virtue which once seems to have fixed itself in Assyria afterwards removed its seat to Media, from thence into Persia and at last came and settled among the Romans. Nothing under the sun is stable or ever will be. Evil succeeds good, good succeeds evil and the one is always the cause of the other. Yet that does not mean that man has to give up his struggle. Quietism would be the death blow of an active life which he extolled—the only life worthy of man. To overcome the inimical influence of Fortune, strength and will power are needed in addition to wisdom. The power of Fortune is great and incalculable but it is not irresistible. If it seems to be irresistible it is the fault of man who does not use all his resources and forces, who is too timid to take up arms against Fortune:

> It is not unknown to me how many have been and are of opinion that worldly events are so governed by fortune and by God, that men cannot by their prudence change them, and that on the contrary there is no remedy whatever, for this they may judge it to be useless to toil much about them, but let things be ruled by chance. This opinion has been more held in our day, from the great changes that have been seen, and are daily seen, beyond every human conjecture. When I think about them, at times I am partly inclined to share this opinion. Nevertheless, that our free will may not be altogether extinguished, I think it may be true that fortune is the ruler of half our actions, but that she allows the other half or thereabouts to be governed by us.[3]

For Machiavelli, then, the conception that Fortune is the ruler of the world is true; but it is only one half of the truth. Man is not subjugated to Fortune; he is not at the mercy of the elements. Though it is not easy to use them in the right way it is possible to devise rules for the great and continual battle against the power of Fortune. But they are very involved and contain two elements that seem to exclude each other. The man who wishes to stand his ground in this contest must combine in his character two opposite qualities. He must be timid and courageous, reserved and impetuous. Only by such a paradoxical mixture can he hope to win the victory. There is no uniform method to be followed at all times. At one moment he must be on his guard, at another he must dare everything. The man who battles fortune must be a sort of Proteus who can change his shape from one moment to the next. He must rely upon both material and mental weapons; he must not neglect the art of war nor must he overlook the art of politics. He who enters the lists against Fortune must understand defensive and offensive warfare and he must suddenly and unexpectedly change from one to the other. Personally Machiavelli is more in favor of the offensive. "It is better," he says, "to be bold than bashful; for Fortune is like a woman who must be teased and treated in a cavalier manner by those that expect to prevail over her." Yet at the end he concludes that the talents required are very rare in men and that is why he holds an essentially cyclical and pessimistic theory of history. There is thus,

. . . No man . . . so prudent as to be able to adapt himself to this, either because he cannot deviate from that to which his nature disposes him, or else because having always prospered by walking in one path, he cannot pursuade himself that it is well to leave it; and therefore the cautious man, when it is time to act suddenly, does not know how to do so and is consequently ruined; for if one could change one's nature with time and circumstance, fortune would never change.

For Santayana mankind is in the first place a race of animals living in the material world. The roots of life and spirit (and politics as well) are in matter. Life and spirit are not the cause of order in the world but its result. Being an animal, man has inward, specific springs of action, called instincts, needs, passions and intents. The precarious order which is attained springs from chaos and pervasive flux which is at the root of everything and from the clash of human passions and intents. It is also the product of the fertility of matter which is the outcome of a thoroughly irrational groping, self-devouring process that only by chance or in certain abstract aspects settles down for a season into constant or calculable order. Existence itself, moreover, since it involves continual lapse and renewal of forms and relations is essentially a blind and involuntary war. Death feeds on life and life feeds on the death of other life. Life cannot take or keep any form without crowding or crushing some other form of life. There is a primaeval war in the jungle before arts arise at all; the stronger plants intercept the rays of the sun and suck up the moisture needed by its weaker neighbors: and this is not malice on its part but the Will to Live. Existence being a perpetual generation involves aspirations and its aspirations envelop it in an atmosphere of light, the joy and beauty of being, which is the living heaven; but for the same reason existence in its texture involves a perpetual and living hell—the conflict and mutual hatred of its parts, each endeavoring to devour its neighbor's substance, in the vain effort to live forever. The greater part of most men's souls dwells in this hell and ends there. Man wishes to exist materially and yet resents the plastic stress, the very force of material being which creates and destroys him.

Man however is not only an animal and a creature of nature but he is also Primal Will and Vital Liberty. Primal Will does not imply intelligence or premeditation. It does imply eagerness to act; it does connote the impulse to feed, to grow, to master and possess everything. Though peace is a precondition for the birth and the pure growth of life, it is not the initial object pursued by it. On the contrary the first sign of life is instinctive or Primal Will: a sudden spasmodic effort to exercise power, and to see what happens. The act if unhindered, and its result if satisfying, become the fixed objects of that will and it becomes thereby "the mortal enemy of everything that might stop such exploits in the future."[4] Budding life is weak and it needs peace and favorable conditions to strengthen it; but when strong and well-knit, life becomes "brave and even truculent." It declares war on all its enemies without knowing who they might be, and if its immediate surroundings are favorable to it, it flourishes in confidence and self-satisfaction. Primal Will or blind initiative of this kind remains fundamental for the organism in all its animal phases; so that a man beneath his intelligent perceptions and arts "retains a pervasive blind courage and absolute willfulness." This private economy of the organic psyche, or the life of the body as he defines it, is deeper than all that it has been forced to concede to and it exercises a pervasive pull over the moral incrustations that in arming the Will for action oppress its basic liberty. Thus, like the hidden forces of a volcano, ignorant energy, which might also be called Egotism, "convinced of its own rightness will burst spasmodically into civil and rational life."[5]

Yet though Primal Will is the impulse to action and power it is nevertheless ultimately impotent. It is "foiled in its blind agitation and devours its own strength in its all-embracing fury."[6] Its needs are never satisfied and it feels what Hamlet called a "plentiful lack" in the empty desire to exist. All our large human units, physical and moral, are therefore tragically transitory and our enacted wills comically cheated by our secret desires. Although we act in society as persons with apparent spontaneity and initiative yet were we really able to have our way not one of us would persevere in the course or in the state in which we actually find ourselves. For our official wills are often false to our natures not so much through hypocrisy as through blind habit and gregarious vagueness. The law of nature at bottom would seem to be that the deepest and most fundamental of human needs can never be satisfied; that the avid chase should recur forever; and that man's vital liberties should be smothered and defeated by contrary powers.

But man is not completely helpless in the face of this inexorable fate which seems to mock and crush his inner consciousness of liberty. Through the Generative Order man's physical powers and passions are modified by society. Training, teaching and contagion to some extent alter his nature. His basic needs, like those for food, companionship and work are met. Customs and traditions, though authoritative, inspire the conscience of the average individual with superstitious as well as prudential fears. Wider influences and allegiances, for instance to a new or foreign religion, are superimposed. Fresh social orders, not blindly imitative or derived from variations in unconscious growth establish express habits and obligations previously unknown. Though government is a modification of war, a means of using compulsion without shedding too much blood, it too rests on such forces as social pressure, spontaneous unanimity and cooperation which tend to attenuate its compulsive character. Ideas flow from the dynamic process of nature which they describe or forecast. Vital liberty, under the discipline of the conditions of life, develops ideal interests such as science and other liberal and economic arts. The marriage of war and play, of religion and magnificence has given the imagination freedom while feeding it on vital and tragic themes.

The Militant Order on the other hand, Santayana defines as an attempt to impose a narrow set of interests on a society. It is in the "sphere of politics and morals, the love of reforming the world from the total mutation that the world is always undergoing."[7] All action, all economic art, exerts force and has effects; but this does not render all action or all economic art militant. The militant impulse springs from that "master passion" that would like to be absolute and to dominate the whole world. It is hostility and hatred toward all dissenting forms of existence. It is war become intentional, self-righteous and fanatical. The militant spirit which is the dominant spirit in politics is not unintended and open to chivalry as is the great war of life. It is blind to its own accidental bias and to the equal legitimacy of all existence. It thirsts to destroy its enemies and to see nothing in the world except its own likeness. The spirit of militancy infects peace, missionaries, politicians and philosophers. It is found in the writing of history. In families and between friends there is also a good deal of unreasonable insistence on dominating one another. Even in each individual there is often a civil war, in which a new passion wars against an old circle of interests, or where in turn the old interests, alarmed, raise a storm of protests against the intruder. The defiance and contradiction of peaceful and complacent conventions, and the appearance of rebellions in the camp of dogmatic moralities and religions all arouse them to furious and militant response. And reason itself plays an eminent militant part in politics, since when it can, it introduces its hard order into the chaos of conflicting customs and quarrels and enters the political arena as an aggressive agent which feels itself capable of achieving social domination.

The militant spirit springs from many sources. It arises from the indecision or self-contradiction of animal will distractedly pursuing incompatible goals at the same time in the same place. It stems from man's extraordinary fertile and redundant imagination, from the grotesque and inconstant images that agitate him and arouse his anxieties. It is driven on by the militant mind which does not see only with its eyes open but when it shuts them, often sees the same thing again, though what it sees is not there.[8] It is set in motion by the great passions and excitements that sweep over mankind and that amount to a kind of madness which is almost a normal part of human life.   It is fed by the latent cruelty and blindness of all competitive life, by the domination of crime over society, by the pride of absoluteness in the human soul, by the radical ignorance of private judgment, by the deep forces of rebellion against reasonable control, by ambition and love of gain, by hot anger and stubbornness. Although it is almost normal to be partly mad, the ideal to be striven for is harmony and sanity.   But this ideal of vital health and harmony is always imperfect, is always a mere crust beneath which mighty chaotic forces are at work.   And it is these mighty chaotic forces allied with the blind irrationality of the will which produce that spirit of fanaticism and militancy which is always threatening the weak ramparts of reason, order and civilization.[9]

Even economic enterprise is a form of militancy though it suffers no moral provocation and is without violent enemies.   Like faction it feels itself to be a virtue, not only for showing courage and initiative but particularly for doing so without blood or vengeance and purely at the call of "some open chance to attempt untried and glorious things."   The nineteenth century not only saw the eruption of faction in the French Revolution and the Napoleonic Wars but it also witnessed, in its second half, the explosion of the faction of enterprise.   This latter explosion by its brilliant feats in science and industry produced a revolution in the equipment of human life and mind and was destined to make a "wholly new era in the relation of mankind to the latent energies of matter."   Yet, in Santayana's analysis, these prophets of enterprise are even more militant than ordinary hunters and warriors.   For the latter are prompted at bottom by mere material needs or material lives while the former desire to improve the world.   The prophets of enterprise do not only seek the exercise of power but want to see mankind adopt their thoughts, obey their precepts and draw forever the line between good and evil exactly where they have drawn it.   They are moved by the ambition and self-confidence to judge and convert the rest of the world.[10]

The third order of society is the rational order.   The rational order defines an attempt to harmonize the most basic interests present in individuals within a society and provide a means of satisfying this harmony of interests.   The rational order ought to exclude militancy even when some people have a basic interest in being militant.   The rational order does not correspond to the ideal society.   It could, however, make the ideal society possible through the conscious harmonization of the interests present in the generative order.   For Santayana, reason is the ability to see "identity, affinity, contrast or irrelevance between essences present in direct intuition."[11]   It is inclusive and harmonizing rather than exclusive and dissonant. It is a new harmony of vital forces. It is a species of insight by which essential relationships are seen to obtain between ideal forms. Rational government in so far as that is possible, is an art, requiring the widest knowledge and the most perfect disinterestedness. It should be steady and traditional yet open to continual readjustments with the natural shifts of customs, passions and aspirations in the world. Though reason cannot define or codify human nature it can yet exercise, under the most ideal conditions, a modicum of control over local and temporal impulses and keep at least an ideal of spiritual liberty and social justice before the public.

Yet this rational order is more of an ideal than a reality. In politics reason seems to play an eminently militant part. The political power "exercised in the alleged service of reason is always exercised by persons, themselves fundamentally irrational."[12]   The life of reason on earth is inevitably distracted. A man harnassed to affairs or intent on his own passions will not see the obvious in their rational, logical order but will rather see their irrational comings and goings or will feel only the active impulses, which as signs, they arouse automatically in his body. The political man is utterly confused when he attempts to be rational. He is ruled by material complications and headlong events. Man lives in a universe that is inhuman and mankind is "too numerous, too various and too unteachable to suffer anything reasonable in politics, in manners or in speculation to subsist in peace."[13]   Reason is the servant of the Irrational Will and is but the keenest faculty of an impassioned psyche. The exuberant radiation of matter prevents any exact harmony from being established among its many endeavors. Every form of Will realized insists on maintaining its ascendancy and of extending it if possible. It clings to what it can achieve without any mercy for the defeats which it may be inflicting on its competitors. Reason is powerless against the presumptions of egotism and ignorance and against that rooted belief with which all animals are born that the world exists for their benefit. Intelligence, though often keen enough, "instead of establishing order among the irrational passions, vital or frivolous, that distract the psyche, hastens as soon as born to devise ingenious ways of satisfying one or another of the passions, regardless of the others in the man himself or in his neighbors and this rape of the intelligence is no less violent in those liberal arts that possess an internal rationality, such as logic, mathematics, music and poetry."[14]   Ordinary rational decisions thus can only make short, clear runs amid the turbid rapids of existence. Reason can only, at best, moderate the fury of the inconstant will, but it cannot control its wanton militancy.

Santayana thus finds liberalism, despite all its intellectual kindness or courtesy to all possible wills, myopic and living in a thankless world. Liberals are the most civilized and culture-loving of beings, the over-ripe fruit of a civilization which they wish to reform. But this civilization has spent its force and is rapidly declining; its conventions have now become empty and its principles have proved false. The wish to reform it is singularly naive. They do not see that the peace they demand was secured by the disciplines and sacrifices that they deplore; that the wealth they possess was accumulated by appropriating land and conducting enterprises in the high-handed manner they denounce; and that the fine arts and refined luxuries they take keen delight in arose in the service of superstitions that they deride and the despotism that they abhor. Although they were no doubt right in believing that the nineteenth century was moving toward the destruction of traditional institutions, privileges and beliefs, the second half of the twentieth century has already made evident that their own wealth, taste and intellectual liberty will dissolve also in some strange barbarism that will think them a good riddance. For Santayana the concupiscence of the flesh and the eyes and the pride of life exhaust and kill the sweets they feed upon; and a "lava wave of primitive blindness and violence must perhaps rise from below to lay the foundations for something differently human and similarly transient."[15]

For Morgenthau politics is stained by corruption, immorality and evil. The corruption, immorality and evil of politics stem from a number of causes. First of all, all action is, at least potentially, immoral and this immorality inherent in all human action is more obviously and to a higher degree present in political action. As Goethe remarked to Eckermann, "He who acts is always unjust; nobody is just but the one who reflects." The very act of acting destroys our moral integrity. For to act is to choose between different equally legitimate demans. Whatever choice we make, we must do evil while we try to do good; for we must abandon one moral end in favor of another. While trying to render to Caesar what is Caesar's and to God what is God's we will at best strike a precarious balance which will ever waver between both, never completely satisfying either, and will usually end at a compromise which puts the struggle at rest without putting conscience at ease. Then too, loyalty to one's nation comes into conflict with our duties to humanity; the father must choose between his children, the friend between his friends, and man between himself and others. Thus the demands which life in society makes on us surpass our faculty to satisfy them. While satisfying one we must neglect others, and the satisfaction of one may even involve the positive violation of another.

The human intellect furthermore is unable to calculate and control completely the results of human action. Once the action is performed, it becomes an independent force creating changes, provoking reactions and colliding with other forces which the actor may or may not have foreseen and which he can control but to a small degree. These factors, which, lying beyond human foresight and influence, we call "accidents" deflect the action from its intended goal and "create evil results out of good intentions."[16] Our thoughts are ours but their ends are none of our own. Our intentions might be good but the consequences of our actions generally are not. In fact, as soon as we leave the realm of our thoughts and aspirations we are inevitably involved in sin and guilt. The fruit of evil grows from the seed of noble thought. Thus those who declare themselves in favor of peace among nations and harmony among individuals usually produce only conflict and war by their action. Men might want to see all men free but their actions put others in chains as others do the same to us. We might believe in the equality of all men but our demands on society make others unequal. Oedipus tried to nullify the oracles' prophesy of future crimes and by doing so only made the fulfillment of the prophesy inevitable. Brutus intended to preserve Roman liberty and brought about its destruction. Lincoln hoped to make all Americans free yet his actions destroyed the lives of many, and made the freedom of others a legal fiction and an actual mockery. Hamlet, conscious of the tragic tension between the ethics of our minds and the ethics of our actions, resolves to act only when he can act as ethically as his intention demands and thus despairs of acting at all and, when he is finally pushed to act, "his actions and fate are devoid of ethical meaning."[17]

The root of corruption, immorality and their concomitant evil stem, Morgenthau argues, from the lust for power. This lust for power manifests itself as the desire to maintain the range of one's person with regard to others, to increase it, or to demonstrate it. Although closely related to selfishness it is not identical with it. For selfishness is still connected to the serving of the vital needs of the individual—food, shelter, security, money, jobs and the like. The desire for power on the other hand, concerns itself not with the individual's mere survival but with his position among his fellows once his vital needs have been served. "The fact is," as Aristotle put it, "that the greatest crimes are caused by excess and not by necessity. Men do not become tyrants in order that they might not suffer cold." The selfishness of man has limits; his will to power has none. While man's vital needs are capable of satisfaction, his lust for power would be satisfied only if the last man becomes an object of his domination, there being nobody above or beside him—that is, if he becomes God. It is this ubiquity of the desire for power which, besides any particular selfishness or other evilness of purpose, constitutes the ubiquity of evil in human action. Here then, is the element of corruption and of sin which injects even into the best of intentions at least a drop of evil and thus spoils it. The transformation of churches into political organizations, of revolutions into dictatorships and of love for country into imperialism are all examples of this tendency.

To the extent to which the essence and aim of politics is power over men politics is evil; for it is to the same extent that it degrades man to a means for other men. It follows that the prototype of this corruption through power is to be found in the political sphere. For in this realm the will to power is not merely combined with dominant aims of a different kind but is the very essence of the ultimate aim, the very life-blood of the action, the basic principle of politics as a distinct sphere of human activity. Politics is a struggle for power over men, and whatever its ultimate purpose may be, power is its immediate goal and the modes of acquiring, maintaining and demonstrating it determine the means and techniques of political action. Although the evil that corrupts political action is the same evil that corrupts all action the corruption of political action is the very paradigm of all possible corruption. Political action is thus incompatible with the rules of morality. For while the test of a morally good action is the degree to which it is capable of treating others not as means to the actor's end but as ends in themselves the test of political success is the degree to which one is able to maintain, to increase, or to demonstrate one's power over others. "It is for this reason alone inevitable that, whereas nonpolitical action is ever exposed to corruption by selfishness and lust for power, this corruption is inherent in the very nature of the political act."[18]

Political action and doing evil are therefore inevitably linked. Ethical standards are always violated on the political scene. It is unattainable for a political action to conform at the same time to the rules of the political art—i.e., to achieve political power and success—and to conform to the rules of ethics—i.e., to be good in itself. Politics is thus "absolutely evil" (Burckhardt), "power corrupts" (Acton), "force is a practical lie" (Emerson) and political ethics is the ethics of doing evil. Politics is, in fact, in the last resort the choice among several possible actions of the one that is the least evil. It is to be as good as one can be in an evil world. Neither science nor ethics nor politics can resolve the conflict between politics and ethics into harmony. Men have no choice between power and the common good. To act successfully, that is, according to the rules of the political art, is political wisdom. To know with despair that the political act is inevitably evil, and to act nevertheless, is moral courage. To choose among several expedient actions the least evil one is moral judgment. Man reconciles his political nature with his moral destiny by combining political wisdom, moral courage and moral judgment. "That this reconciliation is nothing more than a modus vivendi, uneasy, precarious and even paradoxical can disappoint only those who prefer to gloss over and to distort the tragic contradictions of human existence with the soothing logic of a specious concord."[19]

Politics is, then, a battleground between *Virtú* and *Fortuna*, militancy and reason, inherent corruption and the moral impulse. It is far removed from the liberals' and the rationalists' superficial view of it as a kind of market place where reason, compromise, conciliation, moderation, the "greatest good of the greatest number" are bound to emerge victorious in the peaceful competition of interests and ideas. Politics on the contrary has its roots in the dark chaos of Primal Will; is essentially a conflict and mutual hatred of the several parts into which every society is divided, with each part endeavoring to devour its neighbor's substance in the vain effort to live forever; is fuelled by selfishness, the lust for power, greed and ambition; is fed by man's extraordinarily fertile imagination and the grotesque and inconstant images that agitate him and arouse his anxiety; and is sunk in corruption, lies, brutality, evil, deception and self-deception. To deal with politics is to deal with brutal things, for humanity alone will never do. Political action can never be dissociated from corruption and evil. Political action and evil are inextricably linked and ethical standards are always violated on the political scene. The master passion in politics is the desire to be absolute, to impose a narrow set of interests on society. It thirsts to destroy its enemies and to see nothing in the world except its own likeness. It is infected with an element of madness which is always present in all human affairs. The insatiable appetites which torment man drive him to subordinate other men to his voracious will, to use them as means, to violate all ethical norms, and to commit felonies, treacheries and murder.

However, politics is not only beastliness, Primal Will and militancy, corruption and evil. Its elemental harshness and cruelty is mitigated by elements of humanity, reason and morality. By means of the arts of politics peace, law and order are established for brief periods of time. Human improvement and welfare are advanced. Courage, energy and foresight are revealed. Man's blind powers and passions are modified by society. Cooperation and mutual regard overcome for short interludes, the war of each against all. Customs and tradition, social pressure and induced consensus attenuate the compulsive character of government. Ideal interests such as science and other liberal and economic arts are stimulated. Reason exercises for short runs a modicum of control over the blind fury of man's instinctual impulses and even keeps an ideal of spiritual liberty and social justice before the public. Identities and affinities are discovered between contrasting essences. Morality introduces a spirit of concern for others. Civic responsibility and a sense of the common good are developed. And rules and strategies, combining both material and mental weapons, are elaborated for the great and continual battle against the powers of *Fortuna.*

Yet the forces of humanity, reason and morality are ultimately impotent against the forces of beastliness, militancy, corruption and evil. Selfishness, ambition and the lust for power will sooner or later destroy all the barriers set up to contain them. Primal Will will devour its own strength in its all-embracing fury. The forces of militancy and fanaticism will break loose from the bonds imposed upon them. The latent cruelty and blindness of all competitive life, the pride of absoluteness in the human soul, the radical ignorance of judgment will all overflow the banks of custom and institutions and inundate the society. The life of reason on earth is inevitably distracted. Irrational passions will break down the weak ramparts of reason. The militancy of enterprise will drive the forces of production which it has developed by its extravagance and greed into direct conflict with the needs of humanity and the requirements of its own preservation. The corruption and immorality which is the quintessence of political action will continuously inject drops of evil into all its intentions and systematically the evil will spread until it will have contaminated the whole system beyond recovery. In the great and unending battle between *Virtù* and *Fortuna,* the forces of necessity, of the unforseeable and the uncontrollable will relentlessly undermine the forces of freedom, of consciousness, of self-directed energy and movement, spread decay and degeneration and finally topple the most powerful of polities. All political systems sooner or later exhaust themselves and kill the very forces they feed upon. They are all precarious and transitory arrangements and the seeds of their own destruction grow as they do.

CHAPTER 6

ON RATIONALITY AND CAPITALISM

To fully comprehend the modern world, its dynamics and contradictions, we have to try to understand the spirit of another of its most fateful forces—industrial capitalism. Is industrial capitalism rational or irrational, manageable or anarchic, subject to human control or a blind and galloping force which is driving the societies it controls to disintegration and destruction? The future of our civilization might well depend on the answers that will be provided to this complex question.

One of the most comprehensive explanations that has so far been presented and the one which, at least in its most optimistic aspect, has most influenced academic thought is that developed by Max Weber. For Weber modern industrial capitalism is distinguished from all other economic systems by its rationality. Capitalism has been shaped by calculation and sobriety, by cool self-control and frugality, by the requirements of the balance-sheet and its ability to exactly calculate costs and profits, and by systematic and methodical habits. Through the Protestant ethic Christian "worldly asceticism" strode into the market place of life, penetrated the daily routine of life with its methodicalness,[1] elevated rational work into a calling and set men to pursue profit, ever-renewed profit by means of continuous, rational, capitalistic enterprise. The impulse behind capitalism has not been acquisition or pursuit of the greatest possible amount of money. Unlimited greed for gain is not in the least identical with capitalism or its spirit. Nor have daredevil and unscrupulous speculators and economic adventurers been its driving elements. In fact capitalism may even be "identical with the restraint or at least rational tempering"[2] of these irrational impulses. It is methodical rationality that tames the irrational acquisitive drive and becomes the condition of profitability, which in turn is oriented toward systematic, methodical calculation and capital accounting.

The distinctiveness of western culture, characteristic only for itself, is thus to be found in its rationality. Only in the West has science developed as a body of knowledge possessing universal validity. In other civilizations we find observations of great subtlety, as well as empirical knowledge and profound reflections on life and the universe, but nowhere else do we find rational demonstration on the basis of mathematics or precise experiment conducted in laboratories equipped with instruments of measurement. Only the West has developed a rational physics, chemistry and astronomy; and it alone has developed a scientific history and a systematic political science. The rational state with its specialized institutions, its written constitutions regulating political activity, is also unknown anywhere else. While other codifications exist here and there, only in the West do we have a rational jurisprudence, heir to the Roman law, or again such a structure as Canon law. Art too, since the renaissance has been rational in a way without parallel and even the religions practised in the West have systematized their dogma and the benefits of salvation.

The distinctive and fundamental feature of the rationality of Western civilization is that it is not confined to a particular or privileged segment of human activity. It permeates the whole of life. It exerts a permanent action and ceaselessly develops and transcends itself. It renews itself constantly on the basis of new discoveries. Rationality in the form of a progressive intellectualization of life has grown immensely in extent and pervasiveness. This process of progressive intellectualization has stripped the world of charm and poetry and has produced a feeling of "disenchantment with the world." The world becomes an increasingly artificial product of man, who governs it much as one controls a machine. Technology and its corollary specialization, as a result of the ever growing division and subdivision of functions, assume an ascendant position. Man's confidence in his own works grows. As against nature, technology and invention assume ever greater importance. Humanity, ever more confident of its intellectual and rational capacities, seems to have succeeded in exorcising the mysterious and blind processes that have always ruled it.

Rationalization, moreover, is not only limited to the economy, to science and technology and to the arts. It also spreads to government and above all to bureaucracy. The rationalization of government—involving centralization, generalization as well as abstraction of power—brought Western Europe from feudalism through the absolute monarchies to the contemporary state in its democratic form. The rationalization of bureaucracy establishes a system of rational domination and supplants patrimonial charismatic and/or traditional authority. It is based on a number of distinctive principles. Foremost is "the principle of fixed and official jurisdictional areas" which "are generally ordered by rules, that is, by laws or administrative regulations."[3] Ordinary activities become distributed as official duties, and the authority to give commands is distributed in a stable and foreseeable way and replace the random and sporadic character of kinship or patrimonial authority. Methodical provision is made for the regular and continuous fulfillment of duties and for the execution of corresponding rights. And only persons who have the genuinely regulated qualifications to serve are employed in public government. Such a system is always identified as bureaucracy, but the same basic system functions in modern business and is known as management.

From the basic principle of fixed and official jurisdiction flow a whole number of vital practices and criteria. Channels of communication, authority and appeal are regularized. The office assumes functional priority over the person who occupies it. Written and recorded orders are emphasized in place of random, merely personal commands or wishes. The bureau is separated from the private domicile of the official and public monies and equipment are divorced from the private property of the official. Provision is made for the training of expertness in a given office or function. Rigorous priority is given to official as contrasted with merely personal business in the governing of an enterprise. And finally, many activities and functions are converted to clear and specifiable rules which by their very nature have both preceptive and authoritarian significance.

Bureaucracy has a much greater significance for Weber than even this description would indicate. For bureaucratization constitutes for him the most powerful manifestation of the historical principle of rationalization. The growth of bureaucracy in government, business, religion, education and the arts represents that historical process through which we may account for much of what distinguishes the modern from the medieval world. It is the essential and encompassing ambience of modern, Western man. It is an expression of that "organizational revolution" that has led to the replacement of many of the privileges, powers and obligations that formerly were inseparable from property. Administration and organization have now become ends in themselves. Thus the hospital reaches the point of serving not human illness primarily but the hospital, and the university, the church and the labor union all become dominated through processes of rationalization, by their intrinsic organizational goals. Rationalization has in fact become a tidal force in modern history that is sweeping everything before it.

Yet, although Weber saw the process of rationalization as the primary guiding force of the modern world he was also well aware of its ambivalent character and of its baneful effects. Bureaucratic rationality in his view is beset by its own kind of nemesis. From being a force of progress against the traditional order it becomes eventually the seedbed of a tyranny greater, more penetrating, more lasting than anything previously known to history. From being creative and liberating, bureaucratization becomes a force for mechanizing and regimenting society. It creates a world filled with nothing "but little cogs, little men tending to little jobs and striving towards the bigger ones."[4] The soul is parcelled out, men seek for order and nothing but order, become nervous and cowardly if for one moment this order wavers, and helpless if they are torn away from their total incorporation in it. Ruled by precedent, born to carry out regulations, trained for discipline the functionary lacks initiative and is sunk in routine. In education the development of a "meritocracy" based on examinations and diplomas and serving strictly utilitarian needs leads not to the rise of the cultivated man as a well-rounded personality but to the emergence of a technical expert, who from the human point of view is crippled. Instead of leaders and heroes, the bureaucratic way of life produces political philistines and banausic technicians. Depersonalization and routinization lead to psychic proletarianization in the interests of discipline.[5] Rationalized and specialized office work eventually blots out personality, the calculable result, the vision. It destroys grace, dignity, personal creativity, spontaneity and ultimate meaningfulness. Robert Michels described best, in direct line with Weber's perspective, the outcome of the bureaucratic process:

> Bureaucracy is the sworn enemy of individual liberty, and of all bold initiative in matters of internal policy. The dependence upon superior authorities characteristic of the average employee suppresses individuality and gives to the society in which employees predominate a narrow petty-bourgeois and philistine stamp. The bureaucratic spirit corrupts character and engenders moral poverty. In every bureaucracy we may observe place-hunting, a mania for promotion, and obsequiousness towards those on whom promotion depends; there is arrogance towards inferiors and servility towards superiors . . . We may even say that the more conspicuously a bureaucracy is distinguished by its zeal, by its sense of duty, and by its devotion, the more also will it show itself to be petty, narrow, rigid and illiberal.[6]

The modern world of rationality would, in Weber's view, finally lead "to a polar night of icy darkness and hardness." With the fulfillment of the spirit of religious asceticism, material goods would gain an increasing and inexorable power over the lives of men. Victorious capitalism would rest on nothing but mechanical foundations. The pursuit of wealth, stripped of its religious and ethical meaning and unrelated to the highest spiritual and cultural values would finally become associated with purely mundane passions and become a mere sport. The spirit of religious asceticism would finally escape from its cave. At the end of this whole process, Weber saw this possible future for mankind:

> No one knows who will live in this cage in the future, or whether at the end of this tremendous development entirely new prophets will arise, or there will be great rebirth of old ideas and ideals or, if neither, mechanized petrification embellished with a sort of convulsive self-importance. For of the last stage of this cultural development, it might well be truly said: 'Specialists without spirit, sensualists without heart'; this nullity imagines that is has obtained a level of civilization never before achieved![7]

Although Weber's analysis of the driving forces of the modern world contains many profound insights it yet overemphasizes the spirit of rationality, in both its positive and negative aspects present within it. Capitalism was in fact not only shaped by the spirit of rationality but by the blind forces of irrationality. Born in greed and the lust for gain, as Marx so well understood, oozing blood from every one of its pores, driven by the Faustian or Promethean impulse to dominate man and the world and to acquire ever more power over men and things, industrial capitalism is the most explosive and disruptive force that the world has ever seen. Contrary to Weber, the acquisition of the greatest possible amount of money and unlimited greed for gain have been among its chief characteristics. Economic adventurers, dare-devil and unscrupulous speculators, have played a prominent role in its development. The entrepreneur, in Schumpeter's analysis, is driven by the will to conquest, the impulse to fight, to prove himself superior to others, to succeed for the sake not so much of the fruits of success but of success itself. In France, during the Napoleonic period, capitalism was promoted by the state because it found it a potent force against its enemies within and without. In Germany capitalist industrialization was wholly a form of power politics, served the *raison d'état* of the national state and supported Germany's imperial ambitions. The imperious will to power has been one of the main moving forces behind the expansion of capitalism. Wars have stimulated it and power rivalries have nurtured it. In the United States it has not only been motivated by the Protestant ethic but by a form of political capitalism in which success was determined by political and social connections.

Indeed, the industrial capitalist (and the communist state capitalist) is a consumate expression of the power-hungry man described by Hobbes. He is the man driven by nothing but personal interests and the desire for power is a fundamental passion with him. Capitalist society is impelled by a never-ending desire for the accumulation of capital, profit and property. The emergence of this society changed the very conception of property and wealth: they were no longer considered to be the effects of accumulation and acquisition but only their beginnings; wealth became a never-ending process of getting wealthier. Property was transformed into a dynamic new property-providing device. Capitalism is fanned by an "expansion is everything" ideology and the power it accumulates begets a desire for more power. As Marx said in *Das Kapital*: "Accumulate, accumulate, this is the law and the prophets." Cecil Rhodes exclaimed: "Expansion is everything" and he proclaimed that "I would annex the planets if I could." Caught in this world of dynamism and power the capitalist "cannot assure the power and means to live well, which he hath at present, without the acquisition of more" (Hobbes). The progress of capitalist society springs precisely from this pursuit of the highest possible profit, from this obsession with the accumulation of more and more and with the production of more and more. In pursuit of accumulation and profit the bourgeoisie is ready to sacrifice everything and everybody and in the course of driving history into the future it builds up a pile of towering ruins.[9]

The development of capitalism is thus a history of perpetual agitation and turmoil. The capitalist economy is not and cannot be stationary and it cannot expand in a steady or harmonious manner. It is incessantly being revolutionized from within by new enterprise, that is, by the infusion of new commodities or new methods of production or new commercial opportunities into the industrial structure as it exists at any given moment. All existing structures and all the conditions of doing business are always in a process of constant change. Every situation is challenged and upset before it has had time to work itself out. Economic progress in capitalist society means turbulence and disruption. New products and new methods compete with the old methods and means and in this competition the decisive advantage lies with the new. The production of new things or the possibility of producing old things more cheaply signifies death to the old firms and products. This is how "progress" is achieved in capitalist society. In order to escape being undersold, every firm is in the end compelled to follow suit, to invest in its turn, and in order to be able to do so, to plough back part of its profits, that is, to accumulate. Thus everyone accumulates and the capitalist machine continues to hurtle forward, eating up resources, disrupting society and community, violating the environment and producing immense problems which are beyond its capacity to solve.[9]

The dynamics of capitalism began to reach new heights with the "new capitalism" which emerged in the 1920s. The rise of mass production and high consumption transformed and revolutionized the life of the middle class in particular and of the society in general. Propelled by a spirit of perpetual innovation and the creation of new needs on the installment plan by massive advertising, the new forces of technology and consumerism systematically undermined the old Protestant ethic and all its inhibitions. The "higher standard of living", not work as an end in itself now became the engine of change. In place of work and frugality there was a growing emphasis on conspicuous consumption and display. Status and its emblems, not work and the election of God, became the marks of success. The new capitalism furiously promoted a hedonistic way of life, multiplied stimuli and distractions in every direction and loosened the bonds of the old morality. The forces of abundance it un-leashed encouraged prodigality, waste, built-in obsolescence and sybaritic living. The Protestant ethic as a social reality and a life style has been replaced by a new sensibility with its stress on psychedelic experience, extravagant expectations and aspirations which it cannot meet, and apocalyptic moods in all classes. The dynamics of capitalism have produced a counter-culture which challenges the values of capitalism while immersed in its pleasures, has penetrated the heart of bourgeois civilization itself and is now challenging the very values on which it was reared.

The continued pursuit of economic growth by the "advanced" nations is moreover producing a whole series of crises which threaten to tear them apart. Impelled by the boundless ambitions of the technocrats, driven forward by the apparently irresistible momentum which the existing institutions—political, economic and technological—set up toward further economic and technological development, intoxicated by the ideals of economic growth and consumerism, caught in a frenzy of self-seeking and greed, the new industrial revolution is beginning to fissure the physical environment and to produce complex changes of ecological disruption. Industrial pollutants are spreading over land, sea and air. Clamor, dust, fumes, congestion and visual destruction are the predominant features in all our built-up areas. The population ex-plosion is making our overgrown cities uninhabitable and the mounting frustrations of urban life manifest themselves in such symptoms as a seemingly chronic restlessness and discontent, the break-up of families, the growth of drug addiction, obscenity, freak cults and violent forms of protest, self-assertion and defiance. The palpable mass of uniform life, the insect-immensity of the city or beach crowd, induce destructive spasms, a blind need to lunge out and make room. Man becomes a bewildered spectator to what goes on about him, the consumer an uprooted, free-floating, volatile and manipulated creature, the psyche is choked and smothered and the civilization produced by this galloping economy becomes unstable and filled with the most explosive tensions. In fact, our new technology-based civilization is imposing increasingly intolerable strains upon the community and the personalities and testing in the sharpest possible form, man's very capacity to respond to changes which seem to move strongly against the grain of his instinctual needs.[10] Indeed, the increase in noise levels, in the pace of work and commotion, in the intensity of artificial lighting may now be reaching pathological levels and triggering instincts of devastation.

The population explosion and our obsession with economic growth are furthermore threatening the very existence of the technological-scientific civilization which has been constructed over the last two hundred years. Some biologists see a "swarming stage" situation developing which could be terminated either through mass neurosis owing to overcrowding, or through a great increase in predators, or there may occur such a concatenation of events that the population will gradually expand to occupy the whole medium in which it grows and then rapidly decline from the original focus outwards, partly through food shortage and partly poisoned by its own waste products. The same dire consequences confront us in the economic field where the process of unlimited economic growth is going to collide with the earth's finite, renewable and non-renewable resources. Unless an unprecedented revolution in attitudes, activities and class relations takes place, which is highly unlikely, a whole series of studies have warned us that in the next fifty to one hundred years we are going to face a world which will have exhausted its reserves of a large number of its essential metals; will simply be unable to feed its burgeoning populations and will be faced with a holocaust of unimaginable proportions. It is quite possible that the end of the capitalist period will see mankind living in cities which have swollen and crumbled about its ears, see its agricultural lands deteriorate and disappear beneath bricks and mortar, and be forced into the position of having to destroy the remaining fertility of the planet in a vain effort to survive.[11]

However, even if these dire predictions and projections do not materialize precisely in the form in which they have been cast capitalist civilization still suffers from other infirmities which relentlessly eat away at its substance. One of these is the role of money in its system—

the cash nexus that governs relations between men and groups. If the lust for power corrupts relations between individuals and states then the lust for money corrupts the relations between men in capitalist society and injects an element of evil and dissolution into its very existence as a social system. Under capitalism man becomes a commodity and is exchanged, bought, sold and discarded as all other commodities produced by a market economy. Man experiences himself as a thing to be employed successfully on the market. He does not experience himself as an active agent, as the bearer of human powers. His sense of self does not stem from his activity as an independent individual but from his socio-economic role. Chasing after material gain, reduced to selling himself, he eventually discovers that he has lost his very self, that he is like an onion with layer after layer removed and without a kernel. Alienated from himself, suffering from anomie, living in a social order where all human bonds are being destroyed and in a modern state where all the people "are a disorganized dust of individuals" (Durkheim) modern man is seized by panic, neurosis and a feeling of nothingness.[12]

The alienating function of money in the process of acquisition and consumption has been admirably portrayed by both Shakespeare and Marx. For Shakespeare in *Timon of Athens* (Act IV, Scene 3) gold

will make black white; foul, fair;
Wrong, right; base, noble; old, young; coward, valiant.
. . . .
Will lug your priests and servants from your sides,
Pluck stout men's pillows from below their heads:
This yellow slave
Will knit and break religions; bless th'accurst:
Make the hoar leprosy ador'd; place thieves
And give them title, knee, and approbation,
With senators on the bench: this is it
That makes the wappen'd widow wed again;

It is the common whore of mankind that speaks in every tongue to every purpose. For Shakespeare money is the visible deity that transforms all human and natural qualities into their opposites. It is the universal confusion and inversion of things. It is also the universal whore, the universal pander between men and nations. Money, as Marx put it, is the power to confuse and invert all human and natural qualities, to bring about the fraternization of incompatibles. The divine power of money "resides in its character as the alienated and self-alienating species-life of man. It is the alienated power of humanity."[13] A society that desperately worships this "universal whore" transforms loyalty into vice,

vice into virtue, the slave into the master, the master into the slave, ignorance into reason, reason into ignorance and man into a mere object, a thing.

In fact, capitalism or industrialism in all its forms have created a sick civilization. For this is a civilization which has not only rebelled against and rejected the static traditional order but has also rebelled against and rejected the classical and traditional concept of human nature. As against a Plato who counselled that the soul should lead the affections; an Aristotle who described the good life as a cultivation not of some but of all human dispositions but only by limiting each to a Golden Mean; and a St. Thomas who said that the human person should exercise "a royal and politic sovereignty" over the desires, modern man has made desires sovereign and reason is the instrument for serving desires. This modern man, as he has shaped our society and culture, is a being whose desires are limited not by his reason but only by the difficulty of getting more and more satisfaction. The desires of modern man are thus illimitable. In our age our social criterion of progress is that we must encourage and incite ourselves to be forever unsatisfied, to think nothing is enough and to seek the satisfaction of insatiable needs. The desires of modern man have consequently become irrational, are always expanding and forever unsatisfied.

The insatiable desires of modern man have therefore become an unending torture in which "they hunger though they eat, thirst though they drink, long for love though they cannot consummate it, seek and never find, achieve and always fail."[14] Driven by these insatiable desires yet incapable of satisfying them, modern man is confused, anxious, depressed, frustrated, aimless and weary, discontented and increasingly lawless.

Never satisfied and forever seeking the unattainable, he is oppressed by inner confusion, the anxieties of insecurity and a profound unhappiness. Deprived of a rational measure upon his desires he does not conserve his energy but spends it upon unattainable and unsatisfying ends. Lacking confidence in himself, deeply disoriented, his basic impulse is to escape from the pressure of his insatiable desires and from the endless conflicts with other men who are also driven by these same appetites. Actuated by his own inner disorder, driven by fear, inspired by fantasies of hope, he is corraled into organizations and bureaucracies and becomes part of a horde. And this horde of beings without autonomy, of individuals uprooted, isolated and disordered, cannot constitute a coherent society. This horde represents the new barbarism and it has arisen within modern civilization rather than being an invasion from without.

Max Weber and the numberless others who have followed his analysis have not only exaggerated the rationality of capitalism but they have also exaggerated the rationality of science, bureaucracy and management. Science at its best is only knowledge, it is not wisdom—that is, knowledge tempered by judgment. Modern science is not undertaken for its own sake and exclusively for the purpose of knowing. It is not indifferent to purpose and free from function. Pure scientific inquiry should be justified by the knowledge it serves, regardless of its nature. Modern science has on the contrary, become a tool of government, finds its meaning in service to all governments and the huge capitalist and communist corporations and is thereby threatened with the loss of what constitutes it as a distinctive human activity: the distinction between true and false as its central concern. Following Benjamin Franklin in the search for "useful knowledge" rather than Thorstein Veblen's scientist "addicted to the practice of idle curiosity," the modern scientist, a narrow specialist rather than a philosophically oriented scholar, has produced one disaster after another.

Although the modern world worships science and scientific achievements as the ancients worshipped their pagan idols it continues to wander in confusion and uncertainty and to produce catastrophic consequences of which it was completely ignorant in its original experiments and projects. The physicists, for example, who built the atom bombs were completely unaware of the genetic effects of atomic exposure though the evidence of the genetic effects of radiation had been known since 1927. Industrialization, fuelled by science and technology is, as we have already pointed out, radically disturbing our total environment. The irrigation system constructed for the Indus Valley in Pakistan, because of faulty calculations and planning, has resulted in water-logged areas, poisoned crops, and has left behind a white crust of salt. The insecticides and pesticides which have been the pride of our post-war world have poisoned our rivers and created dead lakes. The new era of disease-fighting that began with the sulfas, the anti-biotics and DDT insecticides has produced our cataclysmic population explosion which is threatening to drown us in billions of people we will be unable to feed or support. All this and much more has happened because our scientists and decision-makers have presumed a knowledge which they did not possess and acting out of ignorance and narrow specialization have put the whole world in hazard.[15]

Modern science is thus not a technological Second Coming. Much that passes for science is only dubious philosophy; and much that is held to be "real science" only constitutes confused fragments of the realities by which men live. Our men of science possess no true picture of reality as a whole and are incapable of presenting a true outline of human destiny. Science has become a set of Science Machines operated by technicians and controlled by economic and military men who neither embody nor understand science as creative ethos and orientation. Science has become "scientism" and its technological rationality is in sharp conflict with reason and humanity. The growth of scientific rationality has only produced more pronounced forms of irrationality and has in addition promoted modern forms of myth, fraud and superstition. A high level of technological rationality does not mean a high level of either individual or social intelligence nor does it make for increased freedom. Modern science develops rationality without reason and its technical progress represents at the same time technological idiocy. Through the work of the machine the worker becomes more and more machine-like, dull and spiritless; man's spiritual element, the self-conscious plenitude of life becomes an empty activity; and the more man takes away from nature, the more he subjugates it, "the baser he becomes himself."[16] The rise of science to power and authority has diminished man's humanity, endangered his individuality, banalized his intelligence and threatens him with atomization by unintelligible and unmanageable anonymous forces. The spread of science and technology has in fact led to the deterioration of the human mind in quality and cultural level, to the loss of a sense of wonder and tragedy, to the decline of understanding and wisdom, to an increasing self-estrangement and ultimately to a species of self-extinction.

The rationalization of bureaucracy and management has engendered the same forces of irrationality, mismanagement and idiocy. The process of rationalization has not reduced man to a mere automaton or cheerful robot. Man can never become merely one-dimensional. Man is too refractory and multi-dimensional a creature to be converted to this uniform and homogenized mode of existence. Torn by conflicting impulses, a battleground between contradictory urges, full of itches and fevers, and above all fallible and ignorant, he is simply incapable of establishing, for any lengthy period of time, a completely organized and controlled society. Contrary to what has been claimed by many critics of modern civilization, the forces of technology, organization, mechanization and rationalization cannot produce "a comfortable, smooth, reasonable, democratic unfreedom" (Marcuse) because the men and groups who manage these forces can never escape from the irrational impulses of power and ideology which blind them and corrupt them. Moved by passion, made stupid by routine, obsessed with their own narrow interests, turned rigid and inflexible by the conservative character of all organizations, made machine-like by the world of technology and machines, the rulers of society sooner or later commit those blunders, follies and crimes which undermine if not destroy their own handiwork. And although the conflicts and contradictions built into every society do not necessarily have to lead to the creative transcendence of the old order they do slowly and systematically, drop by acid drop, corrode whatever order might be in existence and finally produce decay and disintegration.

Our modern, rationalized and increasingly bureaucratized world is being eroded by three principal forces.

In the first place we witness everywhere a rising level of incompetence. With few exceptions men are simply bungling their affairs. Everywhere we find incompetence rampant, incompetence triumphant. Appliance manufacturers, as part of their regular policy, establish regional service depots in the expectation—fully justified by experience—that many of their machines will break down during the warrantee period. Millions of automobiles manufactured by the major producers in recent years have been found to contain potentially dangerous production defects. Mass production is turning out more and more goods which are shoddy, which do not work as they are supposed to, and which lack all craftsmanship and durability. Most organizations suffer from a prodigy of wastefulness, corruption, ignorance and indolence. One high school graduate in three, at the least, cannot read at a normal fifth grade level. It is now common practice for colleges to be giving reading lessons to their freshmen. In most colleges a considerable percentage of freshmen cannot read well enough to understand the text-books, and precious few can write a grammatically correct English sentence. Authors cannot write, social scientists do not know social science and English teachers cannot spell. In all organizations we see proclamations penned by administrators whose own office communications are hopelessly muddled. Limitless are the public servants who are indolent and insolent; military commanders whose sheer ineptitude is only matched by their belligerent rhetoric; and governors whose innate servility prevents their actually governing. No wonder schools do not teach, not to speak of bestowing wisdom, countries are misgoverned, economies mismanaged, courts do not dispense justice and affluence fails to produce contentment. All this muddle and incompetence has been brilliantly explained by the Peter Principle, which governs all hierarchies. This principle holds that given any kind of system whose members emphasize achievement and the like, people are sooner or later promoted to the level of their incompetence, and that in time every post tends to be occupied by an employee who is incompetent to carry out its duties.[17]

The problem of incompetence is further compounded by the fact that the men in charge of our major institutions now live much longer than previous generations. While in the past, life expectancy at birth was roughly 27.31 years, now an increasing number of us have a life expectancy at birth that is roughly 70 years. The incompetents thus, have a very long-range future and because of their incompetence, very short-range views of the future. The turn-over of elites is, as a consequence, greatly restricted and we now face the bleak prospect of having incompetenets in power for longer periods than at any previous time in history. The rise of the incompetents to power is one of the most portentous facts of our time. Our civilization is not only going to be destroyed by power and avarice gone berserk but by sheer incompetence.

The second force that has invalidated Weber's projection of a "new polar night of icy darkness and hardness", of a regimented and mechanical world ruled by impersonal and highly expert officials, is that man simply cannot be made into an efficient and calculating robot.   All bureaucracies are beset by petty power struggles and by conflicts of interest, and all bureaucracies are too inefficient and inept to manage the vast problems placed in their laps by modern society.   Split up into numerous organizations with their own organizational interests and commitments, imprisoned in their own narrow specializations, they commit blunder after blunder and arouse the discontent of even an apathetic public. Engaged in empire-building they lose sight of the public interest they presume to serve.   Become philistine and routinized they prod, by their arrogance and bungling, the active minority to discontent and a disgust with the existing order. Unable to elicit respect and support, they spread a general feeling of contempt for those in positions of authority and power.   Crushed by their own forms of meaningless existence they too are infected with a feeling of malaise and desperation.   Incapable of innovation and creativity they can only continue to operate in the grooves which have been dug out by precedent and the inertia of the organizational machine.   The imperatives of organizational behavior limit their flexibility and standard operating procedures introduce distortions and rigidity into all their decisions.   Bureaucracies do not plan or encourage foresight, they at best react to events as they occur.   It is not they who ride the machine but the machine that rides them.   While smothering the forces of spontaneity and life, they are mangled by the vital forces of life.   They are as much master as victim.   The forms and channels which are the very life-blood of their existence suffocate and impoverish them. Holding power at the price of obsequiousness their capacity to deal with affairs is severely limited and their lives pinched and constrained.   Bereft of creativity and vision, our modern bureaucracies in government, the military, education and in the corporations are manned by nervous and cowardly little men clinging to little jobs while fighting for the bigger ones, mutilated in their humanity and floundering in incompetence, conformity and confusion.   In the United States, among other countries, they are also too greedy and corrupt.

The third force that impedes the emergence of a totally rationalized, bureaucratized, mechanized world is the continued presence of the irrational in human affairs. Increasing rationalization neither represents progress nor does it constitute the spread of reason. Although it is based on scientific techniques, it cannot be said to constitute an advance in knowledge in the sense of a better understanding of our way of living. Despite the superficial progress they have brought about in all fields of human activity, rationalization and intellectualization have made no inroads on the empire of the irrational. On the contrary, as rationalization increases, the irrational grows in intensity; the more rationality is pushed forward the greater is the strength of its opposite powers, mysticism and folly of all kinds. The more the various aspects have become rationalized, the more the totality of society seems to be inexplicable. Rationalization only applies to the forecasts which science and technology are able to make by calculating probabilities but it has not been able to affect the irrationality of the affective life or the "ethical irrationality" of the world. Truth, goodness and beauty remain separate and irreconcilable. The effort to harmonize such basic vantage points as economics, politics, morality, art, religion and science is doomed to failure, for no harmony exists between power, need, interest, purity and knowledge. Every choice is essentially a matter of conflict and every choice implies rejection. Moreover, the result of an activity, especially political activity, seldom corresponds to the hopes and original intentions of the agents. There is an inherent antinomy between intention and results. The irrationality of the world finds its clearest expression in the fact that "the purest and noblest intentions may give rise to the most disastrous consequences" and that "it is impossible to perceive how and when an action once initiated will end."[18]

Rationalization and intellectualization have, as we have already indicated, led to disenchantment with the world. The progress of science and technology has presumably undermined man's belief in magic powers, in spirits and demons, but it has also led to a loss of man's prophetic sense, to human spontaneity and independence and to his sense of the sacred. Reality for modern man has become dreary, flat and utilitarian and it has left a great void in his soul, which he tries to fill by furious activity and through all sorts of distracting devices and substitutes. Scientific reason leads in time to its own trivialization. Without strong beliefs or convictions, gnawed at by uncertainty, he attempts to furnish his soul with "the bric-a-brac of religiosity, aestheticism, moralism or scientism,"[19] with a sort of pluralist philosophy which extends a promiscuous welcome to the latest and most heterogeneous maxims from every part of the globe. Mysticism thus becomes mystification, community becomes communitarianism and life is reduced to a series of unrelated experiences. Ignorance and unhappiness, conflict and power-struggles continue to hold sway.

An unbelievable amount of contradiction, furthermore, exists within this society, of structure and structuring, functionalism, applied rationalism, integration and coherence. Its rational aims and pretensions with all its battery of computers, electronic brains, IBM calculators and programming only breed irrationality and technological idiocy. Quantitative and continuous growth does not produce qualitative development. Control over external nature is increasing while man's development of his own nature is stagnating or regressing. Instead of resolving the old contradictions all these instruments and techniques only introduce new contradictions into society. The demands for truth and truthfulness conflict with the absence of any absolute criteria or general code by which to understand and judge. The multiplication of messages, news, and information takes place simultaneously with the spread of loneliness, superstition, silence and cultural impoverishment. The threat of nuclear war and destruction drives men to seek a security which is unobtainable. The incredible means that have been developed to save a sick child or a wounded man and prolong the agony of the dying are the counterparts of the genocides, the population explosions and the famines that have marked our world. Satisfaction and dissatisfaction go hand in hand or oppose each other according to the place or the people. Satiety and a stubborn quest for satisfaction, dissatisfaction and unrest, contradict, confront and reflect each other as they merge. The men of power are irresponsible, ignorant and incompetent; the intellectuals live in a world of make-believe, engulfed in the waters of rhetoric and jargon and are humiliated by having to submit to compulsions and myths in order to climb a few rungs of the social order; the middle classes wallow in packaged satisfactions and are yet aware of being swindled; the workers are trapped in deadening routine and social desperation; and the young reject the society while having no real alternative. Despite its ceaseless superficial modifications our society has no idea of where it is going. In the midst of wealth, in the midst of plenty, above all in the midst of pretensions, life is breaking down all around us. While worshipping balance, honoring stability and venerating coherence and structure, this society is in fact devoted to the transitory, the inconstant, the incoherent, the chaotic and the dynamic and is forever at the breaking point. The society of technology, bureaucracy and consumerism is thus a society of both affluence and want, of squandering and of exactitude and coldness, of frantic change and frigid inflexibility. It is a pseudo-system, a system of non-systems, a cohesion of incoherence.[20]

CHAPTER 7

ON DIALECTICS AND TRAGEDY

It has already been indicated that the most fruitful way of apprehending social reality is by means of the dialectical approach. For us dialectical thought is not a rigid, closed philosophy but a method and perspective. It need neither partake of the excessive rationalism of Hegel nor the extravagant optimism of Marx, though it is ready to borrow whatever is useful from both. It is of course in radical opposition to the scientism of modern social thought and to the positivism of the structural-functional school which will be analyzed later in this study.

Marx and Hegel both found the active element in history in man's "interests", the impelling drive for gain and power and the push toward the fulfillment of his needs. Man, born of nature, driven by will and passion, comes into being, emerges and asserts himself. What he becomes is the result of his own efforts, his struggles against nature and against himself. Man produces himself by his own labor, by praxis, starting from nature and from need in order to achieve the satisfaction of his desires. Everything in society is act, the essence of the human is what it accomplishes. Man as actor creates history, forms societies, builds states, produces techniques, ideologies, institutions, artistic and cultural works.

However, men make their history and their society without knowing how, in a fashion characterized by the ambivalent mixture of knowledge and ignorance, reason and passion, conscious action and blind compulsion.[1] The weaver does not altogether know what he weaves. Man's relations with that which he produces by his work and struggle are two-fold. On the one hand he realizes himself in them. There is no activity that does not give form to some object, that does not have some effect or result which its author finds has satisfied his desires, directly or indirectly. On the other hand—or rather at the same time—man loses himself in his works and objects. He loses his way among the products of his own labor which turn against him and load him down with all their routines, limitations, contradictions and burdens. At one moment he unleashes a succession of acts and events; this is history. At another moment what he has created takes on a life and momentum of its own that limits and subjugates him. Now his own creations bewitch and blind him; this is the great influence of ideology. Now the things he has produced with his own hands—more accurately the abstract things—tend to turn him into a thing itself, just another commodity, an object to be bought, sold and discarded.

The basic issue confronted by dialectical thought is thus the estrangement of man's existence. Though living in a world created by his own labor and knowledge this world was no longer his but rather stood opposed to his inner needs—a strange world governed by inexorable laws, a "thingified world" in which human life is frustrated. This is a world marked by a loss of coherence and liberty, by the numerous conflicts that abound in human living, especially in the conflict between man and nature and man and man. This conflict, which has turned nature into a hostile power that had to be mastered by man and which set man against man, class against class and nation against nation had led to an antagonism between idea and reality, between thought and the real, between consciousness and existence. Man constantly finds himself set off from a world that is adverse and alien to his impulses and desires. The institutions man founds and the culture he creates develop laws of their own, and man's freedom has to comply with them. He is overpowered by the expanding wealth of his economic, political and social surroundings and surrenders to their sway. Men in striving to perpetuate and establish culture perpetuate in the process their own frustrations. The materials that could serve life come to rule over its content and goal and the consciousness of man is made victim to the relationships of material and social production.[2]

Man furthermore lives in a world of discontinuity, limitation and fixity. What tends towards universality and oneness is broken into finite and opposed objects; and the unitary processes of human existence are fractured and broken into discrete and contradictory entities. The concreteness of the experienced world imposes limitations on human potential and is dependent upon the negativity of its objects. This negativity arises because the shaping of the objective world and the creation of its "things" is accomplished by the exclusion of other aspects of reality from its object. The latter are therefore given life and defined by what they are not, by their opposedness and every experienced concrete reality must always contain within itself a negativity that will ultimately destroy it. There is no Being without Nonbeing. The world that man creates is one in which he cannot realize his possibilities, for its falseness has become part of him. His creation has been lost to him and turned against him and that which he made—whether material, social or mental objects— has been expropriated from him by himself or by others and has become alien. The world is false to man because he does not know it and he does not know it because he does not know himself.

The negative, then, constitutes the essential quality of dialectical reason. Negativity is manifest in the very process of reality, so that nothing that exists is true in its given form. All things exist apart from and in want of their truth. The negation that everything contains determines its very being. By virtue of the inherent negativity in them all things become self-contradictory, opposed to themselves and their being consists in that "force which can both comprehend and endure Contradiction."[3] Contradiction is at the root of all movement and life and all reality is self-contradictory. Motion especially, external movement as well as self-movement, is nothing but existing contradiction. A given form of existence thus cannot unfold its content without ultimately perishing. The new, in so far as it emerges, must be the actual negation of the old and not a mere correction or revision. To be sure, the new does not drop full-blown from heaven but must somehow have existed in the midst of the old. But it existed there only as potentiality, and its material realization was excluded by the prevailing form of being. The prevailing form has to be broken through. "The changes of Being" are "a process of becoming other which breaks off graduality and is qualitatively other as against the preceding state of existence."[4] There is no even progress in the world: the appearance of every new condition involves a leap; the birth of the new is the death of the old. Crisis and collapse are thus not accidents and external disturbances but manifest the very nature of things and provide the basis on which the essence of every social system can be understood.

Man consequently does not live in a world of fixed entities but rather in a world of flux, contradiction and Becoming. Development unfolds through conflict, the moving power of history is human passions which produce wholly unintended results, and the structure of reality is a structure of oppositions, of elements that contradict each other and limit each other's possibilities. Things are continually pushing against their opposites, the latter react as contradictions and in moving beyond those oppositions move beyond themselves, hopefully into a new state. Every thesis has not only an antithesis but contains and *is* its antithesis. Everything is the seed of a non-thing and reality is defined equally by the attributes of the things and its relations to what it is not. Stability, as Robert F. Murphy has stated, "is attained through the falsification of reality but underlying this apparent reality is its contradictory non-reality and beyond that is the fusion of the opposites in a restless push toward new forms."[5] Or, if the clash of opposites is unable to produce new forms then the contradictions within that reality can only lead to the decay and disintegration of the existing ones.

The dialectical approach scrutinizes everything it sees and hears about society. Its very nature is question, challenge and scepticism. It asks us to look critically at the neat categories and cliches of commonsense reality. It teaches that reality is self-contradictory and that culturally-given truths may be both true and false at the same time; with its falseness always gaining at the expense of its truth. It requires us to look for paradox as much as complimentarity, for opposition as much as ac-comodation. It seeks to examine phenomena fully and from every angle, to evaluate the contradictions of any proposition and consider any category from the viewpoint of its non-contents as well as its positive attributes.

Above all, the dialectic vision sees history as a mighty drama of conflict between opposing forces and for some, Freud and Simmel among others, essentially tragic. Everywhere we see opposition and dissonance in human affairs. The will to live strives against itself, seeks its own well-being at the expense of others and so constantly sets its teeth in its own flesh. The lust for power sets man against man and group against group in unending contention. The two basic instincts of life and death are in a state of perpetual war with each other; civilization opposes and represses the individual and builds tormenting discontents into the very culture that he creates; and man and nature are locked in violent antagonism. Desire, spiritedness, anger and reason are in perpetual conflict with one another. The demonic and corrupt elements within man are in combat with the moral and ethical elements. Illusion, ignorance and ideology are always to one extent or another in opposition to social reality. God and the devil, light and darkness, good and evil, creativity and tradition struggle for dominance in the world. All social arrangements contain within themselves contradictions and negativities which will ultimately destroy them. Productive forces are in collision with the organizational and property forms which have developed them. Un-resolvable discord, contradictions and conflicts are inherent in the nature of things. In the great struggle between man's understanding and the riddles of the world and his existence each new answer offers only a new question and each new victory only a new disappointment. There is thus no inevitable progress towards the good evident from year to year or from epoch to epoch but only unresolved conflict, which sees today good and tomorrow evil prevail.

Perhaps the German sociologist Simmel best depicted the unending dialectic of human existence. For Simmel social life is characterized by a whole series of dualisms, conflicts and contradictions. Man makes the objects of culture but they become alien to him. He cannot exist without forms but the forms stifle and crush him. Institutions originally considered as means, become ends. Life, vibrating, restless and endlessly self-evolving produces objects that are independent of it and shatters itself on the very object it has produced. Life and activity grate against each other and other life and activities. Individuals come into conflict with groups to preserve their individualities and this conflict is central to the nature of the group and its potential for change and flexibility. The concord, harmony and co-efficacy which help to socialize men must nevertheless be interspersed with distance, competition, and repulsion in order to give way to the actual configuration of society. The solid organizational forms which seem to represent and create society must constantly be disturbed, unbalanced, gnawed at by individualistic and irregular forces in order to attain their vital reaction and development through submission and resistance.[6] Because of our accidental and defective adaptation to our life conditions we preserve and acquire not only as much of the truth as is appropriate for our practical activities but also the lies, illusions and ignorance which are also essential for social existence. Differentiation and separation are an integral part of "sociating" and relating. Closeness to some requires distance from others and the active assertion of difference and opposition are ways of relating. Man has an inward orientation toward himself as a totality but he is pulled outward by his need to become part of a collectivity and to serve its requirements. Both the individual life and the social life are temporary and highly precarious compromises and there is no mutual adjustment and balance of the two spheres. In Simmel's dialectic man is always in danger of being slain by the objects of his own creation which have lost their original human co-efficient and this dialectic is neither characteristic of capitalism, nor of socialism, nor of liberal democracy; it represents the very nature of human existence, the very destiny of civilization.

One of the principal conflicts in every culture is that between form and life become spirit. A culture emerges whenever life produces certain forms in which it expresses and realises itself: works of art, religions, sciences, technologies, laws and innumerable others. These forms encompass the flow of life and provide it with content and form, freedom and order. But although these forms arise out of the life process, because of their unique constellation they do not share "the restless rhythm of life, its ascent and descent, its constant renewal, its incessant divisions and reunifications."[7] These forms are frameworks for the creative life which however soon transcends them. They acquire fixed identities, a logic and lawfulness of their own and this new rigidity inevitably places them at a distance from the spiritual dynamic which created them and made them independent in the first place. Insofar as life, having become spirit, ceaselessly produces such forms which become self-enclosed and demand permanence, these forms become inseparable from life and it could not be itself without them. Yet left to itself life flows on without interruption; its restless rhythm opposes the fixed duration of any particular form. Each cultural form, once it is created, is therefore according to him, "gnawed at varying rates by the forces of life." As soon as one is fully formed, the next begins to form and after a struggle that may be long or short it will inevitably succeed its predecessor.

Life for Simmel must, consequently, because of its essential restlessness, constantly struggle against its own products which have become fixed and do not move along with it. This process manifests itself as the displacement of an old form by a new one. This constant change is the content of culture, even of whole cultural styles and is the sum of "the infinite fruitfulness of life." It also marks, at the same time, the deep contradiction between life's eternal flux and the objective validity and genuineness of the forms through which it passes. Life thus "moves constantly between death and resurrection—between resurrection and death."[8]

This characteristic of cultural processes can be studied in economic change. The economic forces of every epoch develop forms of production which are appropriate to their character. Slave economies, guild constitutions, agrarian modes of labor—all these when they were formed expressed adequately the desires and capacities of their times. Gradually, within their own norms and boundaries, however, there grew economic forces whose extension and development these systems obstructed. In time, through explosive revolutions, he argued, they burst the oppressive bonds of their respective forms and replaced them with modes of production more suitable to the times. Yet, a new mode of production need not have overwhelming energy of its own. Life itself, in its economic and other dimensions—with its drive and its desire for advancement, its internal changes and differentiation—will provide the dynamic for this whole movement. The pulse of life will clash with the forms which it has generated; which demand a validity, which transcend the moment and free themselves from the pulsation which has created them. For this reason life is always in latent opposition to the form. This tension will then sooner or later express itself in this sphere and that; and eventually it will develop into a comprehensive cultural necessity. Thus life perceives "the form as such as something which has been forced upon it." Life would therefore "like to puncture not only this or that form, but form as such, and to absorb the form in its immediacy, to let its own power and fullness stream forth just as if it emanated from life's own source, until all cognition, values and forms are reduced to direct manifestations of life."[9]

Life is as a result inseparably charged with contradictions. Life must either produce forms or proceed through forms. But forms belong to a completely different order of being. They demand some content above and beyond life; they contradict the essence of life with its weaving dynamics, its temporal fates, the unceasing differentiation of each of its parts. Life can thus only enter reality in the form of its antithesis, that is, only in the form of form. This contradiction becomes more urgent and appears more irreconcilable the more life makes itself felt. The forms themselves however attempt to deny this contradiction: in their rigidly individual shapes, in the demands of their imprescriptable rights, they boldly present themselves as the true value and meaning of our existence. And the more culture grows the more audacious the forms become in their opposition to the forces of life.

In this conflict between form and life, life strives to obtain something which it cannot reach. It desires to transcend all forms and to appear in its stark immediacy. Yet the processes of thinking, wishing and forming, can only substitute one form for another. They can never replace the form as such by life which as such transcends the form. The attempt to surmount the forms of culture by the forces of life embodies the deepest internal contradictions of the spirit. Although this chronic conflict between form and life has been acute in many historical epochs, none but ours has revealed it so clearly as its basic theme. The existence of this conflict thus points to the contradictions of our present era. The bridge between the past and the future of cultural forms seems to have been demolished and we now "gaze into an abyss of unformed life beneath our feet."

Another fateful, never-ending conflict in all cultures, according to Simmel, is that between subject and object; which finds its second round within spirit itself. The spirit engenders innumerable structures which keep on existing with peculiar autonomy, independent of the soul that has created them, as well as of any other that accepts or rejects them. Man consequently sees himself as confronting art as well as law, religion as well as technology, sciences as well as custom. Placed on this duality he is now attracted and now repelled by their contents, now fused with them as if they were part of himself, now estranged and untouched by them. In the form of stability, coagulation, persistent existence, the spirit becomes object and places itself over against the streaming life, the intrinsic responsibility and the "variable tensions of the soul." Spirit for this very reason thus "experiences innumerable tragedies over this radical contrast: between subjective life which is restless but finite in time and its contents, which once they are created, are fixed but timelessly valid."[10]

The paradox of culture flows from the fact that the subject of life which we feel in its continuous stream and which drives itself towards perfection cannot by itself reach the perfection of culture. It can become truly cultivated as has been noted only through forms which have become completely alien and crystallized into self-sufficient independence. Culture thus comes into being as a result of the meeting between these two elements, neither of which contain culture by itself: the subjective soul and the objective spiritual product. This meeting is at the root of the metaphysical significance of historical phenomena. Although a number of decisive human activities build bridges between subject and object, these bridges cannot be completed, or if completed, are again and again torn down. Some of these are: cognition; above all, work; and in certain of their meanings also art and religion. The spirit sees itself confronted with an object toward which it is driven by the force as well as the spontaneity of its nature. It remains "condemned, however, in its own motion, as if in a circle which only touches the object, and which, whenever it is about to penetrate it, is abruptly forced back into its self-contained orbit by the immanent force of its law."[11] The basic estrangement of the parties cannot be overcome and the attempts to fuse them remain finite attempts to solve an infinite task.

For Simmel, the starting point and end of his analysis is the deep estrangement or animosity which exists between the organic and creative processes of the soul and its content and products: the vibrating, restless life of the creative soul, which develops toward infinite contrasts with its fixed and ideally unchanging product and its uncanny feed-back effect, which arrests and indeed rigidifies this liveliness. The subjective and objective spirit are thus profoundly opposed to one another. Herein lies one of the fundamental forms of our suffering from our own past, our own dogma, and our own fantasies. On the one hand we have the founder of a religion or an artist, a statesman or an inventor, a scholar or a legislator expressing his essential powers, pouring forth the exuberance of his nature in his work. On the other hand, in the process of his passionate dedication to the cause, with its immanent laws demanding perfection, we find the creative individual become the source of new afflictions. The further the cultural process develops, the more the created shows itself to be the enemy of the creator. Not only can the individual not fulfill himself in his work: in the end his work threatens to destroy him. What life truly and inwardly strives for is nothing other than its own movement and the streaming fullness of it. It cannot bring forth this inner fullness, it cannot enable this fullness to become perceptible in specific creations, except that these very creations become limits for it—firm embankments against which this motion streams and against which it breaks itself.

The "fetishism" which Marx assigned to economic commodities represents for Simmel only a special case of this general fate of the contents of culture. With the increase in culture these contents stand more and more under a paradox: they were originally created by subjects and for subjects: but in the intermediate form of objectivity which they assume they follow an immanent logic of development. In so doing "they estrange themselves from their origin as well as their purpose."[12] They are impelled not by physical necessities but by truly cultural ones which, however, cannot bypass the physical conditions. What drives forth the products of the spirit is the cultural and not the natural, scientific logic of the objects. Herein lies the fatefully immanent drive of all technology as soon as it has moved beyond the range of immediate consumption. Thus the industrial production of a variety of products generates a series of closely related by-products for which there is really no need, and "vast supplies of products come into existence which call forth an artificial demand that is senseless from the perspective of the subject's culture."[13] Thus too in the scientific field excessive specialization and the development of techniques of unsurpassable finesse and methodological perfection turn into micrology, pedantic efforts and an elaboration of the unessential into a method that runs for its own sake. Once certain themes of law, of art, of morals have been created—even if they have been created by most individual and innermost spontaneity—we cannot control the direction in which they will develop. Even language deflects and mutilates not only our expressions but also our most intimate intentions. Objects in their development therefore acquire a logic of their own and because of strict adherence to this logic "our thoughts are led into consequences which are far removed from those originally intended."[14] This is the real tragedy of culture.

For Simmel a tragic relationship—in contrast to a merely sad or extrinsically destructive one—is a relationship in which the destructive forces that are directed against some being spring forth from the deepest levels of this very being; or when its destruction has been initiated in itself, and forms the logical development of the very structure by which a being has built its own positive form. It is the concept of culture that the spirit creates an independent objectivity by which the development of the subject takes its part. This form of objectivity, moreover, possesses a boundless capacity for fulfillment. The infinitely growing supply of objectified spirit thus places demands before the subject, creates desires in him, hits him with feelings of individual inadequacy and helplessness, throws him into total relationships from which he cannot withdraw, although he cannot master their particular contents. Modern man as a consequence feels himself surrounded by an innumerable number of cultural elements which are neither meaningless to him nor, in the final analysis, meaningful. Become richer and overloaded modern culture has everything but owns nothing. Modern man is continuously stimulated by a thousand superfluous items but in spite of all this is not stimulated to expressions of individual creativity. For even from its first moments of existence "culture carries something within itself which, as if by an intrinsic fate, is determined to block, to burden, to obscure and divide its innermost purpose, the transition of the soul from its incomplete to its complete state."[15]

Life is, then, not only shaped by an unending dialectic but is also branded by the tragic nature of human existence. Free and proud man challenges a world which is intrinsically hostile to him and dooms his highest aspirations. Wilfull and presumptuous he is capable of extending himself in a multitude of directions and modes only to come up against the insurmountable limits which inexorably will bring him low. Strong and noble enough to pit himself against the terror and absurdity of existence, the terrible destructive process of universal history, the cruelty of nature, he is capable of soaring to the heights of creativity and plunging into the depths of folly and crime. Flawed and corrupted in his very nature his loftiest endeavors can only culminate in downfall and ruin. Filled with destructive forces that spring from the very deepest levels of his being his acts defile everything he touches. Exaggerating or over-developing one vice or virtue at the expense of the harmonious development of all his faculties he wrecks either himself or the enterprise he has embarked upon. Made arrogant by a noble half-truth or blinded by a one-sided point of view he is driven to frenzy and catastrophe. Capable of outrageous behavior he pays for it by disaster; spoiled by success he loses his mental and moral balance. Intoxicated by victory he is overtaken by defeat. Wrestling with the contradictions and antagonisms at the heart of the world he is sooner or later overcome by them. Moved by the irrational drives of human nature to extend himself beyond the reasonable or the prudent he cracks the very foundations beneath him and splits the earth down to the abyss. The higher the reaches of his power and pride the more terrible and swift the nemesis.

The tragedy of human history consists precisely in the fact that human life cannot be creative without being destructive, that biological urges are enhanced and sublimated by a demoniac spirit and that this spirit cannot express itself without in the end committing the sin of hubris. The lawlessness of human passions must always clash with the ultimate principles of law and order. The anti-traditional mind will always collide with the full-blown tyranny of popular custom and conforming tradition. The vitalities of human life which are both constructive and destructive will constantly defy all those maxims of measure and restraint which for a time constrain them. Life is thus permanently at war with itself and there is no final solution to this perennial conflict between the vitalities of life and the principle of measure, between the creative and destructive energies, between passion and reason, between streaming, exuberant and restless life and the forms and institutions through which they express themselves. The tragic vision reveals man in all his strength and weakness, his freedom and his subjection, his grandeur and his misery.[16]

Civilization is therefore no harmonious, self-adjusting whole but is filled with the most violent inner contradictions and conflicts. Civilization is dialectical as well as tragic. It is no simple event, no peaceful unfoldment. It is rather an act which it is forever necessary to begin anew. No social order or institution is safe from the forces of negativity which are built into it and ceaselessly gnaw away at its foundations. Nothing that exists is ever true in its given form. Civilization can thus never abandon itself to the naive optimism of progress or the perfectability of man. It always threatens to destroy what it has so painfully created. Its social problems can never be definitely solved but must be solved every day anew and crisis and collapse are ever present possibilities. The restless rhythm of life, its ascent and descent, its constant renewal, its incessant divisions and reunifications are always in conflict with the fixed identities and rigidities that forms, institutions, technologies and ideologies assume. All life suffers from the deep estrangement and animosity which exists between the organic and creative processes of the soul and its content and products. The cultural objects which man creates become the enemy of its creator. Every civilization carries within itself, as if by an intrinsic fate, something which is determined to block, to burden, to obscure and to defeat its innermost purpose. All civilizations are accordingly unsatisfactory, frustrating, false and profoundly questionable, and decay and disintegration, ruin and defeat are as inherently interwoven into the plan of the world as success and progress.[17]

PART II

CHAPTER 8

THE POVERTY OF THE
SOCIAL SCIENCES

It has already been indicated that a period of decline is a time when leadership, ideologies and institutions are failing. It is a time when the conventional wisdom has been torn to shreds by events, when elites are incapable of providing that effective leadership which holds societies together, and when the master insitutions have become rigid, inflexible and unresponsive. The break-up of a society's ideology or system of symbols, myths and values, the disintegration of those tacit but deeply lodged assumptions by means of which men try to regulate their conduct, the decline of the quality of its leadership, the failure of institutions to respond to the society's changing needs, the incapacity of elites to handle the new social forces that have emerged—all these attest not merely to the existence of a deep social crisis but to a crisis of civilization. It will now be our task to analyse the principal features of this crisis of civilization.

One of the more obvious symptoms of this general crisis is the condition in which the so-called social sciences find themselves. The study of man is now, and has been for some time, passing through a period of pronounced crisis. The traditional perspectives and explanations have failed at precisely the point in history that demands fullest understanding. The leading schools are all in open disarray, their goals are doubted and their methods, objectivity, and even their motives are being questioned. The political and social upheavals of the last decade and the deeper crisis (some of whose aspects we have already discussed) which lies at their root have shattered the confidence of many who once uncritically accepted the scientific pretensions of the social sciences. The cheerful belief that the university was an independent center of objective scholarship and critical intelligence became incredible when it was discovered that most of the research was financed and controlled by the Pentagon and the C.I.A. The rationality of the political order was less persuasive as American politicians seemed unable to pass, among other programs, a comprehensive gun-control law to stop Americans from shooting one another at home, or to stop an unpopular war in which they ruthlessly shot at others while getting shot at themselves abroad. The concepts of pattern-maintenance and tension-management were found to be less persuasive when societal patterns were cracking and tensions everywhere were mounting. The "end of ideology" theorists became laughing stocks when it was discovered that their theoretical frameworks were nothing more than incautious generalizations of the last years of Eisenhower's surface tranquility and rationalizations for the Western Camp in the Cold War. While social scientists continued to devote great energy to explaining how various agencies ingeniously worked at the political socialization of the society's citizens and future citizens, mobs burnt parts of cities, ethnic rivalries multiplied, alienation spread, disaffection increased, students defied campus rulings and authorities, and a new generation questioned the whole range of civic obligations.

The crisis of the social sciences and its inability to provide us with a theoretical framework for the understanding of our world stems from a number of causes. In the first place, it has now become obvious that the university is not an experimental station of ideas; that it is not in the main an independent institution of reason, dispassionate research and critical judgment but particularly in the social sciences it is the main production center of those ideologies, which masquerade as value-free theoretical systems, that support the existing power structure. The university embedded in and supported by society is nothing more than the hand-maiden of the existing order and the training school of whatever functionaries the status quo requires. In the form of the multiversity it has become a service station for society which teaches in Robert Hutchinson's words "anything we can get anybody to pay for." In the name of service and in return for handsome fees and plush appointments universities and academics have been prepared to collaborate in criminal bombing campaigns, espionage, deceit and all the corruption connected with the struggle for power. In the study of the Third World, for example, "area specialists" and "experts" on modernization have produced what Gunnar Myrdal has described as a literature essentially motivated by diplomatic considerations and by the requirements of national power and international power competition. In the cause of service the university has been willing to do whatever society will pay for, and this had led it to surrender one of the indispensable characteristics of wisdom: moral discrimination. Serving the state and the business corporations, acting as the champions of the official society, the university has progressively come to resemble nothing so much as the highly refined, all-purpose brothel Jean Genet described in his play *The Balcony*.

Another crucial reason for the failure of the social sciences to comprehend our world and for the general lowering of the level of social intelligence has come from their attempt to apply the methods of the physical sciences to the study of society and politics. This "scientistic" approach is based on the belief that the problems of social life are in essence similar to the problems of physical nature. It claims that the social sciences can understand the facts of society in the same way in which the physical sciences can understand the laws of nature and that while the latter, by using the knowledge which they have acquired, can dominate nature and harness it to their own ends, the former can use their knowledge to create a gigantic social mechanism which can be placed at the command of the political and economic masters of society.

However, three basic distinctions between the social and the physical world defeat the scientistic conception of society. First of all, in the natural world, we deal primarily with typical situations and typical phenomena as such. In the social world we have to try and understand a great, complicated and delicate social organization representing a vast array of phenomena of all kinds filled with all sorts of bewildering contradictions, conflicts and tensions. Furthermore, the social scientist can never be a completely detached observer of social events. While the natural scientist is capable of being much more detached in his study of the phenomena of nature, he does not, as a general rule, involve his religious, moral, political, social or economic biases in his investigations of a particular problem. The social scientist's methods and results however reflect these biases and are implicated in the very act of his social investigation. All the social sciences, as we have already shown, are tainted by an ideological taint. Finally, the natural sciences deal with lifeless matter, and even where they deal with human beings or living matter they deal with them as some sort of mechanism. They do not deal with or understand the blind instincts and passions that drive man, the fact that man is both an irrational and rational being. They do not see that of all living beings in the universe man is the most complex one; and that the methods used to study less complex organisms cannot be applied to the study of the human condition. It is for these three reasons, among others, that the analogy between the natural and social sciences simply collapses.

Scientism, furthermore, is incapable of understanding the problems of power, of political conflict, of ideology, of war and revolution. In its view the existence of all the problems of politics is assumed to be primarily the result of the lack of information and political knowledge, of lack of skill in the handling of social and political situations. All these political phenomena are presumed to be the product of accidents or are considered deviations from the rule of reason which ought to dominate the life of man. In fact, all these political problems arise not from ignorance, which scientism is supposed to remedy, but from deep-seated conflicts of interests, from certain basic antagonisms which are inherent in every social order, and which no amount of scientific knowledge can eliminate as such. Wisdom, knowledge and political skill may, under favorable circumstances, solve these problems for a time, but there is no scientific device that can solve the problems of war, of class conflicts, of freedom, of authority, in the same way in which the problem of, say, the internal combustion engine has been solved.

The problem of the combustion engine was solved when the scientists dealing with it found the formula as a result of which the internal combustion engine could be built, and once the formula was found, the natural scientists could forget about the problem of the internal combustion engine and direct their attention to other projects. Political problems, however, are not of this kind; they cannot be solved by the invention of a mechanical formula which will allow mankind to forget about their existence, and turn its attention toward a problem which has yet not been solved. Being projections of human nature into society, mankind's basic political problems can never be permanently solved. Scientism overlooks the fact that those who must solve human problems are also human beings, and that there is no relying on human beings. Man's essential political problems will always remain with him; they can only be restated, manipulated and temporarily resolved and each epoch has to come to terms with them anew.

In fact, the ideal of scientism as applied to politics is to eliminate politics altogether from social life. In place of politics it seeks to substitute rational manipulation, professional administration and social engineering. Scientism assumes that if only the right formulae can be found, that once the right mechanical devices have been applied, then the political domination of man by man, the violent clashes of human collectivities and man's irrationality will disappear as temporary aberrations from the rule of cooperation and reason.[1]   Disregarding human complexity, unaware of the self-contradictions of the human will, pursuing incompatible goals at the same time and in the same place, ignoring the grotesque and inconstant images that agitate man and arouse his anxieties, scientism reduces man to a machine, society to a computer or some other mechanical contraption, human selfishness, passions, dreams, fears and delusions to mathematical formulae, history and the social sciences to a collection of trivial facts and data and the language of politics and sociology to a barbarous jargon.* Wittgenstein's castigation of philosophers is apposite to the practitioners of scientism: "Philosophers constantly see the method of science before their eyes, and are irresistably tempted to ask and answer questions in the way science does. This tendency is the real source of metaphysics, and leads the philosopher into complete darkness."

Another approach that has greatly contributed to the stultification of the social science imagination and to the impoverishment of political and social thought has been the one associated with what has been called "methodism." Rejecting traditional political theories, sweeping the floor of the mind of all the accumulated knowledge of the past and levelling it in the process, the "methodist" approach constructs a "straight road" in Descartes' phrase which enables the devotees of methodus to follow a prescribed series of mental steps in their investigations. If political philosophy and theory stressed the arduous difficulties awaiting those who sought truth, the methodists or methodologists emphasize the economy of being methodical, extol the utility of the easy and familiar paths[2] and point to the advantages of adhering to the beaten path which they have laid down rather than "blazing a new trail" in the search for understanding.

The methodist, thus, does not search for wisdom but for a "kit of tools" or a "bag of tricks" with which to acquire "scientific knowledge." He seeks "truth" that is economical, replicable and easily packaged and this is to be obtained through research "manuals," "handbooks," and a check list or inventory of do's and don'ts. Instead of cultivating political understanding and teaching students of politics to become sensitized to the enormous complexities, predicaments, uncertainties and drama of the political order, the methodists are engaged in the search for ever better "research skills" and spend their time teaching

---

* As Kathleen Knott has written: "Jargon is a parrotlike or mumbo jumbo imitation of the precise classifications of the physical and mathematical sciences. A language is a jargon when its references claim an objectivity, an agreement about a definition, that does not exist."

sampling, interviewing, coding, analysis, etc. This kind of scientific education leads to narrowness and rigidity, and produces men who, as Thomas Kuhn pointed out, can only practice "normal science," that is, the acknowledged science of the profession, the science that is based on whatever orthodoxy prevails at any particular moment. The behaviorist school, which is the principal representative of methodism, has not only introduced the engineering approach into political thought with its inputs and outputs but has reduced political knowledge to a knowledge of techniques and to neatly devised, mechanical schemata which are presumed to explain the whole complicated world of politics. It in fact represents a flat-earth view of society.

Academic knowledge has, therefore, ceased to be a bold and personal pursuit of truth and has become instead the accumulation of so-called correct information and interpretation. Following settled procedures and explicit rules most of the scholarly work by this school is timid, mediocre, trivial, conservative and conducted in terms of the professionally sanctioned methodologies and research procedures. Few academics dare to stand alone and articulate a personal view of political and social reality. Indeed, the whole concept of "replicable" research assumes that an original mind is neither wanted nor needed: for another academic can emerge with the same conclusions if he only follows the rules and goes through the same or similar motions. Less and less knowledge now emanates from poring over books in libraries or from isolated reflection which nourishes all creativity. Research is now conducted in laboratories or through "interviewing" and is then processed by the newest technological inventions. Tape-recorders and computers are now accepted instruments of knowledge-production. Not only does this elaborate machinery aid scholarly research but it provides the mechanism whereby what passes for credible research can be produced in suitably visible quantities. Using equipment consequently becomes "a way of imparting a material sub-structure to one's methodology; the machine actually materializes the method."[3]

Contemporary scholarship as a result inhabits a world of barren reality and utopian pretention. Instead of cultivating the qualities crucial to theorizing—curiosity, concern, the juxtaposition of contraries, and wonder at the variety and subtle interconnections of things —it encourages a mania for data which is meaningless in itself, formal abstractions which have no connection with social reality and conformism to the prevailing fashions. It resembles more the world of bureaucratic sterility than that of intellectual creativity. Without a sense of history or tragedy, its approach is superficial and without depth. It is highly significant, for example, that the organizing notions on which game-theory, communications models and mechanical systems rest are essentially history-less. Having cast aside many of the speculative insights and inherited learning that were the peculiar glory of Western man, modern social science has become the perfect instrument for an age of mechanism, big organizations, technological idiocy, and of rationality without reason. Modern social science substitutes caution for intellectual adventure, the obvious and the trivial for a critical analysis of contemporary reality, graduates calculating servants of power, and while trying to shape a society of regular and predictable behavior it in fact functions in one marked by breakdown, with its political systems sputtering and its communication networks infiltrated by deafening and incoherent sounds.

Another approach which has blinded the social sciences and prevented them from understanding social reality in all its complexity is the structural-functional approach. This approach in both sociology and political science has constituted the rise to prominence of a "new scholasticism: of formal theory centering on the construction of generalized political and social systems carefully insulated from empirical reality."

The central notion in Talcott Parsons' phantasmagorical conceptual construction is that of a system defined as a set of functionally interdependent elements. For him the world is one and must be made safe in its oneness. Its oneness in fact is the world's most vital characteristic. Its parts therefore take on meaning and significance only in relation to this wholeness. For Parsons it is not the divisions in the world, its negations, internal contradictions and class conflicts that were its deepest realities but its unbroken oneness. Making conceptual distinctions is thus not an end for itself but a way of providing routes to the whole.

Social systems can, according to him, be described and their processes analyzed in terms of four highly general sub-systems of human action—the organism, personality, social system and cultural system. This classification is an application of a general paradigm which can be used throughout the field of action and can analyze any action system in terms of four functional categories: 1) that concerned with the maintenance of the highest "governing" or controlling patterns of the system; 2) the internal integration of the system; 3) its orientation to the attainment of goals in relation to its environment; and 4) its more generalized adaptation to the broad conditions of the environment—e.g., the non-action physical environment.[4]

Adopting this notion of action Parsons has worked out and elaborated classifications of the types and structures of social action in a language which has been described as a bad translation from the German. In terms of the paradigm which has been set forth, Parsons distinguishes four sub-systems of a society. The first sub-system is that which is formed by the institutions responsible for "pattern-maintenance" and "tension-management," or in other words, with the institutions concerned with socialization, education and pre-eminently with religion. The second is that composed by the institutions concerned with "integration" or the maintenance of differentiating norms and rules: these are primarily legal institutions—courts, the legal profession, the police. The third is the political system, which has responsibilities for collective goal-attainment; and the fourth is the economy, which has the function of adaptation to the physical environment (that is, production). Each sub-system, furthermore, has its own sub-system performing for the sub-system the same basic function as the sub-systems severally perform for the main system, so that there was an overall "nesting" process of systems within systems. And to complete the process there were inputs and outputs continually being fed from one sub-system to another, and there were feedbacks.

Parsons additionally analyzes the social systems with the aid of his four major pairs of pattern variables. These are: 1) Affectivity/Affective Neutrality; 2) Universalism/Particularism; 3) Ascription/Achievement; and 4) Diffuseness/Specificity. The first pattern variable poses before an actor in a situation the choice between immediate gratification of his impulses and self-restraint; the second places before the actor the choice of treating the objects in a situation in accordance with general norms covering all objects in that class which is designated universalism; or he may deal with them according to their standing in some particular relationship to him or his collectivity; the third variable, also identified as a choice between quality and performance, distinguishes between ascribed status, acquired with no effort, like a family name, and achieved status acquired through personal activity; the last of the pattern variables is used to distinguish between a relation that involves a very limited claim by one person on the other and a relation that involves wide and unspecified claims on both sides.

These pattern variables were according to him not only capable of characterizing and classifying exhaustively orientations, roles and value patterns but were also the switch points which directed action along one course rather than another and by separating one course of action from another kept the whole system working. In particular, they provided the means whereby disruptive elements could be prevented from destroying the social and normative order which was of the essence of all societies. For Parsons the primary elements that assured the maintenance of social structures are not material interests but normative elements, especially religious values and norms.

The sharpest focus of Parsons' analysis of social systems, however, is on the self-maintaining processes that govern them, the order-maintaining mechanisms inherent in them. His "social system" is a social world with its own ramifying network of defenses against tension, disorder and conflict; force your way into one and another springs up, ready to absorb the shock. This system's stability may be contingent, but it is never fragile. What is emphasized is its almost endless capacity to contain and nullify shock; what is laboriously displayed is an intricate and interdependent network of mechanisms that ties together the system's energies within itself, that efficiently distributes it to stress points and that never wastes any of it. The Parsonian social system thus is one whose "equilibrium" once established is conceived to be perpetual and whose essential reality is believed to be its inner coherence rather than the conflicts, tensions and disorders that are merely considered to be secondary disturbances or aberrations. Conflict, tension and disorder are never seen to derive from the necessary and inevitable requirements of social life. And the actors who play roles in this system have an extraordinary plastic potentiality for conformity. The socialization process produces individuals who are supposed to completely fit into the society, who need never be constrained and who always act willingly out of an inward motivation. The individual is, in fact, conceived of as an entirely "social creature," as an empty, hollowed-out container that depends entirely upon experience in and training by social systems. There is no conflict between individual and society.

The Parsonian social world furthermore is one where men use power benignly on behalf of the common interest and collective goals and where power differences rarely tempt the stronger to take more than morality dictates. The polity is conceived of "as a social sub-system theoretically parallel to the economy,"5 in which 1) power is treated as analogous in the polity to money in the economy; 2) power is viewed as a generalized medium of interchange in the polity, that is, as a circulating medium; and 3) in which power, like money, is seen as an "input" that can be combined with other elements to produce certain outputs useful to the system as a whole. He thus opposes, in his analysis of the concept of power, what games theorists call the "zero-sum" conception (particularly as it was used by C. Wright Mills in *The Power Elite*) according to which the power of some involves the powerlessness of others, because this view implies the existence of divided interests and conflict in society. He chooses rather to define power as the capacity of the social system to get things done in its collective interest; this enables it to put the emphasis upon an overriding collective interest and upon the integration of the system through common values, while playing down any discordant interests or internal conflicts. The Parsonian system is, in brief, a perpetual motion machine.

Conflicts and disorder are therefore viewed not as part of the necessary order of things; they are more nearly similar to the fortuitous illnesses of the body than to the aging body's certain infirmity and inevitable death. Parsons operates with the assumption that there is nothing inherent in a social system that will bring it to an end, seriously disrupt it, continuously subject it to stress and strain or even radically change its structure from time to time. For Parsons the social system is immortal.[6]

The most consistent and systematic functionalist in political science is David Easton, though he might not altogether agree. Yet his "systems approach" in politics is an interesting variant of functionalism that has had great influence among political scientists. Indeed, Easton might almost be considered the political scientists' Parsons, for their work is similar in many respects, though Easton claims that the sources of his thinking lie elsewhere—in what is called "general systems theory," an approach to analysis developed by a small group of scholars with a strong bias to biology and mathematical analysis. Like Parsons, Easton too has searched for a "general" theory, a unified conceptual framework for the analysis of political life. And like Parsons, again, he is concerned with order and stability, with equilibrium and with the "persistence" of political systems in a world of change and stress.

Discarding the definition of politics as the study of power, Easton comes up with a definition of politics that states that political science is concerned only with the "authoritative allocation of values or policies"[7] for a society. The allocation of values means all those kinds of activities involved in the formulation and execution of state policy. The "policy-making process" or the "political system" consists of a web of decisions and actions that allocates values and the taking and implementing and revision of policy decisions. Authority in his definition is that which makes a policy "authoritative." This happens "when the people to whom it was intended to apply or who are affected by it consider that they must or ought to obey it."[8]

The basic elements in his conceptual structure are amazingly simple. There is a political system operating in an environment. There are inputs to the system (demand and support) and outputs from the system (decisions and actions of authorities). There is feed-back; a "loop" connects authority and membership so that responses of members are communicated to authority and can generate further action by authorities. The basic unit of policy is the inter-action, and more specifically, the inter-action arising out of the behavior of members of the system when they are acting as members of the system. The concept of the "system" is defined in purely analytic or nominal terms. A system, in Easton's terms, comprises any set of inter-actions that an investigator finds interesting. There need be no empirical connections among them.

In the category of inputs, *Demands* provide the raw material or information which the system must process and the energy needed by the system. Demands arise either in the environment (external) or within the system itself (internal). The environment includes other systems within the total system (society)—ecology, economy, culture, personality, social structure, demography, etc. Each of these constitute the major set of variables in the setting that helped to shape the demands entering the political system from the outside. But there is also another aspect of inputs, *Support.* This is the energy in the form of action or orientations (states of mind) which promotes or hinders a political system, or the demands and decisions which are needed to keep the system running. It exists when we say that a man is loyal to his party, attached to democracy or infused with patriotism. The area of support arises from three objects. Firstly, the political community: members must be ready to support the peaceful settlement of demands and there must be a high degree of national unity or "consensus." Secondly, the regime: members must support the rules of the game— the constitutional principles which legitimate action and provide authority. Thirdly, members must support the actual government if it is to perform the concrete tasks of negotiating settlements: force is not enough.

Easton next discusses the mechanisms of support, and it is here that he deals with outputs. By mechanisms of support is meant the means of maintaining a constant flow of support for the system. Outputs can be mechanisms of support if the policy decisions made within the political system meet the day-to-day demands placed upon it. There may also be inducements, positive or negative (that is, sanctions) and these will vary from system to system (democratic or totalitarian) and indeed within each broad category of systems. Governments or, in another domain parties, need not meet all the demands even of the most influential supporters; they could call upon a reserve of support —consensus or party loyalty. But some demands of the influential members—individuals or groups—must be satisfied if the system is to maintain itself.

Another mechanism of support is politicization. This is the process of manufacturing support, of political socialization—the equivalent of "general socialization" in societies. The patterns of political life

are learnt by the members of the system; they assimilate political attitudes and orientations. Those expectations are reinforced by a common
network of rewards and punishments and by means of the communication of myths, doctrines, ideologies, philosophies, etc. which influence
all members. The system thus comes to be accepted as legitimate.[9]
Although Easton recognizes that the political system is subject to
"stresses" which may be due primarily to lack of supports or to excess
of demands, his whole emphasis is on the political system's contribution
to "boundary maintenance" of the social system as a whole. All systems
thus by implication have a built-in tendency toward equilibrium, the
steady state, homeostasis, adjustment and balance.[10] His theory deals
more with the statics than the dynamics of politics. Its bias toward
stability and order and to system-persistence makes it impossible for
his theory to understand those forces that unbalance, disturb and destroy
political orders.

Committed to the prevailing political system and its normative
premises the contemporary political science which he helped to fashion
has, as he himself admitted, "failed to anticipate the crises that are upon
us."[11] And its excessive concern with system maintenance perspectives
has blinded it to the brutal realities of politics.

The system theorists and equilibrium theorists thus present a view
of society that is lifeless, bloodless and abstract to the point of unreality. Parsons and Easton, and many more could be singled out, reject
as we have shown, the concept of power as the central notion of social
life. Having rejected the concept of power they are simply incapable
of understanding the social divisions in the world, its irrationalities,
negations, internal contradictions and class and group conflicts. Because
there is power, i.e., because there are rulers and ruled, there are always
inequalities of participation in the regulated game of the political process. In every society it is the strong that rule and the rule of the strong
generates the opposition of the weak. Power always implies non-power
and therefore resistance. The dialectic of power and resistance is the
motive force of history. From the interest of those in power at a given
time we can always deduce the interests of the powerless and with them
the movements of conflict and change. Here is the nexus where norms
and values are laid down, called into question, modified, called into
question again and degenerate. It is the framework within which the
great drama of human societies is played out. Power produces conflict and "conflict between antagonistic interests gives lasting expression to the fundamental uncertainty of human existence, by ever giving
rise to new solutions and ever casting doubt on them as soon as they
take form."[12] Legitimacy thus amounts at best to a precarious pre-

ponderance of power over the resistance it engenders. Of all states, equilibrium is the least likely, a freakish accident rather than the general rule.

Societies and social organizations are, furthermore, not only held together by consensus but by constraint, not only by universal agreement but by the coercion of some by others. Institutions exist to protect men from the evil of their fellow men rather than as monuments of consensus. Although it is useful to speak of the "value system of a society," such characteristic values or ideologies as we have already suggested are ruling rather than common, enforced rather than accepted at any given time. Norms are established and maintained by power and their substance reflects the interests of the powerful. As conflict generates change, so does constraint generate conflict. Conflict is therefore ubiquitous, as constraint is ubiquitous wherever human beings set up social organizations. In a highly formal sense it can be claimed that it is always the basis of constraint that is at issue in social conflict. Order in society is consequently not obtained by consensus but by constraint and the selective application of sanctions and because there is no certainty there has to be constraint to assure some liveable minimum of coherence. The failure of the ruling class to assure coherence leads either to the revolutionary overthrow of the society or to its degeneration.

The structural-functional-equilibrium model is thus essentially a Utopian model of society, comparable to the Utopian future envisioned by Marx but in this case applied to the prevailing bourgeois democratic order. In terms of this model, society is a neatly-functioning whole, sharp conflict is absent, universal consensus rules, everybody plays his role, equilibrium reigns and justice is assured. Children are born and socialized and allocated until they die; new children are born and the same happens all over again. Power is exercised on behalf of the whole society and with its support. Political decisions are basically the expression of a common or general will. Power is not a zero-sum game but a currency of which every citizen has his share. A universal system of participation, an undisturbed flow of communications characterizes the political process and its inherent "justice." The society adapts to changing environmental conditions and to internal processes of social differentiation through feed-back processes, input-output relations, and through manifestations of the flow of power in a system of support and initiative. Equilibrium is maintained by the regular occurrence of certain pattern-processes. The system is essentially self-sufficient, internally consistent, self-regulating and closed to the outside. Of course, this system is not static in the sense of being dead; things take place all the time; but happily they are under control and they all help to maintain the precious equilibrium of the whole. Things not only take place, they function and as long as they do all is well. There is in fact nothing inherent in the system that can seriously disturb it or disrupt it. The system is immortal.

The only thing wrong with this model, however, is that is has never existed and is not likely ever to come into being. The whole vast super-structure of concepts that has been raised does not describe social reality, the propositions do not explain the dynamics of social life and from the models nothing follows. Its claims to science are mere pretention. Its elaborate and specialized vocabularies are a substitute for thought. Its obvious failures can be read in the crises, disturbances and revolutions of the age. It has been unable to explain the demonic nature of power, the blindness of ideology, the subconscious and pri-meval forces within man which resist and defy complete socialization, the irrationalities which are at the heart of things, the corruption and evil of politics, the dialectics of social life, the rise and fall of elites and societies and the basic tragedy of human existence. Produced in a temporary period of tranquility it has no relevance to our era of anxiety, disruption and decay. Those educated in its precepts simply cannot understand our age; nor can they act as guides through its social mine-fields. Complacent and conservative, abstruse and mechan-ical, serving the status-quo rather than analyzing it, its intellectual poverty is only exceeded by the power its adherents have gained in our academic institutions, by their tenacious refusal to relinquish it and by their stubborn refusal to learn from experience. An elite which has accepted its basic assumptions simply cannot possess the intel-lectual resources, sophistication and depth to respond to the problems of the age and the marks of ignorance and defeat are branded upon its forehead.

CHAPTER 9

THE FAILURE OF LIBERAL DEMOCRACY

The multiple crises that confront our age spring not only from the revolutionary technological and economic transformations that have uprooted and disoriented millions of people but also arise from the failures of political institutions and of the political imagination. Today as in the thirties the liberal ideology and the liberal political system are under attack. The supposedly "revolutionary" issues of the present day—black rebellion and urban poverty in America, university crises and student rebellions throughout the West, breakdown of urban services and government, bureaucratic ossification, maldirected economic priorities—are all merely the outward symptoms of a much deeper moral crisis. The very legitimacy of liberal government itself—which is to say, the right and competence to rule—has been called into question. There is no longer a secure belief, as there once was, that liberalism either deserves to resolve the multiple problems that face us or that we can go on living as we have been doing.

All the basic tenets of liberalism have been exploded by the inherent development of liberal society itself. Its essential faith in the marketplace, in the beneficent outcome of the free play of ideas and popular forces has been shown up to be an absurd myth. The free play of market forces has not produced the Good but has strengthened Privilege and the Power of the Strong. Political competition between parties and institutions has not made government more responsive to its constituents but has created an unimaginable and remote governmental power which seems to feed upon itself on the one hand and personal impotence and gnawing dissatisfaction on the part of the mass of the citizens on the other. Mass democracy and universal suffrage have degraded the political process. The spread of mass education has neither reduced prejudices, superstitions nor ignorance nor has it raised the general level of knowledge or of understanding. Humanism as an educational program does not in any way correlate with humane social conduct. Liberalism's emphasis on individual rights and freedom has not led to the greater self-perfection of the individual nor has it made him more virtuous or moral. Material abundance has neither produced human happiness nor satisfaction. Its belief in and encouragement of scientific reason and its offspring technology has produced a mad disordering of the world and of man's relationship to his total environment.[1]

The crisis of liberalism that is now so apparent is not the crisis of nineteenth century laissez-faire liberalism but of its twentieth century reformist variant. It is the crisis of what Theodore Lowi has aptly called interest-group liberalism.[2]   Interest-group liberalism is the amalgam of capitalism, statism and pluralism that has replaced the laissez-faire liberalism of the nineteenth century and that its champions believe can manage the highly complex economies and mass societies of the twentieth century. In terms of this theory, group competition has replaced market competition, self-regulation now takes place through politics rather than economics, and a plurality of well-organized interests able and willing to use power has now emerged alongside the state. The entrenchment of interest-group liberalism has finally led to the acceptance by the capitalist class of statism and positive government, has vastly expanded the role of administration and organization within government and without; and has created a ubiquitous network of autonomous groups through which power and control are allegedly widely distributed.

The pluralist ideology which is the principal exponent of interest-group liberalism is based upon a number of postulates. First, it holds that since groups are the rule in markets and elsewhere, imperfect competition is now the rule of social relations. Second, the method of imperfect competition is not really competition but a form of it called bargaining. In this bargaining situation the number of participants is small, the relationship is face to face and the bargainers have "market power", which means that they have some control over the terms of their agreements and can administer rather than merely react to their environment. Third, since class solidarity is supposedly absent, bargaining becomes the single alternative to violence and coercion in industrial society. And last, if the system is stable and peaceful, as it ought to be by definition, it proves the self-regulative character of pluralism. It is therefore the way the system works and the way it ought to work.

Although pluralism's acceptance of positive government first puts it at an ideological pole opposite capitalism in reality there is very little difference between them. Capitalism and pluralism have not really been synthesized, they have merely absorbed each other. Pluralism is just as mechanistic in its outlook as orthodox Smithian economics. If Adam Smith believed that competition between freely contracting individuals in the marketplace tended toward a benign equilibrium then the pluralists believe that pluralist competition tends toward a similar equilibrium and that its involvement with government can only produce good. The utilization of government is simply one of the many ways groups achieve equilibrium. Pluralist equilibrium and organized group bargaining is consequently really the public interest. In actual fact the pluralistic embrace of government turns out to be, in its own way, as anti-governmental as capitalism. For pluralism does not involve government in the making of positive decisions but it has been reduced to nothing more than another set of interests, and one that is particularly solicitous of business needs.

Interest-group liberalism and its pluralist ideology thus have not basically changed the character of capitalist society. Organized groups, it is now more than obvious, are no more virtuous than private individual firms or groups and might even be more rapacious and rigid. The regulatory agencies that have been set up to supervise the activities of certain industries have become the protectors of the industries they are supposed to regulate and have generally done little that is clearly unacceptable to these industries. Even when the purpose of a program is the uplifting of the underprivileged the administrative arrangement favored by interest-group liberalism tends, in the first instance, toward the creation of new privilege instead. Urban redevelopment programs based upon the federal support of private plans tend only too easily to become the means by which the building industry regularizes itself for its own profit and benefit. In the case of the poverty programs of the 1960s not only was power delegated to community action groups, ad hoc local bodies, newly created agencies, but also the responsibility for finding solutions, and the result was not the solution of the problem of poverty but the emergence of a group of privileged managers of the poverty interest. As programs are split off and allowed to establish self-governing relations with clientele groups, professional norms are usually elaborated governing the proper ways of doing things. These rules-of-the-game heavily weight access and power in favor of the existing interests just as American parliamentary rules-of-the-game have always tended to make Congress a refuge for classes in decline. In the imperfect competition or bargaining that takes place between organized groups the strong have become stronger, the middle groups have been squeezed by the more powerful and the weak have become weaker. The lion always gets the lion's share.[3]

The failures of interest-group liberalism are most evident in the sphere of income and power distribution. The poorest fifth of the United States population receives only 4 percent of the nation's annual income and the next poorest fifth only 11 percent while the richest fifth gets about 45 percent and the fifth at the top over 20 percent. Inequality of assets is even greater: 1 percent of the people controls more than one-third of the country's wealth. Although many Americans now own some stocks 2 percent of all individual stock-holders own about two-thirds of stocks held by individuals. The same inequality exists in the business world. Of the almost two million corporations in America one-tenth of one percent controls 55 percent of the total corporate assets; 1.1 percent controls 82 percent. At the other end of the spectrum, 94 percent of the corporations own only 9 percent of the total assets. Even the public economy is unequal, for the poor pay a larger share of their incomes for taxes than other groups; people earning less than $2,000 pay fully half of their incomes in direct and indirect taxes as compared with only 45 percent payed by those earning $50,000 or more. Moderate income groups are not much better off; people earning $8,000-$10,000 a year pay only 4 percent less of their income than those making $25,000-$50,000.[4]   It has in fact been estimated that despite fifty years of increased government intervention, supposedly "confiscatory" taxation, welfare statism and the rest, the United States has seen no dramatic change in the concentration of wealth and income during this whole period.[5]

Interest-group liberalism has not only been unable to provide social justice but it renders government impotent. Liberal or social democratic governments which are more or less the same thing, are unable to plan. They are bountiful in plans but irresolute and incompetent in planning. Liberalism has become a doctrine "whose means are its ends, whose combatants are its clientele, whose standards are not even those of the mob but worse, are those the bargainers can fashion to fit the bargain."[6] Delegation of power has become the alienation of public domain—the gift of sovereignty to private satrapies. The pluralist notion that a system built upon groups and bargaining is self-corrective has been disproved in practice. Imperfect competition or oligopoly produces, contrary to Galbraith's analysis, not countervailing power but accomodating power. Imperfect competition can only occur at a level that injures too many people and excludes too many groups from the society's benefits. Sentimentalizing the group, the group member and the interests, interest-group liberalism undermines the public welfare, corrupts democratic government by making it the instrument of interest-groups with all their financial and political resources and breeds the new pathology that infects our society.

Moreover, government by and through interest-groups is in its fundamental impact conservative in almost every sense of that term. It is a system uniquely designed for the maintenance of the existing state of affairs. The kind of society created by interest-group liberalism is socially static. It has little political vitality. A fully group-organized society loses much of its capacity for change. Organizations are shaped by organizational imperatives and these imperatives produce organizational conservatism. Conservatism is literally built into the nature of organization itself. In this sense one can say that formal groups are inherently conservative regardless of the nature of the goals and of the organizations or the previous position of its members. Leadership is naturally oligarchic and the organizations become highly bureaucratized and rigid. Regardless of its commitment to particular goals, the established organizations will resist other organizational forms or approaches to attain those same goals. Organizational maintenance replaces every other possible goal. Risk taking is smothered, innovation and creativity is stifled, entrepreneurship withers and independence is penalized. "The highly organized groups that abound in our society seem to present a picture, not of dynamic equilibrium, but of a society that is running down, a society in a state of decadence."[7]

The Western world however is not only beset by a crisis of liberalism in all its forms but also confronts a crisis of authority. Although democracy offers the people an opportunity to choose their rulers at prescribed intervals it in no way implies "government by the people" with all minority dominations eliminated. It does not intrinsically demand the weakening of authority; it only requires that authority be founded on the consent of the people. This consent has, as we know, at exceptional moments been given to men of strong authority. Pericles is an ancient example of this; Lloyd George, Churchill and de Gaulle are instances from recent times. Nevertheless there is something in democracy that tends to undermine authority. This debilitation of authority is produced by a number of factors characteristic of a democratic system.

In the first place, democracy is the theory of sovereignty which specifies no qualifications for governing except that of numbers. Momentary desire, passing caprice and merely average taste are made supreme. It puts the power of choosing its rulers into the hands of an undifferentiated and easily manipulated multitude. Democracy has thus always tended to undermine uniqueness and creativity. It is insensitive or hostile to cultural excellence and independence of mind and character. It prevents, as Tocqueville put it, original minds and energetic characters from rising above the crowd. In achieving political equality it erodes away the social and cultural bases of human greatness. Theory and philosophy are despised or neglected and technique and technicism are glorified. Large and noble themes are jettisoned in the general preoccupation with the useful, the finite and the average. The individual is lost or overwhelmed by the sheer number of his "equals" and is filled with a sense of his own "insignificance and weakness."[8] Moved by an exaggerated taste for useful gratifications and a devotion to the present, democracies tend to an equal disregard for the past and the future. When these are combined with the worship of success in place of fame and of competitive achievement in place of individual ambition the results are, Tocqueville finds, conducive to a restlessness that breeds melancholy:

> To these causes must be attributed that strange melancholy which often haunts the inhabitants of democratic countries in the midst of their abundance, and that disgust at life which sometimes seizes upon them in the midst of calm and easy circumstances. Complaints are made in France that the number of suicides increases; in America suicide is rare, but insanity is said to be more common than anywhere else. These are all different symptoms of the same disease . . . In democratic times enjoyments are more intense than in the ages of aristocracy, and the number of those who partake in them is vastly larger; but, on the other hand, it must be admitted that man's hopes and desires are oftener blasted, the soul is more stricken and perturbed, and care itself more keen . . . [9]

Democracy has also tended to make uniformity a surrogate for "equality", and the populace is, as John Stuart Mill pointed out,[10] particularly effective in penetrating and policing private life in order to assure that uniformity prevails. The popular ethos and social pressures over personal beliefs enslave the individual. Public opinion presses with enormous weight upon the mind of each individual and surrounds, directs and weakens him. As men grow more alike, each man feels himself feebler than all the rest. Lost among the sheer numbers of the crowd he mistrusts himself as soon as it assails him. Made uniform by all the vast collective forces of the modern world the average individual becomes more weak, more narrow-minded and dependent. Manly candor and masculine independence of opinion which constitute the outstanding features in distinguished characters are rarely to be seen. And it becomes more difficult to find the highest talents and virtues among those who are in authority.

By reducing traditional social inequalities and by destroying the idiosyncratic and the exclusive democracy, furthermore, helps clear the way for the operations of the market and for the bureaucratic impulse. There is no doubt that it supports one of the principal instruments of our present system, the mass. The goods produced for the market are placed beyond effective criticism or judgement, regardless of their ugliness or the injury they do to individuals and societies, by the fact that they could not be produced, and their manufacturers could not make profits, if they were not purchased and in this way sanctioned by the people. The great private and public bureaucracies could not function without the "organization men" who staff them and the masses who support them. And much of the mass culture produced by the system is impregnable despite its outrageous vulgarity, because "it is what the people want." The elevation of the masses as the arbiters of taste reduces the very level of civilization to the lowest common denominator and sows the seeds of degeneration.

Another factor is the reluctance of the multitudes to support for long, as Glenn Tinder has argued, "the discipline and tensions of great leadership."[11] When circumstances do not absolutely demand otherwise, and very often not even then, a people is apt to empower men of meager energy and imagination; and even in times of crisis they may be won over by the demagogue who instigates and is carried to power by popular prejudice and hatred. Thus the roster of peacetime democratic leaders demonstrates the tendency of the people to empower mediocrities. In ancient Athens, for example, after Pericles' death, the principal leaders of the city were Nicias, passive and unexciting and the demagogic Cleon. Looking at the matter from the side of the government, it can be said that democracy minimizes the obligation to lead. It raises to power those who are ready to be subservient to the unexamined prejudices and preferences of the multitudes and to the practitioners of "permissive exploitation." Democracy thus offers an opening, if not an invitation, for men to seek power merely for its prestige and its material rewards and not from the capacity or the will to take a part in historical existence. The men who attain power are neither able nor willing to change thoughts and values, or to play lofty historic roles but are merely satisfied to subordinate themselves to the ignorant and pliable mass. There are very few democratic political leaders with any inward assurance as to how our civilization is to be changed and guided. They simply do not know where they are going, because strictly speaking, they have no fixed road, no predetermined trajectory before them.

Operating in a world of mass disintegration and spiritual and intellectual impoverishment, mass democracy as a socially organized dissipation of social awareness must necessarily be opposed to the exercise of authority. Social conditions which eliminate solitude and reflection, which transfer decisions to groups rather than to individuals and which surround all actions in routines, not only tend to limit the opportunities for assuming and for feeling the weight of authority, they tend to root out men of the type who desire and can bear the burdens of authority. Thus, genuinely personal authority does not accord well with the major forces and institutions of industrialism or democracy. Technology and industry demand a calculable environment, as secure as possible against the intervention of personal will and initiative. Managers of course are needed; but they do not have the independence of character, the historic imagination, which is a quality of true authority, and their main qualification in any case is impersmnal routine efficiency. Thus too, genuinely personal authority does not accord with a society which lives by the poll, market research and by the phantoms of mass opinion.

Authority is weakened by many other factors. The exaggerated respect for expertise, which is one of the most striking characteristics of industrial society enhances the tendency of the people to mistrust, or to fail to recognize mere sagacity or wisdom. Identifying narrow expertise with political and intellectual superiority our mass democracies pay no attention to the discriminating power of wisdom. The concept of wisdom, in fact, can now be hardly seen or heard. Relying on expert advisers, who are the prototypes of the mass-man of our age and who have mostly been wrong in the bargain, leaders tend to escape reflection and the burdens of decision. Vesting leadership in committees and other group organizations comes to replace character and insight. In the sphere of intellectual and spiritual activity, the impulse toward understanding is severely damaged by the organization and the spread of group research projects, in which the place of the solitary individual thinker and scholar is taken by a committee or a group of students working for a professor. All of these—the pandering to mass tastes and prejudices, the degradation of the person by the machine process, the reverence of the expert and the tendency to substitute bureaucratic order for personal reflection and choice—are illustrations of the decline of authority which the democratic system makes inevitable.

The decline of political authority in our modern democracies has even graver consequences for our civilization. For one thing, it is the principal cause of our paralysis in the face of the ominous conditions that confront us. For another, if a people is not capable of identifying with and of paying some attention to the governing minority which alone can conceive and plan historical action it is condemned either to immobility or to blind and uncontrollable movement; and if a society has no respect for the creative minorities capable of original insight and communication it is condemned to ignorance and confined to the insipid and the purely private. The weakness of authority thus leads to the depersonalization of the world. If persons are deprived of command, if the men in power are no longer capable of thinking and acting in behalf of the community in relation to the great world then the world loses personal meaning and orientation. Personality means the attainment of a certain healthy degree of coherence and integration. Only through integration which comes through the creative actions and inspiring words of living men can life and society rise above the level of the impersonal and the mechanical. Thus the decline of authority means "either that society is dismembered by centrifugal forces, its various segments losing touch with all central purpose and outlook; or else it sinks into mechanistic and merely habitual order."[12]

The decline of political and spiritual quality therefore appears to be associated with all those forces of mass disintegration—whether as causes or effects—which are so apparent as we look around us. The rise of the businessman and then of the multitudes with the displacement of the older governing groups; the loss of that grasp of reality which is expressed in a statesman's imagination, an artist's vision or a philosopher's wisdom; the impoverishment of the individual in huge bureaucratic organizations; in all of these one can observe the failure of personal command. The logic of the overall situation becomes obvious. The level of personal life is so low that freedom becomes purely formal and devoid of meaning. It is a freedom which is both empty and oppressive. Man is exalted by precept but degraded in practice. Personal existence becomes helpless, frustration and resentment increase, the community is fractured, men tend to flee from themselves and from concern with public affairs, states become ungovernable and society is plunged into nihilism and decadence.

CHAPTER 10

THE ILLUSIONS OF TECHNOCRACY

Another manifestation of Utopian thinking is to be found among those who have become infatuated with and enthralled by the technological achievements of the post-World War II period. According to this group of thinkers the advanced sectors of mankind, with America in the lead, are now about to enter a novel metamorphic phase in human history. This new revolutionary era, shaped by the new technologies which have emerged during the last twenty-seven years, will produce a mutation, potentially as basic, though in a telescopic form, as that experienced through the slow process of evolution from animal to human experience. No aspect of man's existence—his self-consciousness, his patterns of interaction and his very biological structure itself—can escape being revolutionized by the new technological and scientific forces that have been released. Mankind according to these prophets has now within, or almost within, its grasp new powers over itself and its environment that will radically transform the whole character and meaning of human existence. Running through all their speculations there is the sense that an age is ending and that something new and portentous is about to begin. However, as we shall see, this new and portentous era might yet turn out to be something completely different from what these ideologists and prophets imagine it to be. Instead of inaugurating a new stage of civilization it might only be completing the final stage of the old one and instead of launching a new stage of human evolution it might only be preparing the conditions for a new, modern version of the Dark Ages.[1]

Many names have been given to this putative new society. For Ralf Dahrendorf we are living in a post-capitalist society in which what counts is not ownership but authority and which is ruled not by capitalist or managerial elites but by governmental elites.[2] For Amitai Etzioni we are now in a post-modern era. The modern period ended with the radical transformation of the technologies of communication, knowledge and energy that followed World War II. The "active" societies which he sees as replacing the former modern societies will be aware, committed and potent; will provide a comprehensive over-layer of societal guidance; and will be responsive to its changing memberships and "engaged in an intensive and perpetual self-transformation."[3] Herman Kahn sees the long-term multifold trend of western culture toward increasingly sensate (empirical, this-worldly, secular, humanistic, pragmatic, manipulative, explicitly rational, utilitarian, contractual, epicurean, hedonistic, etc.) cultures and even toward a late sensate culture which has a very pronounced tendency toward cynical, nihilistic, superficial, transient, disillusioned and alienated forms of cultural expression and social behavior.[4] According to George Lichtheim, our contemporary industrial society is increasingly post-bourgeois with both the bourgeoisie and the proletariat fading out.[5] For Kenneth Boulding we are at the start of the post-civilized era, or the technological and developed society. The distinctive characteristic of this new period is the consciousness of, using Teilhard's phrase, the noosphere, the sphere of knowledge, as the premise for the social direction of society and the achievement of social as against individual self-consciousness. Society would now be guided by social and mental evolution rather than by the adaptive biological or social evolution of the past.[6] Marshall McLuhan sees the new civilization as based on a single aspect of technology—the new electronic media, which he holds constitute not merely new methods of communication but a total new environment that will radically alter everything from politics to social behavior.[7] Jacques Ellul concludes that technology per se will determine the future; in his opinion we are entering into a new era of "technological society" wherein technology is no longer an instrument for pre-existing human purposes but has become an end in itself, controlling both men and their society.[8] Many theologians speak of the age coming into being as "post-Christian" or marked by "the death of God", while Harvey Cox hails the advent of the "technopolitan era".[9] All are agreed, however, that as a result of technological factors we are leaving the industrial era of bourgeois society behind and entering a radically new world.

More than a decade ago a theologian who regarded with dread "the end of the modern world" even spoke of the coming of "technological man".[10]

One of the leading ideologists for this notion of a new society is Daniel Bell. In a series of essays he has tried to elaborate the leading features of what he calls the "post-industrial society," the first stage of which America is now experiencing. This post-industrial society can be characterized in several ways. In the first place, this new society is no longer primarily a manufacturing economy. The service sector (comprising trade, finance, insurance and real estate; personal, professional, business and repair services; and general government) now accounts for more than half of the total employment and more than half of the gross national product. America has now become a "service economy"—i.e., the first nation in the history of the world in which more than half of the employed population is not involved in the production of food, clothing, houses and automobiles and other tangible goods. As a consequence of this, the manual and unskilled worker-class is shrinking in the society, while at the other end of the continuum the class of "knowledge-workers" is becoming predominant in the new society.

However, what is crucial in the new post-industrial society is not just the shift from property or political criteria to knowledge as "the base of new power" but a change in the character of knowledge itself. What has now become decisive for society, he claims, is the new centrality of theoretical knowledge, the "primacy of theory over empiricism" no less, and the codification of knowledge into abstract systems of symbols that can be translated into many different and varied circumstances. Every society, he fancifully claims, now "lives by innovation and growth,"[11] and it is theoretical knowledge that has become the matrix of innovation. With the growing sophistication of simulation procedures through the use of computers—simulations of economic systems, of social behavior, of decision problems—we have the possibility for the first time of nothing less than large-scale "controlled experiments" in the social sciences. These in turn will permit the society to plot alternative futures in different courses and to greatly increase the extent to which it can choose and control matters that affect its life.

All these developments, furthermore, transform the university, where all this theoretical knowledge is sought, tested and codified in a disinterested way (sic) into the primary institution of the new society. If the business firm was the key institution of the past hundred years, because of its role in organizing production for the mass creation of products then the university and the research corporations, the industrial laboratories and the experimental stations will become the central institutions of the next hundred years, because of their role as the new sources of innovation and knowledge. The husbanding of talent and the spread of educational and intellectual institutions will thus become of primary concern for the society. Not only the best talents but eventually the entire complex of prestige and status will be rooted in the intellectual and scientific communities. The predominant men of the future are going to be the scientists, the mathematicians, the economists and the engineers of the new computer technology.

This new society will be one which will recognize the fact that men have the technological and scientific possibility "of controlling the changes in their lives consciously, and by social decision."[12]   Through the new "intellectual technology" which has been mentioned—systems-analysis, simulation, game theory, decision theory, programming and other methods hitched to the computer—society is able to lay out a new compass of the rationality of means. Social change is therefore now a process of direct and deliberate contrivance. Men now seek to anticipate change, measure the course of its direction and impact, control it and even shape it for predetermined ends. The "transformation of society" is no longer an abstract phrase but a process in which governments are actively engaged on a highly conscious basis. The emergence of planning in the western countries, whether it be target plans, indicative planning, induced investment or simply economic growth or full employment is an example of this process. Rationality, planning and foresight are thus all the hallmarks of the technocratic age which has already made its appearance. In place of the old world view and its traditional and customary religious, aesthetic and intuitive modes, the technocratic mind-view emphasizes the logical, practical, problem-solving, instrumental, orderly and disciplined approach to objectives and relies on a calculus of precision and measurement and on the concept of a system.

Although these new elites do not as yet constitute the ruling class of the society they do constitute the major centers of a new powerful constituency within it. The break-up of the former property system has led to the rise of new elites whose technical skill forms the basis of their power and prestige. Knowledge and planning—military planning, economic planning, social planning—have now become the basic requisites for all organized action in the modern world. The members of this new technocratic elite, with their new techniques of decision-making (systems-analysis, linear programming and program budgeting) have now become essential to the formulation and analysis of decisions on which political judgments have to be made if not with the actual wielding of power itself. They are the first products, in fact, of a new system in the recruitment of power (just as property and inheritance were the essence of the old system). The norms of the new intelligentsia —the norms of professionalism—are a departure from the hitherto prevailing norms of economic self-interest which have guided the former business civilization. And in the upper reaches of this new elite —that is, in the scientific community—men hold significantly different values which could become the foundation of a new ethos for such a class.

A more lurid variation of Bell's model has been advanced by Zbigniew Brzezinski. According to him America is now becoming a "technetronic" society, i.e., a society that is shaped culturally, psychologically, socially and economically by the impact of technology and electronics, particularly computers and communication.[13] In this new society "human conduct will become less spontaneous and less mysterious— more predetermined and subject to deliberate programming." Man will increasingly possess the capacity to determine the sex of his children, to affect, through drugs, the extent of their intelligence and to modify and control the personality. The human brain will acquire expanded powers, with computers becoming as routine an extension of man's reasoning as automobiles have been of man's mobility. By the end of the century computers will reason as well as man and will be able to engage in "creative" thought; wedded to robots or to "Laboratory beings," they could act like humans. The human body will be improved and its durability extended even to the age of 120.

Cybernetics and automation will revolutionize working habits with leisure becoming the practice and active work the exception—and a privilege reserved for the most talented. The achievement-oriented society will give way to the amusement-focussed society, with essentially spectacular spectacles (mass sports, T.V.) providing an opiate for increasingly purposeless masses. These millions of uncoordinated citizens, supervised and controlled, will however, easily be within the reach of magnetic and attractive personalities effectively exploiting the latest communication techniques who will be able to manipulate their emotions and control their reason. The information-revolution, including expensive information storage, instant retrieval and eventually pushbutton visual and sound availability of needed data in almost any private home will furthermore transform the character of institutionized collective education. The new means of communication will create an extraordinarily interwoven society, in continuous visual, audial and increasingly close contact among almost all its members—electronically interacting, sharing instantly in most social experiences, prompting far greater personal involvement and with their consciousness shaped in a sporadic manner fundamentally different from the literate modes of transmitting information of the industrial age. The growing capacities for calculating instantly most complex interactions and the increasing availability of biochemical means of human control "increase the potential scope of self-conscious direction and thereby also the pressures to direct, to choose, and to change."[14]

The profoundest change, however, is going to take place in the intellectual community itself. The largely humanist-oriented, occasionally ideologically-minded intellectual dissenter, who saw his role largely in terms of offering social critiques is now being rapidly displaced either by experts or specialists, who become involved in special government undertakings, or by the generalists-integrators who become in effect "house-ideologues for those in power, providing over-all intellectual integration for disparate actions." A community of organization-oriented, application-minded intellectuals relating itself more effectively to the political system than their predecessors will thus serve to introduce into the political system concerns broader than those likely to be generated by that system itself and perhaps more relevant than those articulated by outside critics.

Moreover, he argues, the rapid pace of change will put a premium on anticipating events and planning for them. Power will consequently gravitate into the hands of those who control the information, and can correlate it most rapidly. The universities will therefore become an intensely involved think-tank, the source of much sustained political planning and social innovation. Our existing post-crisis management institutions will probably be increasingly supplanted by pre-crisis management institutions, the task of which will be to identify in advance likely social crises and to develop programs to cope with them. All these developments, he admits, could encourage tendencies during the next several decades toward a technocratic dictatorship, leaving less and less room for political procedures as we know them today.

Although Robert Heilbroner does not belong ideologically to the group we have been considering, his carefully calculated flirtation with what he calls socialism leads him to some of the same conclusions. For him too, contemporary capitalism is being slowly but systematically undermined by the new revolutionary power that has arisen within it —the veritable explosion of organized knowledge and its applied counterpart, scientific technology. Like the first manifestations of the market in the medieval era, the river of science and technology must cut its own channel through the existing social landscape and profoundly alter the prevailing terrain. Though science and technology do at first impart an immense momentum to capitalism they are basically incompatible and in long-term conflict with its fundamental working arrangements.   These twin revolutionary forces create social problems that require non-market controls to correct or forestall; exert a steady push from many levels and areas of the economy in the direction of the society of organization; and renders less relevant and effective the market ties on which that system is ultimately founded.   By pushing the frontiers of work from the farm to the factory, then from the factory to the store or the office and now from store and office "into a spectrum of jobs whose common denominator is that they require public action and public funds for their initiation and support,"[16] science and technology speed capitalism along the general path of planning and control.   The incorporation of technology into the working mechanisms of the capitalist system thus ultimately undermines it.

However, science and technology have an even more profound and critical effect on the capitalist system.   The idea of science directly challenges the ideas of capitalism which, based as it is on acquisitiveness and money-making, has always suffered from the moral ambivalence in which these activities have been held.   Capitalism has never served as a powerful avatar of the social imagination.   By way of contrast, science and its technical application is the "burning idea" of the twentieth century, comparable in its impact on men's minds to the flush of the democratic enthusiasm of the late eighteenth century or to the political commitment won by communism in the early twentieth.   In a lyrical passage whose irrelevance is now so evident a mere seven years later, he writes that "the altruism of science", its "purity", the awesome vistas it opens and the venerable path it has followed have won from all groups, and especially from the young, exactly that passionate interest and conviction that is so egregiously lacking to capitalism as a way of life.[17]

Science in modern society, in America as well as in Russia, thus carries a near-religious ethos of conviction and sacrifice.   The new elites arising within these societies owe their ascendancy and their allegiance in large part to science.   The scientific cadres proper, the social scientists, the government administrative personnel, even the military all look to science not merely as the vehicle of their expertise but "as the magnetic north of their compass of values".   In fact, the primacy of scientific discovery as a central purpose of society, a raison d'être for its existence, perhaps even as an instrument for its religious impulses, will become the central goals which the scientific community will ultimately impose on the society.   To partake in the adventure of the scientific mission or its technical realization will become as dominating a motive for the future as the wish to participate in economic adventure is at present, and he has no doubt that the distribution of social resources and privileges will reflect this basic orientation toward scientific exploration and application.

This new scientific civilization which he envisages will not only exalt the scientific mission but will also place a great emphasis on rational solutions to social problems that are today not yet subject to human direction. Not only economic affairs (which should become of secondary importance) but the numbers and location of the population, its genetic quality, the manner of social domestication of children, the choice of life-work—even the very direction of life itself are all apt to become subjects of scientific investigation and control. Indeed, "the key word of the new society is apt to be control".[18]

Although he does not lay out the routes and timetables by which this new scientific elite is going to become the "new lord and master" of society he is yet convinced that this is the direction which history is bound to take in one form or another. What is certain, however, is the profound incompatibility between the new idea of the active use of science within society and the idea of capitalism as a social system. The conflict between the two he finds does not lie on the surface, in any clash between the immediate needs of science and those of capitalism. It lies, rather, in the ideas that ultimately inform both worlds. The world of science, as it is applied by society, is committed to the idea of "man as a being who shapes his collective destiny;" the world of capitalism is committed to an idea of man as one "who permits his common social destination to take care of itself." The essential idea of a society built on "scientific engineering" is to impose human will on the social universe; that of capitalism to allow the social universe to unfold as if it were beyond human interference.

Thus, as compared with the activist philosophy of science as a social instrument, the inherent social passivity of capitalism becomes archaic and eventually intolerable. The "self-regulating economy" that is its highest social achievement stands condemned in his eyes by its absence of a directing intelligence, and all the small steps that have been taken to correct its deficiencies only reveal the inhibitions placed on the potential exercise of purposeful thought and action by its remaining barriers of ideology and privilege. In the end, capitalism is "weighed in the scale of science and found wanting not alone as a system but as a philosophy."[19]

For Alvin Toffler, the flamboyant journalistic popularizer of futurism, we are now moving from an affluent society into a super-industrial society. This super-industrial society is one characterized by movements of ever accelerating change, which are influencing the way we relate to other people, to things, to the entire universe of ideas, art and values. The flood of ever-accelerating change buffets nations and individuals, influences our sense of time, revolutionizes the tempo of life and affects the way we "feel" the world around us.

This explosive process of change is creating not an extended, larger-than-life version of our present society but a new society. It is a revolution which is shattering institutions and power relationships. What is occurring now is not only a crisis of capitalism but of industrial society itself, regardless of its political form. We are simultaneously experiencing a youth revolution, a sexual revolution, a racial revolution, a colonial revolution, an economic revolution and "the most rapid and deep-going technological revolution in history."[20]   This revolution is sending a flow of newness into the lives of countless individuals, confronting them with unfamiliar situations and first-time situations. Reaching deep into our personal lives the enormous changes ahead will transform traditional family structures and sexual attitudes. They will smash conventional relationships between old and young. They will overthrow our values with respect to money and success. They will alter work, play and education beyond recognition. They will unleash a spectacular, elegant yet frightening scientific advance. Man will be slammed against the non-routine and the unpredicted. And by so doing the problems of adaptation will be escalated to a new and dangerous level.

Without entering into a discussion of all the science-fiction innovations which he and the scientists he consulted project for the future, it is necessary to analyze some of the more salient transformations that he argues follow from the emergence of the super-industrial society.

In the first place, the process of high-speed change is producing a human being who is a "permanent transient"[21] living in a "high transience society." Transience is the new "temporariness" in everyday life. Relationships that once endured for long spans now have shorter life expectancies. Lives, things, places, people, ideas and organizational structures all get "used up" more quickly and men have an almost tangible feeling that they live, rootless and uncertain, among shifting sand dunes. Men's relationships with things are thus increasingly temporary. Society becomes a buy, use and throw-away society. Buildings disappear overnight, and the faces of cities can change completely in a year. The economics of permanence are replaced by the economics of transience. Planned obsolescence impels the consumer toward rented, disposable or temporary products. All these shufflings and reshufflings introduce a "dazzling dynamism into the everyday life of the individual and heightens still further the sense of speed, turmoil and impermanence in society."[22]

Another feature of this new society is its nomadism. Never in history has distance meant less. Never have man's relationships with place been more numerous, fragile and temporary. Throughout the advanced technological society and particularly among those whom he characterizes "as the people of the future" (managers, scientists, technicians, etc.) commuting, travelling and regularly relocating one's family have become second nature. Figuratively, we "use up" places and dispose of them in much the same way that we dispose of Kleenex or beer cans. We are in fact witnessing an historic decline in the significance of place in human life. Thousands of scientists and engineers move back and forth from job to job like particles in an atom. As technological change roars through the advanced economies, outmoding whole industries and creating new ones almost overnight, millions of unskilled and semi-skilled workers find themselves compelled to relocate. The result of this vastly increased mobility is a growing "loss of commitment", increasing anxiety and depression among many who find it difficult to adjust to ever new surroundings and for the most severe cases the development of abnormal mental content and breaks with reality.

This new super-industrial society is also affecting the nature of organization and bureaucracy. Toffler rather naively believes that what we are now witnessing is not "the triumph but the breakdown of bureaucracy."[23] We are seeing the arrival of a new organizational system that will increasingly challenge and ultimately supplant bureaucracy. This new organization of the future he called "Ad-hocracy". Instead of bureaucracies with neatly arranged tables of organization we are now in the midst of a permanent organizational revolution. The seemingly permanent structures of many large organizations, often because they resist change, are now heavily infiltrated with task-forces, transient teams and ad hoc groups whose members come together to solve a specific problem and then separate. These ad hoc groups and "non-routine organizations" are playing havoc with the traditional conceptions of organization as constituting more or less permanent structures. Although throw-away organizations, ad hoc teams or committees, do not necessarily replace permanent functional structures, they do change them beyond recognition and drain them of both people and power. Instead of people filling fixed slots in the functional organization they now move back and forth at a high rate of speed. When this process is repeated often enough, he argues, the loyalties of the people involved are altered, the lines of authority are shaken up, responsibilities shift and vast organizational structures are taken apart, belted together in new forms and then rearranged again. What is now within our grasp, no more and no less, is a kind of organizational ability that is alive with intelligence, alive with information and at its maximum completely flexible.

A society of instant food, instant education and instant cities, is also a society of instant images. It is one engaged in a more rapid turnover of the images and image-structures of our brains. The new communications technology, for example, upstages and replaces celebrities at an accelerating rate and makes leadership in all fields more unstable than it has ever been before. Our relationships with the images of reality upon. which we base our behavior are growing on average, more and more transient. Life styles change with incredible rapidity. Fads come and go at a dizzying pace. Widely held mental models of reality are attacked by new counter-models of reality. Carefully engineered medium-messages hammer at our senses and communications people constantly work to make each instant exposure to the mass media carry a heavier informational and emotional freight. Nations advancing toward super-industrialism are engaged in a frantic process of fabricating images and then ruthlessly destroying them. One art style supplants another at a furious pace. Ideas come and go at a frenetic rate. Today change is so swift and relentless in the techno-societies that yesterday's truths suddenly become today's fictions and the most highly skilled and intelligent members of society admit difficulty in keeping up with the deluge of new knowledge—even in extremely narrow fields. In education, in politics, in economic theory, in medicine, in international affairs, wave after wave of new images penetrate our defenses and shake up our mental models of reality. The result of this image-bombardment is "the accelerated decay of old images, a faster intellectual through-put, and a new profound sense of the impermanence of knowledge itself . . . "[24]

All these changes and bombardments to which man is subject produce in the end what Toffler describes as a state of "future shock", which in fact is a state of "present shock." For despite all his heroism and stamina, man remains a biological organism, a "biosystem", and all such systems operate within inexorable limits. There are discoverable limits to the amount of change that the human organism can absorb, and by endlessly accelerating change without first determining these limits, we are submitting masses of men to demands they simply cannot tolerate. We throw them into the peculiar state of future shock, which is the "distress both physical and psychological, that arises from an overload of the human organism's adaptive system and its decision-making processes.

Put more simply, future shock is the human response to overstimulation."[25]

Different people react to future shock in different ways. The symptoms range all the way from anxiety, hostility to authority and seemingly senseless violence, to physical illness, depression and apathy. Its victims, depending upon the stage and intensity of the disease, often manifest erratic swings in interest and life-style, followed by an effort to "crawl into their shells" through social, intellectual and emotional withdrawal. They feel continually bugged and harassed and seek desperately to reduce the number of decisions they must make. If you overload the environment with novelty you thus get the equivalent of anxiety-neurotics. High change and novelty induce men to behave irrationally and act against their own interests. Our image of reality becomes distorted and we suffer from confusion and a blurring of the lines between illusion and reality.

However, future shock does not only produce physical illness. It attacks the psyche as well. The striking signs of confusional breakdown we see around us—the spreading use of drugs, the rise of mysticism, the recurrent outbreaks of vandalism and individual violence, the politics of nihilism and nostalgia, the sick apathy of millions—all can be understood better by recogning their relationship to future shock. Faced with the need to make new, faster and as yet "unprogrammed" decisions, moreover, the techno-societies confront a decision-making crisis. Masses of men feel themselves harried, futile, incapable of working out their private futures. The conviction grows that the rat race is too tough and that things are out of control. The uncontrolled acceleration of scientific, technological and social change subverts "the powers of the individual to make sensible, competent decisions about his own destiny."[26] The United States, in fact, exhibits all the qualities of a nation suffering from a nervous breakdown.

What, then, are we to make of the apocalyptic visions held out to us? Are we truly at the beginning of a new metamorphic phase in human history? Is bourgeois society about to disappear? Is a new "technological man" about to take the place of industrial man and manage the new future? To compare the predictions made by the "speculators" we have cited with the reality that we see all around us should make evident in what direction the world is moving.

Now there is no doubt that we live in a world of accelerating and explosive change. Man's ability to master his environment has seemingly vastly increased. Science and its technical applications have captivated more minds. Space flights, nucleic acids, body transplants, the computer, nuclear energy and television have all profoundly affected the way we live, think and act. The standard of living has risen dramatically for many millions of people in the advanced societies. Cybernetics and automation have already revolutionized working habits. The human brain (not the mind, it should be noted) has acquired expanded powers through computers. Man's relationship with place has become numerous, fragile and temporary. A service economy in which more than half of the population is not involved in the production of food, clothing, houses and automobiles and other tangible goods has probably come into existence, though there is still some doubt about its actual composition. The number of scientists, mathematicians, economists and computer-engineers has skyrocketed as compared with the past. Planning on the part of the state and the corporations has spread. New techniques of decision-making (systems analysis, linear programming amd program-budgeting) have been invented and applied and new bureaucratic, scientific, technological and academic elites have emerged as new centers of power and influence.

However, all these changes have not created a "new post-industrial society" or a "post-capitalist society" or an "active society" or a "post-civilized era." Technology has not provided the basis for a wholly new society, nor has it become the integrating element in a new civilization. All these transformations constitute merely an extended, larger-than-life version of our present society, but have in no way created a new civilization and are unlikely to do so. These changes, novel as they have been, have not produced a new society for a number of reasons.

In the first place, the new bureaucratic and technological elites are simply incapable of constituting a new ruling class. These new elites are essentially a service class, defined by their service relations to authority. These are men and brains for hire, commodities to be bought, sold and discarded. At best they can only be the narrow and specialized managers of society but not its leaders. Unlike the nineteenth century bourgeoisie or the feudal aristocracy they have no independent base of economic power and thus no secure base of personal authority. They lack that "feel" for command, that spiritual independence and intrepidity, that bold and broad historical perspective which shapes a new ruling class and provides it with the creative resources to lead a society. The norms of professionalism which are supposed to represent the new elite's contribution to the new civilization are in fact the norms of the bureaucratic ethos—duty, service and loyalty—in other words, values of subordination, not of autonomous domination. Although all these new elites belong to the ruling class because their roles are roles of authority, these new elites as such *are* never the ruling class. Their latent interests aim at what exists; but what it is that exists is not decided by them but given to them. They are dependent on forces beyond their influence or control. Brzezinski's revealing description of the new group of intellectual experts as "house-ideologues for those in power" is true for all the other elites that have come forward in the post-war period. These are not new commanding groups but servants of power, forced by their very circumstances to sell their talents to the political and economic masters of society, whoever they might be, and to serve the goals they set. They are merely a reserve army of talent, and it is only necessary to know these men to realize how eager they are to barter away their pedestrian knowledge and their fragile integrity in order to obtain the financial rewards which are offered, and the fleeting recognition which follows their acts of intellectual servitude and betrayal.

Secondly, it is simply not true that the economy is coming more and more to be dominated by a technical and scientific elite. Although the number of persons classified as professional and technical has increased rapidly over the past few decades—so that we even now face a glut of PhDs without jobs—they still represent only a tiny minority of the nation. And what is even more important, they are not the ones who set the standards for the society or who make its major decisions. Their economic position is controlled by the continuing dominance of the mores and laws of bourgeois man. What the United States, or any other advanced society, produces or communicates is still determined by the profit motive and by what the market will accept; it is a function of popular demand stimulated by advertising, and of government expenditures determined by political decisions and by the balance of political forces. Government economic policy is not shaped by technical considerations, by some objective standard subject to scientific verification, but still mainly reflects the interests of the dominant business class and the political ability of business and labor to promote the objectives of particular industries at the expense of the public good. The bourgeoisie is still in the saddle.

The rise of the supposed new elites does not stem from any radical transformation of bourgeois or industrial society. The limited prominence which they have attained springs from the fact that they are concentrated in a few areas of high visibility. The industries in which the scientists and technicians play the greatest role are the highly publicized and politically crucial defense and space industries. The heaviest emphasis on scientific and technological innovation is concentrated in the war economy and the industrial-military complex. This is the home of the new elite, if it exists at all. As President Kennedy noted in his 1963 economic report: "The defense, space and atomic energy activities of the country absorb about two-thirds of the trained people available for exploring our scientific and technological frontiers." It is in these areas where the physicists are and where the ratio of PhDs to production workers is so fantastically high. These new elites have been nurtured by war preparations created by the war economy and have served it faithfully. In the rest of American industry such scientists as it employs are engaged in producing some new variants of an old detergent, or in creating fat-free ice-cream. It need only be mentioned that this heavy concentration of scientific and engineering resources in the American war economy has severely injured the civilian sectors of that economy and has even resulted in America falling behind Europe and Japan in consumer technology.

Then again, the so-called new techniques of decision-making first applied to defense and space activities have been, to put it charitably, less than a success there and even less successful when applied to other aspects of the economy or to the solution of social problems. The Vietnam war has completely discredited the pretentions of those who assumed that human behavior could be predicted and rationalized. Although systems engineering has built rockets, missiles and new weapons systems it has accomplished even these technical goals at costs which far exceeded their original estimates. Hundreds of billions of taxpayers' money have been lost in cost overruns. Systems analysis and PPBS (Planning Programming Budgeting Systems) have had little success with urban problems, job-corps training problems and related projects.[27] Keynesianism and macro-economic planning have failed to solve the problems of unemployment and inflation and some economists feel that running an economy to order may be beyond the power of analysis of present-day economists.[28] The technical revolutionizing of education that many electronic and related firms hoped to spearhead has not taken place in face of the diversity and complexity of the school system and the teachers' fears of innovation and change. The social sciences have dismally failed to understand, among many problems, those relating to education, welfare and social planning. The scientist, removed from his own area of specialization, is usually as ignorant and as foolish as the most vulgar laborer. And the Chairman of the Commission set up to study the workings of the Pentagon, that citadel of the new technology and managerialism, said in 1970, that the Defense Department was now "an impossible organization to administer" and that "we are amazed it works at all, it's so big and cumbersome under the present organizational structure." Summing up his impressions of the Department's operations he said: "Everybody is somewhat responsible for everything, and nobody is completely responsible for anything. So there's no way of assigning authority, responsibility and accountability. There is nobody you can point your finger to if anything goes wrong, and there is nobody you can pin a medal on if it goes right, because everything is everybody's business and, as you know, what is everybody's business is nobody's business. They spend their time coordinating with each other and shuffling paper back and forth and that's what causes all the red tape and big staffs in the department. Nobody can do anything without checking with seven other people."[29]

Our modern, advanced industrial societies are thus, as we have already shown in our chapter on "Rationality and Capitalism," not guided by either rationality or the "purity", "altruism" or "objectivity" of science. They are most certainly not engaged in a process of "direct and deliberate contrivance". They are in fact a peculiar compound of technological and organizational rationalization—i.e. of rationality without reason—and of irrationality, mismanagement, unbelievable contradictions and self-destructiveness. The technological and functional changes of the post-war period have merely introduced new elements of dislocation, uncertainty, confusion and disintegration into our societies. The flood of change that has swept over us has subjected man to new anxieties and tensions, both individual and social, and has overloaded the human organism's adaptive system. Elites are disintegrating, our images of reality have become more and more distorted, the lines between illusion and reality have become more and more blurred, consensus is cracking, men are acting more and more irrationally and against their own interests, millions of people are losing faith in the honesty and efficacy of their institutions and feel themselves in the grip of forces they can neither understand nor control, and our capacity to make sensible and competent decisions has drastically declined. The growth of tribal gang warfare, the spread of nomadism, the abandoning of the cities, the ephemeralness of things and relationships, the incipient breakdown not only of law and order but of the comforts and services of material civilization, the coexistence of indolence and luxury, all presage the coming end of a civilization. We are witnessing in fact not the birth of a new civilization but the disintegration, varying naturally from country to country, of our existing industrial, bourgeois society. The modern age is sliding into pathology and decadence and at the end might sink into the abyss of a new Dark Age "made more sinister," as Churchill put it in 1940, "and perhaps more protracted by the lights of perverted science."

CHAPTER 11

THE FAILURE OF SOCIALISM

The general crisis of our civilization is expressed not only in the degeneration of the existing bourgeois, democratic order but in the lack of any viable alternative to it. The decadence of bourgeois society is paralleled by the decadence of the proletariat and of all the Socialist and Communist parties that speak in its name.

Karl Marx's analysis of the role of the proletariat in history has been completely invalidated by events. In terms of this analysis the proletariat was a new star on the historical horizon and its grand historic mission was to supersede the bourgeoisie as the ruler of a new socialist or communist society. This responsibility had been placed upon it, according to Marx, because it represented the dynamic contradiction within the existing bourgeois order. On the one hand, so this analysis ran, the workers suffered the concentrated horrors of industrial society "in their most inhuman form," and they were denied "even the appearance of humanity." On the other hand, this "irremediable and imperious distress" forced the proletariat to revolt out of practical necessity. By rebelling against its own inhumanity the proletariat rebelled against inhumanity itself; and while emancipating itself it would automatically emancipate society, whose class divisions it was destined to abolish.[1] Out of this struggle a new, liberated humanity was to emerge and mankind would pass from the "kingdom of necessity to the realm of freedom."

The history of the proletariat during the last hundred years and more however, has turned in a verdict which refutes this Marxist diagnosis and prognosis. Its course during this time has shown what it is capable of, but also indubitably what it has been unable to accomplish.

The proletariat has been capable of acting in a whole variety of modes and directions. It has shown great courage and self-sacrifice in fighting for its right to organize. It has been militant in the struggle for its economic interests—shorter hours, higher wages and fringe benefits of all kinds. In a few countries it took the lead in the movement for democratic rights and universal franchise. In Germany the anti-clerical Social Democrats defended the Catholic victims of Bismarck's *Kultur-Kampf*; in France socialist workers rallied against the anti-Semitism of the Dreyfus case; in England the uneducated mass was a driving force for the expansion of education; in France in 1968 it rocked the foundations of the Gaullist regime by organizing a general strike; in East Berlin, Budapest and Gdansk it challenged the Communist masters of society in violent street battles; and in every western nation, the working class has been a leading champion of the welfare state, of national health schemes and of social security. And in the Communist countries parties rule in the name of the proletariat while in fact, as we shall see, pursuing policies which have nothing to do with the original goals and aspirations of socialism.

Yet, although the proletariat has, on rare occasions, been a revolutionary force and for longer periods a reformist force it has never been a revolutionary class. It lacks that indispensable element that makes it possible for an opposition class to counterpose itself to the existing ruling class—political capacity. It has never been able to secrete from within its own ranks that leadership which would be faithful to its interests and would defend them boldly, imaginatively and tenaciously. The proletariat is either too easily coopted into the existing system through higher living standards and welfare benefits as has happened under modern capitalism, without however reducing its inchoate discontent, or it is too impotent to create a new society. Unlike the bourgeoisie, whose role the proletariat was supposed to have duplicated, it lacks the property, the riches, the education and cultivation which the former accumulated over centuries before it came to power. The bourgeoisie understood how to take hold of society, how to spread its own system and values throughout the community, and thereby assure its economic and political supremacy. This, precisely, is the task which the proletariat has shown itself incapable of undertaking.

The proletariat, in reality, is essentially a subordinate class. Its place in the process of production dehumanizes, degrades and stupifies it. Condemned to monotonous labor it becomes monotonous and narrow in its thinking and aspirations. The impotence of the worker is not merely a stratagem of the rulers but the logical consequence of industrial society. "Votaries of the dinner pail" as Veblen described the trade-unions, they have no comprehensive social vision valid for the whole society. Members of the working class are, furthermore, more likely to be authoritarian in their attitudes than members of the middle class.[2] While the proletariat everywhere is still reformist on economic issues and is still capable of waging militant economic struggles it is at the same time more authoritarian on such issues as civil liberties, minority rights and any form of deviant behavior. Its extreme nationalism and xenophobia are notorious. The working class has not only supported Communist parties but has also given its devotion to Nazi labor unions, to Salazar, Varga and Peron and many other "populist fascists". In the United States George Wallace has tapped many sources of support from the working class—even among the most "sophisticated" like the U.A.W.—for his racism and demagogy. Many American labor leaders are even more reactionary in their attitudes and style of life than the leaders of Wall Street. The lower strata are suggestible, simple, sentimental, credulous and easily manipulated. The emergence of the labor movement to a position of power constitutes in fact a further sign of social decline. It has inaugurated the age of the masses with their vulgar and dull tastes, their low cultural standards and their worship not only of the common but of the commonplace. Its highest ideal is that set by the average man. We have witnessed during the last fifty years not only the dissolution of the myth of progress but also the myth of the liberating power of the proletariat.

The Social Democratic parties which are its principal representatives in such Western countries as Great Britain, Germany and the Scandinavian lands, have not only failed to "reform" or "civilize" or "tame" the capitalist system in which they function but have become embedded within it. The measures which they have advocated and which they have to some extent realized—the Welfare State, state intervention in the economy, full employment for brief periods—have not basically changed the class relations of capitalist society. Large pockets of poverty still continue to exist, the inequality of income between the top strata of society and the vast majority of wage and salary earners has not markedly decreased and the Keynesian efforts to manage the economy have not been as successful as it was once claimed they would be.* The

---

* According to the "official social commentary" on the conditions of Britain, 1 percent of the British population today still owns 30 percent of the nation's wealth despite all the progressive taxation since the days of Lloyd George (James Reston, *New York Times*, Dec. 8, 1972).

Swedish "paradise" has been found to be populated with all kinds of maladies and discontents. The Social Democratic parties are as committed to the ideology of unlimited economic growth, with all its attendant evils, tensions, and conflicts and dangers as are the capitalist rulers of our civilization. They offer no alternative to our run-away industrial system but at best merely hope to further improve the material position of their supporters within it.

In reality, the welfare state which emerged after the Second World War is not so much the handiwork of the socialist parties but is the consequence of the shocks and dislocations of the Second World War and of the measures which were taken, particularly in Britain, to mobilize the society for the war effort and of the initial fear of Russian Communism. Forced to adapt itself to the conditions of a siege-economy, the Conservative-led British government of that time was compelled to initiate policies which would produce greater social cohesiveness within the national society. Rationing schemes thus reduced the significance of money in the sharing out of available food and necessities and made for greater egalitarianism. The tremendously high taxation which had to be enforced further helped to reduce the economic gaps between the classes. New and far-reaching administrative systems made possible the swift transfer of purchasing power from citizen to citizen, and from citizen to state. The need to equip a great army necessitated a system of controls which produced a revolution in British economic life that turned Britain "into a country more fully socialist than anything achieved by the conscious planners of Soviet Russia".[3] A plan for universal social security was worked out by Sir William Beveridge. New educational reforms were submitted. A Ministry of Town and Country Planning was set up. The achievements of the post-war Labor government as even R.H.S. Crossman was forced to admit, in the *New Fabian Essays*, only "marked the end of a century of social reform and not as its socialist supporters had hoped, the beginning of a new epoch." And at the end of the first Labor government's term of office, after they had consolidated and implemented a great many of the promises of the war administration, its leaders had become "exhausted volcanoes", bereft of ideas and energy and fit only for rejection by the electorate.

The Social Democratic parties have failed to fulfill the hopes, which at one time they held out, to be the leaders of a new epoch of social development because they feel themselves to be, in the very depths of their being, merely the junior partners of the ruling classes of the societies in which they function politically. They only constitute a safe political alternative for the management of capitalist society. Instead of changing the system they reinforce it. Stemming from the trade unions, some sections of the professional and middle classes and from those groups of intellectuals who for one reason or another are not altogether at home within the established order, they lack that psychological self-confidence and strength to act as an authoritative ruling class for the society as a whole. They suffer from a feeling of inferiority. They stand too much in awe of their "betters"* and they are by nature conservative, slow moving and slow thinking. These are men incapable of doing great harm (except by neglect and mismanagement) but are not up to doing great good either. Without energy, confidence or originality they rely like Harold Wilson on the cheap tricks and deviousness of the political game and recruit the mediocre, the timid and the conformist into their leadership. They are, by and large, satisfied with the large crumbs that they have extracted from the existing order. Although they sometimes desperately try to assume a technocratic image they are at bottom deeply and sentimentally attached to middle class society with all its regressive myths and fixations. Democratic Socialism—and of course, all other parties as well—require men of great stature, rulers of unprecedented authority and statesmen of broad vision to manage the affairs of our highly complex society but instead it has produced pygmies, rulers of unprecedented lack of authority and pathetic political opportunists and incompetents.

One instructive example of Democratic Socialism which has deviated from the west European pattern is to be found in Israel. Originating in the oppression and ferment of the towns and villages of Eastern Europe, developing in a backward and desolate country, the task of Israeli socialism was not to reform an ongoing capitalist society but to create a new social order. Israeli socialism thus provided the nationalist movement of Zionism with the principal components of its ideology, shaped the political elite which took command of the leadership of this movement and through its novel social experiments—kibbutz, Histadrut and other institutions—left its mark on Israel's social structure.

Israeli socialism began its career in the early years of this century with a profusion of zealous ideals and aspirations. From A.D. Gordon whose teachings were a curious amalgam of cabbalistic mysticism, prophetic messianism, populist agrarianism and Tolstoyan socialism it received the philosophy of the religion of labor. To him and his followers physical labor on the land assumed an almost transcendental meaning and provided most of the psychological satisfaction commonly

---

* Labor's Deputy Prime Minister, I was told by one of his colleagues, felt awkward and ill at ease when introduced to one of Britain's leading millionaires, though he himself, while he held office, in fact possessed much more power and prestige than any mere millionaire.

supplied by religion. Through hard physical labor man would be redeemed, a new Jewish personality forged, the land liberated and a new human species created. The Marxist-influenced *Poalei Zion* Party (Israel Workers' Party) introduced into the movement the concept of the working class as the vanguard of the national movement and even the creation of a society based "on the public ownership of the means of production" (through the waging of a class struggle).[4] The *G'dud Avodah* (Workers Brigade) members of the *Third Aliyah* (Wave of Immigration) aimed at the conversion of the entire country into one great kibbutz, owned and self-governed by all its members, whether engaged in agriculture or industry; and in 1925 they went even further and envisaged "the establishment of a national center of labor for the Jewish People and a Communistic Society in the country."[5] The Zionist Youth Movement, *Hashomer Hatzair* (The Young Guard) which later became the *Mapam* Party came to the country with a strange collection of ideas derived in varying proportions from Marx, Freud, Buber and other apostles of the then fashionable *Jugendkultur*. Strongly influenced by the German *Wandervogel* movement with its romantic worship of nature, its cult of eroticism and contempt for bourgeois values it hoped to create "a new land of Israel free from the shackles of European capitalism and of the diaspora."

All these pioneering currents, however, were not only shaped by their different ideologies but what is even more important they all shared certain personal characteristics which were to influence the very ethos of the society, particularly in its pre-independence period. Revolutionaries, romantics, adventurers and utopian dreamers, they were all inspired by a spirit of self-sacrifice and puritanical dedication to collective goals. Politics was for them not merely a party program but a way of life based on self-realization. Life they considered to be a perpetual striving, an incessant ordeal. Like so many of the young Russian populists they were obsessed with the urge to conquer themselves, to reshape their personalities after some great ideal and to find meaning and purpose through great deeds. They worshipped youth, strength, life, liberty and "intoxicating beauty". Ideas had to be lived and not merely talked about. Living lives of "this-worldly asceticism", extolling the virtues of nature, frugality and noble poverty, they fanatically rejected even the external features of the old existence. Such features included alcohol and frequently tobacco, the cinema, dancing and even decent table manners. Jackets and dresses they despised. Neckties were banned. The clothes they wore were unadorned and demonstrably proletarian in a Russian style. They were, in short, determined not merely to establish a safe haven for Jews but a new paradise as well, "a kingdom of saints," purged of luxury, injustice, inequality and evil.

An additional important facet of their ideology was their insistence on self-government and membership participation in all decisions affecting their group. Nachman Syrkin, another one of their ideologists, hardly saw the need for a civil service, in his vision of a federation of producers-cooperatives controlling the economy of the future Jewish commonwealth. In his plan, all men of merit would be summoned to the capital for special temporary duty and then return home to their village communities.[6] The spirit of the *Third Aliyah*, as we have noted, was passionately anti-authoritarian. Its members regarded formal government by professionals as anathema. The new *chalutzim* wanted to be free men, operating in federated, voluntarily established communes of like-minded members and subject to the most direct kind of participatory democracy. No man should be master; all men must have an equal share in government. They conceived of the entire country as a network of cooperative or collective agricultural and industrial associations with a minimum of coercion and a maximum of voluntary, reciprocal engagement by free yet committed individuals.

Spurred on by all these varied, though closely related ideologies, these socialist groups and parties came to be responsible for an unprecedented revolution in Jewish life. Out of their ranks emerged a ruling elite with the necessary capacities for political leadership of the Zionist movement and later of the Jewish State. Faced with a reactive and hostile Arab nationalism, whose nature they hardly understood and whose deep roots they stubbornly refused to recognize, they were soon enough compelled to establish underground defense organizations and to prepare themselves to battle for their rights by "blood and fire". They forged a class of economic entrepreneurs with some of the qualities required for the economic development of this undeveloped land. Performing the triple roles of political and military leadership—though in the military field they were joined and from 1945-1948 even surpassed by the right-wing terrorists—and economic entrepreneurship, Labor Zionism became the strongest power-bloc in the new State. Unlike the Social Democratic parties of Europe, Israeli socialism was not only a political and trade union movement but the leader of society with the economic and political resources to stamp its imprint upon the community. It shaped a social order, constructed a labor economy, created a state, built an army and set a pattern of politics and society, of habits, passions and prejudices that add up to a national character in the making.

Contemporary Israel, however, bears little resemblance to the dreams and ideals of the early pioneering generation. Instead of a society of self-governing equals Israel is dominated by a power elite stemming precisely from the pioneers who came to the country during the Second and Third *aliyot*. This power elite comprises the political leadership of the country, of the Histadrut and of the party; the economic leaders of the enterprises established by the *Histadrut* (the Labor Federation) which employs about one quarter of Israel's capital and manpower and the leaders of other *Histadrut* institutions like the Sick Fund and the trade unions; the heads of the various state enterprises, particularly in the defense establishment; and the top strata of the bureaucracy, including the army. Although this power elite does not have a monopoly of power, having to share its dominance with a smaller but rapidly growing private economic sector, with other competing political groups and with a corrupt, politically extremist religious establishment, it is still today the dominant though rapidly decaying power grouping within the society.

This Israeli power elite constitutes a kind of "labor bourgeoisie" which has been chiefly responsible for the establishment and defense of the state and for the economic development of the country. This is an elite not of private wealth but of power, based on the public wealth of the labor movement, of the state and of the tremendous foreign financial resources collected by the Zionist movement, and on the extraordinary resources of patronage which it commands. It has been responsible for the establishment not of a socialist society but of a modern society, characterized more and more by the petty-bourgeois values it had originally rebelled against but which are now returning in full force. Israel has now become a society intoxicated by the desire for material goods—above all the automobile—and the status they are supposed to bring. All those turbulent energies that formally impelled them to challenge the desolation are now poured into consumerism, careerism and the army. Instead of Israel influencing the diaspora whose decadent ways it had once rejected it is the diaspora, particularly the way of life and values of the American Jewish community, that is influencing Israel. The deliberate simplicity and economic equality of the pioneering "way of life" is now giving way to an imitation of American styles of dress and entertainment (extravagant barmitzvahs and weddings and gala dinners) and American prestige symbols (outsize automobiles, for example) are accepted by Israeli capitalist and socialist leaders alike. Israel is becoming a class society like any other, marked by the same inequalities, with a sub-class of poor, consisting of about 20 percent of the population living below the poverty level, and softened only by the considerable welfare services which it provides. In its own small way, Israel is becoming a distorted and less efficient copy of America. Ben-Aharon, the former controversial Secretary-General of the *Histadrut*, charged that government policy had produced "socialism in reverse by expropriating public funds for the enrichment of a few. This policy endangers our very existence . . . by polarizing the nation into rich and poor. We live in an unreal situation, created out of Hollywood. Our living standards are based on funds mobilized for Phantoms and immigrant absorption, and those close to the coffers get rich. Public money gets wasted and the nouveau riche wax fatter like a cancer in the national bloodstream."[7]

The power elite that rules Israel combines within itself a peculiar combination of qualities. On the one hand this is an elite of Lions and Foxes, of single-minded fanatics, of man "mad for a purpose", of builders and entrepreneurs, of stubborn fighters and clever opportunists. On the other hand, this is also an elite irremediably stamped by its small town origins, its lack of education, its closed-mindedness, its intolerance and anti-intellectualism. The former heretics, only partially and superficially emancipated, show a total indifference toward religious coercion and in their old age tend to return to the archaic religious symbols and values of their orthodox grandparents. They are both contentious and bureaucratic, factious and authoritarian. The political system of proportional representation places great power in the hands of the party machines, penalizes independent thought and independent personalities and encourages political conformism. Obsessed with power, greedy for the privileges and perquisites of office, they are now becoming an increasingly routinized, conservative elite out of touch with the social realities they have engendered and incapable of bold and creative initiatives either at home or abroad.

The contradictory qualities which characterize the elite also mark the rest of Israeli society. The economic system is a network of islands of initiative and entrepreneurship surrounded by a sea of inefficiency, mismanagement and waste. The majority of Israeli capitalists and the managers of labor or cooperative concerns concentrate most of their initiative and mental effort not on running their enterprises effectively but on obtaining favors and exclusive support from the government. The main competition to be found in the upper echelons of the Israeli economy is for "ever new kinds of assistance undreamt of and unanticipated by others."[8] The quality which ensures success is not entrepreneurial daring or productive effort but the cultivation of "connections", erecting a facade and currying favors. Israelis want the benefits of the "affluent" society but are unwilling to undertake the hard work and to practice the modern skills that this entails. The bureaucracy, which is intimately involved with economic activities, is a by-word for arrogance, nepotism, contempt for the public, lavish expense accounts, influence peddling and inefficiency. What Ben-Aharon said of the situation he found within the Histadrut economy when he took office is true of most of the country's institutions. He described it thus: "The vested interests, the bureaucracy, the laziness—lazy thinking! They are afraid to try anything new—afraid of intellectual risk."[9]

The rapid development of the consumer society has also led to the growth of a mass culture as its necessary complement. Its theater is a provincial copy of Broadway. The cinema is a place of refuge for almost all Israelis. Most of the best sellers from the West find a ready reading public. Its radio and television programs are mainly filled out with variety material and "light music"—interlaced with commercials. The latest fashions are quickly adopted. The most sought after value is recreation, perceived as the pleasure of excitement, supplied externally. The modes of mass culture are however consumed not only by the masses of the society but by its privileged sectors and has even infiltrated the kibbutz movement. Except for a few independent and critical thinkers, completely without influence, its academic life is in the grip of mediocrity, its style of thought copied from America and its academics are most eager to serve the needs of the state and the army. Its students are apathetic and only interested in their careers. The Jews, Edmond Flag tells us, are characterized by concern with the terrestrial world, some being attached to life in order to ennoble it, others to exploit it. In Israel, the trend toward ennoblement is now being submerged by other trends—the desire for "normal" life, the thirst for material abundance and cheap pleasures and the hunger to live well.

The kibbutz movement too has been affected by all the developments that we have described. There has been a decline in the population of the kibbutzim. From constituting 7.5 percent of the whole in 1947, it fell to 5 percent in 1955, 3.7 percent in 1959 and 3.1 percent in 1966.[10] Its creative energy has ebbed, it no longer occupies the center of the stage and it has been thrown onto the margin of events. Turning more and more toward industry, the kibbutzim are now affected by the problems of the distance between the decision makers and those who carry out the decisions, the fragmentation of labor and the alienation of labor. Employing hired labor they profit from the "surplus value" that this hired labor creates. Although the kibbutz still practices a form of direct democracy, with the weekly meeting of members the chief deliberative body of the group, yet even in this area changes are taking place. The growth of different branches of production, the need for professional knowledge, economic and technical expertise and specialization are all weakening the spirit of participation. The feeling is growing that the important decisions affecting the life of the community are no longer really made at the general meeting but elsewhere, by special committees, by those responsible for the various branches of the kibbutz's activities and by the secretariat. The result is scepticism, apathy and less regular attendance by the members and the development of a bureaucratic elite within the kibbutz itself with its concomitant privileges, limited though they still are at present. And, though the kibbutz has proved itself to be an effective form of economic organization it has neither produced a "new man" nor a "new socialist culture."

All these changes, however, have not affected the desperate patriotism of the average Israeli. Though his social ethic may be distorted his nationalistic feelings are more intense than among most peoples. 90 percent of Israel's young men and 50 percent of its young women readily serve in the army. Surrounded by neighbors who openly express their enmity to the state, haunted by the traumatic experiences of the Holocaust, the people of Israel are ready to make every sacrifice for their country's security.

In fact, is is precisely in the military sphere that Israel has scored its greatest successes. By a strange and ironic twist of fate, the Israeli state, which was shaped by socialist idealists, utopians and even pacifists, is now known the world over for its military prowess, for its talent in the waging of war, for its fighting spirit and for its export of quality weapons. The army and the scientific and industrial establishment linked to it are the most modernized institutions in the state. Faced with the ever present challenge and unrelenting competitiveness of the Arab armies surrounding it, the Israeli army has been compelled to be superior and more efficient than its likely foes, or else it and the state will cease to exist. Thus, an ethos has been created in the army different from that in civilian life. Political nepotism is not as prevalent as it is in civilian life. Selection for positions is usually based on merit. The efficient and daring officer is generally preferred to the routine performer, although the euphoria induced by the 1967 war led to a dangerous slackening in military alertness and to a politicization of the high command. Ability is, in most cases, the accepted standard for choosing the leadership. Even the manner of speech and the kind of relationships that prevail between its members are different. Discussions within army circles are more clear and direct. The dichotomy between words and intent and between intent and execution is smaller. It need only be added that this kind of "modern" efficiency has only been made possible by the authoritarian methods which are the very life-blood of an army organization and that its efficiency has so far only been tested against decadent and backward Arab forces.

However, Israel's military success in four major battles against the Arabs, its steadily increasing military strength and its need to devote such a disproportionate amount of energy and resources to defense problems has had a warping effect on the outlook of the ruling elite and on the society's spiritual and ethical life. Caught in the dynamic of its struggle with its intransigent, hysterical and nihilistic Arab neighbors, Israel too has become a country "possessed" by its security problem. The battles it has waged have created by their own inner logic a momentum toward reliance on military solutions and even toward expansionism. From 1967 to 1973 it was determined to maintain most of the territories it had conquered in the 1967 war and to keep under its control the one million Arabs living in the occupied territories. Rigid and unyielding in their diplomatic posture, become intoxicated with success and infected with the arrogance of power, its leaders are reluctant to explore the fragile possibilities for some sort of co-existence which might be possible with their enemies. Having tasted the fruits of military and political success they seemed to enjoy the unhindered opportunities they had until October 1973 for ruling over another people. Unwilling to grant the Palestinians of the occupied territories some form of national independence, Israel now practices a highly original form of "an enlightened and intelligent colonialism." Israel passed in an amazingly short period from "utopia" to a mini-empire.

All these developments have been steadily eroding the values on which Israeli society was built. Dependent on American support it became, particularly during the Nixon administration, a vociferous champion of the Cold War and of America's barbaric policies in Vietnam. The original Zionist philosophy which had postulated that a nation and a country could only be built by the hard work of its own citizens is now being flouted as more and more of the manual and unskilled work in Israel is being done by Arab workers from the occupied territories. A new class of foremen, contractors and "patrons" has arisen who invade the West Bank and Gaza to enlist the Palestinian inhabitants to work in Israel under their supervision. Watching all this happening, the under-privileged Israelis, most of whom are Oriental Jews, to preserve their pride, prefer to remain the poor wards of society rather than to take the jobs now in the hands of the Arabs. New vested groups closely connected with the military establishment—construction and building companies, land speculators and investors, contractors for the defense sectors and innumerable others connected with the defense system—all "tend to encourage the government to keep the territorial status quo and prevent any steps that might bring about withdrawal from the territories."[11] The continued growth of the defense budget and the preoccupation with security matters is, furthermore, preventing the Israeli government from devoting its full energies and resources to the solution of the country's pressing domestic problems. Violence, crime and marginal ways of life are spreading rapidly among youth and even adults. Financial corruption has proliferated into every sector of the society, including the army itself. Israeli society is "gradually becoming anarchic and wild" and is showing all the symptoms and dangers that threaten the existence of urban and technological societies in other countries. Political differences and genuine public debate slowly expired as security, national fanaticism and national unity became the common denominator of all the political parties in the period between 1967 and October 1973. Although it has revived again as a result of the 1973 earthquake, it has still not made a basic dent in the military and political consensus that governs Israel. The flag of security has steadily replaced the flag of social reform. Thus Israel's obsession with security has inevitably led to the decline of intellectual life, the erosion of the quality of the society and of the quality of social, economic and educational development, to political rigidity, immobility, mediocrity and to dangerous and suicidal impulses.

The development of Labor Zionism and of the state during the last seventy years or so shows only too clearly the power of realities over dreams, the corruption to which every movement and people is heir, and the feebleness of man in the face of the power-lusts, the greed and the irrational passions which drive him.

Of course, the most successful examples of what passes for socialism are to be found within the communist regimes. The party regimes that now rule in Russia, China and the other Communist countries were at first inspired by the noblest of ideals. Influenced by Western European Marxism, as in Russia, the revolutionaries thought of themselves as the representatives of a new epoch of human development. Although Russia itself, as they recognized, was not yet ready for socialism, the Russian Revolution which they saw coming and for which they organized themselves would be the signal for a European and world revolution, and backward Russia would then be the inspiration for a new historical breakthrough under Marxist leadership. In place of the formal democracy of bourgeois society, they would establish a system of direct democracy through the Soviets, with its representatives not only elected but subject to recall at any time. Workers would control production and distribution, bureaucrats would receive pay not exceeding that of a workman and the old bureaucratic apparatus would be smashed. Through economic planning, direction, rationality and control would be imposed upon the economic system. The method of total public ownership would replace the chaos and greed of capitalism with one purposefully directed toward human needs and welfare. The temporary proletarian dictatorship, in the interest of the majority, would ultimately lead to the withering away of the state itself. A class society would be replaced by a classless society and Russia would be cleansed of its "Asiatic" and "barbaric" features and raised to new heights of cultural achievement.

Over fifty years of Communist rule in Russia have completely shattered all these utopian hopes and expectations. Communism in Russia can now be seen for what it is. It is not a new stage of post-capitalist historical development and it is not a socialist alternative to bourgeois society. Communism is essentially a movement for the modernization of Russian society. The positive objective of modern communism is not to remove social conflicts or to create an egalitarian classless society but to overcome Russia's own backwardness. Its essential role has been to duplicate the work performed by early capitalism in the west, naturally within its own Russian setting and by employing its own very special Russian methods. Communism under Stalin, for instance, was an amalgam of a ritualized Marxist or Marxist-Leninist ideology with Russia's primordial and savage backwardness. Its basic driving forces, however, are the same as those which have impelled capitalism —economic growth for the sake of growth—and in Russia economic growth was also strictly subordinated to the growth of state power. On the one hand, communism is a second and much more effective edition of the Petrine regime and on the other, it constitutes a form of state capitalism, with the state performing the tasks of economic accumulation and economic development that the private bourgeoisie performed in the "free enterprise" economies of the West.

The Russian state is not ruled by the workers or the peasants but by a new power elite which has emerged from all the revolutionary upheavals. This new ruling elite, presiding over a clearly articulated class society, is not an elite of wealth but an elite of power, with its power stemming from its control of the party which is its chief instrument of rule and from the party's dictatorial control of the state with all its instruments of force and coercion, and of the state-controlled economy. It is not wealth that creates power but power that engenders superior status and the material rewards of office. The creation of this new elite has been its greatest achievement. Sprung from the most ambitious sections of the "people", barely one generation removed from the village, this elite is crude and primitive, arrogant and with a pronounced feeling of inferiority and infected with the barbarous cruelty which has always been a characteristic of Russia's rulers and political traditions. It is an elite of builders and entrepreneurs (though at a Russian tempo), bureaucrats and technocrats. Its specialty, however, is large-scale organization and the party through which it operates is still probably the best organized of political movements.[12]   It is therefore a highly effective political elite, in the Russian tradition, ever ready to sacrifice economic goals to the political objectives of holding power and of maintaining and expanding its multi-national empire.   The governance of this huge realm is not only Russia's greatest problem but has always been the chief business and largest industry of Russia. That it has been able, until now, to lead its vast domains as an effective political unit suffices to give to the present rulers of Soviet Russia tremendous weight in the world.

However, the society which has emerged after over fifty years of travail and upheaval is one marked by obvious contradictions, weaknesses and irrationalities. Its planned economy was able to industrialize the country and to build an awesome military machine at unprecedented human costs and sacrifices, but its consumer sector is snarled in inefficiency and mismanagement. Its planned economy has not been able to avert pollution, ecological dislocation and other evils of industrialism. Its agriculture is hopelessly disorganized and backward and its peasantry apathetic and morose. The new proletariat which has emerged, half-peasant and half-urban worker, is disoriented, still half-dazed and out of place in this new environment. Drunkenness is even a greater problem that it ever was. Absenteeism, theft of government property and the primordial Russian sloth are all rampant. The new professional middle class that has been trained, though "passively discontented," is more interested in protecting and improving its material privileges than in trying to actively reform the regime. Although a small and heroic intellectual opposition has come to the fore, in the mass this middle class is so mediocre, its thinking is so bureaucratized, its initiative so crippled by regulations and its lives are so gray that it constitutes no serious danger to the regime. And, despite the fact that its non-Russian nationalities—Jews, Ukrainians, Georgians, Tartars, Lithuanians and others—are beginning to stir, the iron bands of dictatorship are still strong enough to be able to hold this sprawling and fragile empire together.[13]

The regime that now rules the Soviet empire has now become essentially conservative, mitigated only by the slow movements toward economic growth and higher living standards which have mollified this still passive people. The present Communist Party is no longer a revolutionary party in which individual courage, resourcefulness and initiative make for advancement but is constituted in such a way as to welcome the obedient and the pliant and to weed out individual talent. Its chief interest is to maintain itself in power and to enjoy those prerogatives equivalent to those associated with wealth under capitalism: luxury, convenience and prestige. It is not any particular doctrine or tradition that motivates it, nor is it attached to any special personality or leader. It is power and power alone that shapes its outlook and behavior. The regime has no particular desire either to restore the horrors of Stalinism or to persecute the intelligentsia as such. It only wants everything to go on as before—authority is to be respected, the intelligentsia to behave in public and no disturbance of the system by dangerous and unfamiliar reforms. It is prepared to grant small concessions when pressed too hard and to apply moderate doses of repression when the situation demands it, but its deepest desire is for stability and order. It hopes that this combination of slow reforms, higher living standards and a tight grip over the polity will enable it to maintain itself in power for a long time.

It is only in the field of foreign policy that the regime shows dynamism and more or less consistent motivation. Its foreign policy objectives are, however, neither shaped by the ideology of Marxism-Leninism nor by that of international revolution. The ideology that moves it is that of Great Russian nationalism, with its inherent cult of force and expansionist ambitions. Its enemies are not class enemies, e.g., world imperialism and anti-communism, but national enemies, e.g., Chinese and Jews. Glorying in its new formed national power, appealing to the chauvinism of the Russian people, desirous of contacts with the West but suspicious of its possible disruptive consequences, the ruling elite concentrates its energies with deep purposefulness on the consolidation and expansion of Russia's imperial power. Pouring vast resources into its own "industrial-military complex" it is determined to maintain its position of supremacy in Eastern Europe, encircle China, expand its influence wherever that is possible, join the United States as a global power and even surpass it in time. Although this kind of nationalistic policy is at present eliciting support for the regime, in the long run, as we have already noted, it must undermine the bases of the regime's strength. Obsessed with imperial power, driven by all kinds of messianic pretentions and illusions the Soviet regime is in danger of straining its society to such an extent that not even all its numerous police forces will be able to prevent its disintegration in the future.

The Chinese experiment under Mao Tse-tung has from the beginning been even less formally influenced by Western Marxism than Russian Communism was. At every stage of its journey further to the east, Marxism became more diluted and more adapted to its national environ-

ments. Chinese Communism, as is transparent by now, is a unique
Chinese instrument for the modernization of China's massively backward peasant society and for the development of Chinese national
strength, consciousness and pride. It is the most effective Chinese
response to the disruptive impact of the West, deeply rooted within
Chinese traditions and mores and it can only be understood in terms
of its Chineseness rather than in terms of its so-called and borrowed
"Marxism-Leninism-Stalinism."

The Chinese Communists, after a whole series of trials and errors,
have elaborated a special Chinese path to modernization. It is industrializing at a slower, less catastrophic pace than the Russians or the
West did; it places more emphasis upon agricultural development; it
has relied more on persuasion than on terror; in its system of management it has given greater initiative to rank and file participation; and
its Yenan experience of guerrilla warfare has played a more important
role as a model of conduct for the rest of the society. The Chinese are
thus now, after the upheavals of the Cultural Revolution, trying to
integrate the cities with the countryside and to make the urban areas
and industries serve the countryside. City-based factories are being
urged to engage in agriculture, while mechanization of farming and
the construction of small machine-tool industries on rural communes
are encouraged. The policy, in short, is to continue with urban industrialization while at the same time consciously developing rural industries.

However, the most important developments that are taking place are
those which are affecting the peoples' mentality and its system of values.
A whole nation has been set to work and the Protestant ethic of work
"as a high calling" is being inculcated into all strata of society. A spirit
of this-worldly asceticism permeates the nation. Self-reliance is stressed,
initiative and achievement encouraged and austerity and frugality
enforced. Attacking the old and deeply-rooted bureaucratic mentality
with all its arrogance and sense of superiority and also in order to keep
them in contact with the masses, state and party cadres are compelled
to spend some time working in either factories or on the farms. Practical
work and academic studies have been combined. The intellectual and
cultural gulf separating the urban and rural areas is being narrowed.
As against the Taoist and Buddhist view of man "in nature" the regime
stresses the view of man "over nature", and against the Confucian idea
of "harmony with nature" the emphasis is now on the "war against
nature" which the people are being called upon frantically to undertake. The model of a Communist man is not defined in terms of his
being—as part of a stable tradition—but in his becoming through

learning, toil, criticism and self-criticism and struggle. It need only be added that these dramatic transformations in fundamental cultural values and basic motivations are among the most momentous changes being introduced into China, far more significant than its material efforts in industry and agriculture and at the same time the prerequisites for their continued material success.

Yet, all these policies and values, it must be clearly understood, do not make China some sort of model socialist society. These are all merely a Chinese variant of modernization and of state capitalism. Material incentives have been restored to increase productivity. Politics, as the Chinese say, is in command. The reconstituted party, with strong army representation, is still the principal dictatorial force that guides, manipulates and rules this immense country with all its overflowing millions. Purges and other convulsions take place frequently. The Maoist cult of personality, while in effect, was a repulsive expression of the most primitive form of mass indoctrination and mass control. Creative thought, outside the fields of economics and military science, is rigidly controlled. A mental monotone has been imposed upon the country. All thought, all ideas—past, present and future—are twisted, rolled out and flattened into a few simple slogans which are hammered incessantly and insistently into the minds of the people. The individual personality is completely subservient to the group and the collectivity. Though the Chinese ruling elite is, by virtue of the country's cultural traditions and history, more cultivated and sophisticated than the Russian or the American, and though Chinese society is probably the most egalitarian in the world, it is still a class society with its leading strata enjoying not only power but all the material benefits that power brings. Its further economic development, which is now being pushed with greater vigor than ever before, can only intensify the class differentiations that now exist and bring China closer to the conditions that now prevail in the more highly industrialized societies.

The Chinese revolution is indubitably one of the most momentous events of contemporary history. A highly civilized, energetic and creative people has "stood up" after over a century of humiliations, invasions and foreign intrusions. This is, despite all the socialist pretensions and fulminations of Chinese propaganda, a nationalist revolution, committed to modernization and the social transformation of its own society and not an example of advanced socialism. It is a combination of revolutionary modernization with Chinese nationalism, interweaving old patterns with new motifs. Its turn to a collectivistic economy is in line with the old Confucianist distrust of individual initiative and the profit motive; and its style of ruling can only be understood in relation to the crucial importance of the bureaucracy in China's imperial past. It is now beginning again to emphasize that tradition should be used intelligently and prudently and that they should "Let the past serve the present." In foreign policy it is motivated by the same power-drives as are all other nation states, its self interests take precedence over every other consideration and its behavior is no less egotistic and cynical. The Chinese Revolution is an historic event for China and the world but it is not the beginning of a new stage of socialist development.[14]

Socialism in all its forms is thus a failure and constitutes no challenge or alternative to modern industrial civilization. Its ideal of a classless society is pure utopia. Every social movement is dominated by Michel's iron law of oligarchy. The mass is incapable, because of its inherent impotence, to rule either itself or society. Instead of the self-emancipation of the people we have everywhere the rule of new bureaucratic elites. Wherever socialism acquires supreme power it merely replaces one ruling class for another, one mode of oppression for another. The oppressed have continued to remain an object of history, a pawn rather than a new liberating force. Nationalization of the economy and a system of centralized planning are neither more efficient nor more rational than the capitalist market economy. The Social Democratic parties of the West are mere adjuncts of the capitalist order, small men with small minds. The state capitalist or state socialist (if one prefers that appellation) regimes of the communist world are the mere instruments for catching up with the advanced industrial capitalist societies. Modernizing and industrializing, nationalistic and imperialistic, they mirror the cultures which have shaped them. In Russia, the regime is still crude and primitive. In China its traditional cultivation is mixed with ruthlessness and mental conformism. In Vietnam its extraordinary heroism is combined with the utmost readiness to kill and be killed. Their values and ultimate aims are essentially those which have motivated the capitalist system and as we have already seen, their ultimate aim of material abundance does not and cannot bring a new flowering of the human personality and of human freedom and creativity but only adds new evils, conflicts, contradictions and dangers to the old stock of human infirmities.

However, socialism has had an even more insidious effect on history. By elevating the masses it degrades civilization. Excellence is disparaged, mediocrity enthroned, vulgar appetites stimulated and a spirit of rancour encouraged. The entry of the masses into the historical arena has lowered the level of culture. It has produced the mass man, the day-to-day man, without lofty ideals or ambitions, his inferior ego inflated, his concern with his own selfish interests encouraged and his head stuffed with all the rubbish of mass culture. Interested only in material improvements and material benefits the masses become fodder for industry, commerce and advertising. Our mass societies stifle experiment and adventure and blast every budding novelty and seed of genius with their omnipresent and fierce stupidity. Their encouragement of uniformity quenches the thirst for new outlets, for more perfect, even if alien achievements, and reveals a mind dead to the ideal. Mouthing the insipidities about human progress and perfection, devoid of a long memory and bereft of an historic conscience, the mass men produced by socialism and by capitalism—instant men from the slums or the progenies of newly acquired power or learning—have simply not acquired the experience or the depth necessary for the creation of a new civilization or for the preservation and improvement of the existing one. Socialism in the underdeveloped countries represents the most effective method of building modern societies; in the developed world it is one manifestation, among others, of the spreading barbarism and decadence.

CHAPTER 12

THE DECADENCE OF MASS SOCIETY

The failures of our ruling elites and of our leading ideologies to manage or comprehend the explosive forces of the twentieth century have produced a state of contemporary decadence in which we have our being. The fears of decline that have haunted the leading minds of the Western world for the last fifty years or more have now become the stuff of everyday reality. In 1975 many people, including many Americans, were possessed by a growing feeling that an age is withering, that a civilization is in the process of collapsing. The bourgeois civilization that began to emerge with such confidence and energy in the sixteenth century and that then gathering force and momentum swept to the triumphant heights of the nineteenth century is now beginning to collapse with a bang and a whimper. We are witnessing the end of the bourgeois epoch of history, the passing of the modern age.

Viewed in the broadest historical perspective it is possible to see decadence, as Spengler, Berdayev and others saw it, as the triumph of civilization over culture. Culture predominates in young societies awakening to new life, grows like a young organism endowed with exuberant vitality and represents a new ideology and world outlook. It involves the original creation of new values, of new religious symbols and artistic styles, of new intellectual and spiritual structures, new sciences, new political systems, new moral codes. Culture is always aristocratic and based upon quality rather than quantity. It stresses austerity and duty, honor and service, reflection and excellence. It emphasizes the individual rather than the organization, original creation rather than preservation and duplication, prototypes rather than mass production, an aesthetic outlook upon life rather than an ethical one. The energy of culture man is directed inwards and awakens his latent inner potentialities and powers. It is the product of men of genius, of great creators and trail-blazers, and of a rising ruling class.

However, every culture in the process of flowering and becoming more complex and refined exhausts its creative forces and spirit. It is torn apart by the inner contradictions which it generates. No culture can always remain on the heights where it is born but must inevitably descend and fall. It is powerless to sustain its high level of quality and the quantitative principle overcomes it in the end. All cultures at a certain stage of their development disclose the principles and actions which sap their own spiritual and social foundations. The creative energy of culture is dispersed and decline sets in because culture is incapable of developing eternally or fully realizing the aims of its creators. Culture having lost its original force becomes civilization.

One of the chief features of civilization is manifested in its desire for unlimited expansion. The energy of civilization man is directed outwards. He is driven by a will to "new" life, to power and dominion at all costs. An age of imperialism usually denotes the end of a culture. The weaker the creative forces become the stronger grows the lust for world domination. Empires rest on dead bodies, amorphous and dispirited masses of men, on aimless megalomania, the scrap material from a great history. Imperialism is civilization unadulterated. The expansive tendency as Spengler has suggested is a "doom, something demonic and immense, which grips, forces into service and uses up the late mankind of the world-city stage, willy-nilly, aware or unaware."[1] The will to universal domination therefore disintegrates and melts the historical collectivities belonging to culture. The ravenous imperial will contains the seed of death. Imperialism, as Berdayev has argued, "in its uncontrollable development undermines its own foundations and prepares the transition to socialism, which is likewise governed by the universal will to power and organization and which is thus a further stage and manifestation of civilization."[2] Both imperialism and socialism are consequently the expressions of a deep cultural crisis. They represent the triumph of civilization at the expense of culture and then bring with it the vulgarization or the loss of the splendid forms created by culture. It is civilization tainted by machine oil and all the defects of a technical society.

Another characteristic of civilization is represented by the triumph of technique and materialism.   Civilization is inevitably dominated by economics and is by its very nature technical.   It considers the organization of power and technique as the authentic approach to a realization of "life".   Supposedly practical, utilitarian and "realistic" it devotes all its energies to the irrational accumulation of profit and to the superficial enjoyments to be had from "life".   Its sole aim is the enjoyment of life in its immediate manifestation.   Civilization's chief pursuit is the establishment of security and economic wellbeing for as many people as possible and in the process it crushes individuality and exuberant creativity and leads to the sway of the masses and the mechanical.   It gives itself up to the torrent of hedonism and is engulfed by it.

Civilization is therefore dominated by the power of money.   It is fascinated and tormented by money, its power and glory, its delusions and devastations.   The money-power rules and corrupts the mass media, the parliaments and the universities.   In the 1972 American elections, for example, over $400 million were spent in an extravaganza of commercials, frantic cross-country airplane flights, underhanded activities of all kinds, theatrics, gimmickry, and the careful programming of applauding crowds.[3]   A society dominated by economic interests and motives is by its very nature unfit to grapple with the great problems which determine its destiny.   For, while politics, at its highest, must be concerned with the public interest, economics is self-regarding.   Political power sacrifices men for some common ideal, however distorted, but economic power merely wastes them away.   Life comes to mean, not a waxing in strength for great tasks but a matter of the "greatest happiness of the greatest number," of comfort and ease, of bread and circuses.   The standard of living dominates the style of life and its inhabitants are possessed by its individual and communal apparatus.   Those whose lives are devoted to the acquisition of purely economic advantages—as the Carthaginians were in ancient times and the modern West, with America in the lead, is in ours—are correspondingly incapable of purely political thinking.   That is why the great economic groupings of the present day (e.g., big corporations and labor unions) pile one political failure on another.   Through money, democracy becomes its own destroyer, after money has destroyed the intellect.   A civilization intoxicated by economic interests is one that systematically undermines the qualities on which a high culture can be built and sustained.

Civilization is as a consequence, by its very nature "bourgeois" in the moment of its complete triumph.   It is synonymous with the civilized will to organized power and enjoyment of life.   The spirit of civilization is that of the middle classes with all their greed and their concern with the ephemeral, the momemtary and the corrupt. To be a bourgeois, therefore, is to be a slave of the material and an enemy of the higher creations of the human spirit. The perfected European and American civilizations gave rise to the industrial-capitalist system, which represents not only a mighty economic achievement and development but also a culture phenomenon which destroys culture. It is anti-philosophical, mechanistic and fictitious. Its automatism, technique and mechanism rob life of humanity and meaning. The divorce of economy from life, the exaltation of economics as the highest principle of life, the technical interpretation of life and the fundamental capitalist principle of profit transform man's economic life into a fetish. The capitalist system sows the seeds of its own destruction by unleashing vast irrational appetites and ambitions which it cannot fulfill. Labor and life lose all creative purpose and meaning and as a result it produces discontent, alienation and an indictment against its whole system. Socialism is the penalty it pays. But socialism carries on the work of civilization and reflects its bourgeois principles; it aims to develop civilization still further without infusing it with new values. Thus, industrial civilization manufactures fictions, inevitably undermines the discipline and motivating principle of labor, violates the environment, disrupts the human personality and in these ways prepares its own downfall.

The triumphant advent of the machine, introduced by capitalism, has furthermore produced a profound change in the relationship between man and nature and hence in his social environment and ultimate destiny. Life now loses its organic character and natural rhythm; man is separated from nature by an artificial environment of machines, by the very instruments of his intended domination of nature. Rebelling against the ascetic ideals of medievalism man discards both resignation and contemplation and determines to dominate nature, organize life and increase its productive forces. This, however, does not help to bring him into closer communion with the inner life of nature. On the contrary, by mastering it technically and organizing its forces man not only becomes further removed from it but produces a backlash of nature which begins to mock and undermine his achievements. Organization proves to be the death of organism. Life becomes increasingly a matter of technique. The machine leaves its mark upon the human spirit and all its manifestations. Civilization comes to rest on a mere mechanical foundation. Its speculation and art tend to become increasingly technical in character. It transforms the metaphysical into the physical, the inner into the outer, the adventures of the mind into the adventures of technocracy. Religion ceases to be a matter of belief and becomes largely verbal, ritualistic and an economic and political machine. Specialization is developed at the expense of human integrity. Everything becomes absorbed into the endless recurrence of the same. Man loses himself in mere facts and their banality. Civilization represents par excellence the triumph of technique over mind, imagination and the individual.

In place of the eighteenth century city of culture, which still retains some connection with the living tradition, civilization produces the "megalopolis" in which life has lost its roots, no longer possesses vital rhythm and has descended to a level of general uniformity. In these "barrack cities" vast assemblages of people live on top of each other, each a stranger to the other, each jostling and rubbing against the other, their life a meaningless repetition of purely mechanical tasks and vulgar, brutal diversions. Overcrowded and overgrown, congested with traffic, deafened with noise, tawdry and chaotic, the megalopolis breeds its own special kind of pathology. This manifests itself not only in the statistics of crime and mental disorder but in the enormous sums spent on drugs, sedatives, stimulants and tranquillizers that "help" the "lonely crowds" of our great cities to adjust to the vacuous horrors that are being planned for them by greedy speculators and property developers and by governments without civic or historic pride. Ruled by the forces of materialism and commercialism the modern megalopolis, that stone sea, marks the end of organic growth and the beginning of a process of daemonic development, soulless and artificial, extravagant, cancerous and life-destroying.

The economic, technological and political forces of the age of civilization fashion a new human type—the mass-man. The appearance of the mass-man, as Ortega y Gasset has argued, is one of the formidable facts of the period in which we live. The mass-man is the average man. Instead of making great demands on himself, piling up difficulties and duties, as does the man who belongs to the "creative minority", he demands nothing special of himself, lives only for the moment, imposes no effort on himself toward excellence and is a mere buoy that floats on the waves. This commonplace man with his commonplace mind has now acquired the assurance to proclaim the rights of the commonplace and to impose them wherever he wills. Instructed only in the techniques of modern life without being educated in them; innoculated with the pride and power of modern instruments but without understanding the awesome power they possess or the immense problems they pose, the mass-man gives the impression of a primitive man suddenly risen in the midst of civilization. Common, inert and ubiquitous, immobile and ravenous, he "crushes beneath him everything that is different, everything that is excellent, individual, qualified and select."[4]

Thus anybody who is not like everybody, who does not think like everybody, is either eliminated or reduced to silence and impotence. Of course, it is clear that this "everybody" is not everybody. Everybody was in the past the complex unity of the mass and the divergent, specialized creative minorities. Today, however, "everybody" is the mass alone and this includes the elite as well.

The mass-man is to be found not only among the working classes but throughout all the ranks of society. The new middle classes, employed in our large corporations, government bureaucracies and universities, have been turned into mass men. Without property, which could provide them with an identifiable area of freedom, the members of the new middle classes live lives of perpetual dependency. Its members are employees and their livelihoods are always contingent on the approval and good will of the organizations which employ them. Such a class will inevitably be cautious, conventional, superficial and attuned to the sensibilities of those around them. Controlled by the organizations by which this class is employed, its members become part of the function they perform. The individual is regarded with indifference. No one is indispensable. He is not himself, having no more genuine individuality than one pin in a row, a mere object of general utility. Those most effectively predestined to such a life are persons without any serious desire to be themselves. In order to advance he must be able to make himself liked. He must persuade and at times corrupt; he must hold his tongue, circumvent and lie when necessary; and avoid showing any independence beyond that which might be required. Slaves of their functions, deracinated and reduced to the level of a thing, the new middle classes have no sense of rank or difference, are immersed in the multitude and bereft of genuine human attributes.

The mass civilization which dominates us is ruled by elites which have also been infected with the values of the mass. The elites are coordinated by the very masses they lead, they are nothing but the complement of the many. Although the elites perform different and higher functions they are but others in essence with the many. The elites can only reach their influential positions by becoming the functionaries of the masses, through being attentive to their wishes and by never running counter to their demands. They do not regard themselves as being endowed with independent selfhood but merely as the exponents of the multitude which backs them up. At bottom they are as powerless as the masses they are presumed to lead, only marginally of greater competence than the managed, the executants of whatever may be re-echoed by the average will of the multitude. What they are is not measured by an ideal, is not related to the genuine needs of the society, but is based upon their conceptions of the fundamental qualities of mankind as manifested in the majority and as dominant in action. History is thus now dominated by the masses rather than by richly developed individuals. Mass society has no place for the self-made and creative personalities, nor has it any desire for independence and originality in either the management or conduct of life. Neither liberty of external action nor freedom of internal judgment have any unique value for it. A system devised by geniuses is now run by morons. Now the result of "leadership" of this sort is inextricable confusion and mismanagement. At the parting of the ways in the life-order, as Jaspers has noted, "where the question is between creation or decay, that man will be decisive for new creation who is able on his own initiative to seize the helm and steer a course of his own choosing—even if that course be opposed to the will of the masses. Should the emergence of such persons become impossible, a lamentable shipwreck will be inevitable."[5]

Modern technology, political democracy and popular education have, furthermore, produced a mass culture—to give expression to the mass society. The old upper class monopoly of culture has been broken. In place of a high culture created for a small audience of taste and cultivation we now have a mass culture manufactured either by businessmen for profit in the capitalist West or by party bureaucrats for the maintenance of their power in the communist East. While a work of high culture, however mediocre, is an expression of feelings, ideas, tastes and individual vision, a work of mass culture has neither style, individual vision nor feelings or ideas. Mass culture offers its customers neither an emotional purgation nor an aesthetic experience for these demand an effort of the imagination and the intellect. The modern assembly line relentlessly churns out a standardized product whose modest aim is not even entertainment, for this too involves life and thus effort, but merely distraction. It may be stimulating or soporific but it must be easy to digest. It asks nothing of its audience for it is totally subordinated to it. As T.W. Adorno has put it "Distraction is bound to the present mode of production, to the rationalized and mechanized process of labor to which . . . the masses are subject . . . People want to have fun. A fully concentrated and conscious experience of art is possible only to those whose lives do not put such a strain on them that in their spare time they want relief from both boredom and effort simultaneously. The whole sphere of cheap commercial entertainment reflects this dual desire."[6]

Mass culture is thus the direct product of mass production. On the one hand, mass production has produced a mass of shoddy goods, increased leisure time and raised the real income of the poor, but on the other it has impoverished life. It has not only deindividualized life and drained each of our ends of meaning as we achieved it, but it has also inexorably excluded all art and anything of significance when it has been unable to reduce it to popular culture and diversion. The great mass of consumers determines what is to be produced. Producers and consumers alike go through the mass production mill to come out homogeneous and decharacterized. The mass media must omit all experience and expression the meaning of which is not obvious and approved. They can never question man's fate where it is questionable —they cannot sow doubt about an accepted style of life or the approved conventions of the society. They also cannot touch those experiences that art, literature and philosophy deal with—authentic and significant human experience presented in authentic and significant form. For to do so would be to present experiences which are paradoxical, difficult, challenging and at any rate not easily understood. Art is not concerned with making the conventional and accepted more conventional and accepted—it is precisely after this point that art begins and the mass media stops.

All the mass media in the end alienate people from personal experience and, though appearing to reduce it, they intensify their moral isolation from each other, from reality and from themselves. The offerings of the mass media impair the capacity for meaningful experience. While art can deepen the perception of reality, popular culture, in both its middle- and low-brow forms, veils it, diverts from it and becomes an obstacle to experiencing it. Immersed in meaninglessness, fatigue and non-fulfillment, the masses who are bombarded by the mass media are permeated with dull feelings of weariness and emptiness, futility and apathy. External stimuli are unable to fill the void of their lives. Bored and frustrated they seek diversion. But diversion, however frantic, cannot relieve the boredom which streams from non-fulfillment —just as the company so unceasingly pursued cannot stave off loneliness. Trying to waste time, time wastes them. Their monotonous existence depletes them psychologically and leaves them drained and powerless, torn between despair and boredom and filled with frightening potentialities for violence and anarchy.

The mass society that has emerged in our time is thus inchoate and uncreative. Its members are neither related to each other as individuals nor as members of a community. Its atoms cohere not according to individual choice or tradition but in a purely mechanical way, drawn together by the magnet of their common properties. Its morality sinks to the level of its most primitive members and its taste to that of the least sensitive and the most ignorant. Yet it is precisely these masses who are regarded by the rulers of mass society as the human norm. On the one hand they are treated as a medical student would treat a corpse he is about to dissect and on the other they are flattered and pandered to. But these masses are, rather, man as non-man. He is the man who has been reduced to a solitary dot, uniform with all the other dots that go to make up the mass society. He is sunk into stereotyped experience and he cannot detach himself in order to observe much less to evaluate it. He has no project of his own and only fulfills the routines that exist. The vast populations who now inhabit the wastelands of the modern world have lost the power to be individuals and have become a powerless, frustrated and nerve-wrecked mass.

The growth and expansion of mass society has additionally affected the worlds of learning and the arts.

Mass literacy has, as ought to be more than apparent by now, lowered the general level of culture and understanding. The majority of people who have learned how to read and write during the last hundred years have made very little use of it for their own enlightenment. The amount of ignorance in the world has in no way decreased as compared with the past. The vast expansion of higher education has led to a catastrophic lowering of academic standards. The universities now turn out hordes of graduates whose smattering of knowledge is a danger to themselves and to the society. The stretching out of schooling, made necessary by modern industrial conditions, has led to its increasing thinness. Educational incapacity has become one of the most serious problems facing our modern world. The purveyors of learning, moreover, the teachers and potential teachers have also been infected by the standards and values of mass society. The Higher Capitalism has invaded the campus and the most successful faculty members have become entrepreneurs of research, lavishly funded by government and foundations. The project rather than the serious book, the institute rather than the classroom, have become the principal identifying marks of this new breed. What passes for scholarship has become an adjunct of power. The most successful teachers, scholars and intellectuals have in fact become idea-mongers, people whose principal talent consists in their ability to disseminate those general ideas that have become respectable and popular. Instead of the older specialist-scholar who may have learnt more and more about less and less, these new intellectuals avid for publicity, say less and less about more and more. Corrupted by their search for worldly success and approval, our modern intellectuals and scholars have degraded learning and betrayed the high calling of independent scholarship and thought. Most of our successful scholars and intellectuals have gone on a trip to

Hog Island—the place where Norman Podhoretz had finally "made it" and found paradise—and have given their souls not for the conquest of a whole world but for free food and drink.[7]

The inflation of society, the expansion of the mass media, the growth of higher education, have all diluted the quality of intellectual life. In the universities men and women who formerly would have been fortunate to have become clerks have now become academics. Instead of seeking truth they accumulate what passes for correct information and interpretations. Lacking personal security and self-confidence they are incapable of thinking for themselves and accept whatever passes for the current orthodoxy. In this world of increasing intellectualization the people who dare to form their opinions and tastes independently become fewer and fewer. The superficially revolutionary character of our times only hides a dreary expanse of intellectual stagnation. Our most daring minds and most outstanding people have only been toying with the most shallow and frivolous ideas. Everywhere we see laziness of thought and imaginations captivated by routine and outworn categories. With a few exceptions, the performance of the intellectuals during the last fifty years has been generally characterized by cowardice, opportunism, dishonesty and irresponsibility. Ruled by opinion and the latest fad the minds of the intelligentsia have been corroded and literacy has fallen apart into a state of general decomposition.

However, some of the clearest expressions of decline and decadence are to be found in the arts. All the arts are in a state of pattern dissolution. They show no unity of topic, style and objective. Eclectic and unintegrated they present an incoherent potpourri or hash of all sorts of topics, styles and objectives. The break-through to functional forms in architecture has thus quickly enough given way to machine-like buildings which are peeling and aging more rapidly than the huts of the peasants in the Middle Ages. The revolt against the limitations of the traditional framework of the octave scale has not only led to experiments in atonality, however monotonous the sounds they produce, but to the even more monotonous and pervasive rhythms of rock and roll, with all its barbaric cries and sounds manufactured by the latest technology. In painting and sculpture the work of art as a "cultural object" has been dissolved and the distinction between subject and object and between art and life erased; and both have been decomposed into spaces, environments, motions, media-mixes, happenings and the creation of "man-machine" interaction systems. Modern art is not only characterized by absurdity and extravagance but it has become the respectable salesman of the commerce of chaos.

The literature of the past two decades has perhaps most clearly touched the nerve of the age. In reading the literature of the period one has the feeling of a world infected by madness and leading toward some cosmic disaster. The world is represented as having lost all coherence and consistency, the absolutes have vanished, and man lives unawares on floating ground. Many of their protagonists are schizoid, insanity rather than normalcy has become the touchstone of reality. The individual is protrayed as a mere thing batted back and forth by the fanatical pettiness of huge and impersonal institutions. The events that are described seem to be gratuitous and the line between good and evil no longer exists. The phenomena of every-day life assume a grotesque appearance. They wrinkle and disintegrate, they crack; and man seems to fall into a bottomless abyss. Some see the modern world, and America in particular, as a delusive wonderland of colliding forces where love as often as hate leads to violence. For others the excremental vision has become tactile. And there are individuals who see the world of thieves, rapists and murderers as the only honest world, for here the profoundest and most forbidden human impulses are expressed in direct, primitive terms. The tremors of apocalypse, warning of some impending holocaust, have penetrated the modern sensibility.[8]

According to George Steiner, among others, the old verbal culture is in decline and there is everywhere a general retreat from the word. The primacy of logic is now drawing to a close. Rhetoric and the arts of conviction which it disciplines are almost in total disrepute. The democratization of high culture has adulterated the products of classic literacy. More and more of the informational energy required by a mass consumer society is being transmitted pictorially. A large segment of mankind between the ages of thirteen and twenty-five moreover, now lives immersed in a throbbing sound culture where activity such as reading, writing, private communication, learning, previously framed with silence, now takes place in a field of strident vibrato. The decline of the old verbal culture, the increasing importance of the language of mathematics and the idiom of the computer, the spread of pop and rock music as the lingua-franca of youth, all presage the emergence of a diminished or post-culture. The high culture based on privilege and hierarchical order and sustained by the great works of the past and the truths and beauties achieved in the tradition destroyed itself in two world wars. We are now living in a cruel "late stage in western affairs" marked by feelings of disarray, by a regress into violence and moral obtuseness, by a central failure of values in the arts and in the graces of personal and social behavior. Confused and bombarded modern man is suffused with fears "of a new 'Dark Age' in which civilization itself as we have known it may disappear or be confined to the small islands of archaic conservation."[9]

The catastrophes and transformations of the modern age have thus had the most pronounced effects on the life and condition of man in this period of human history. Two world wars have annihilated decisive reserves of intelligence, of nervous resilience and of political talent. Our culture, as T.S. Eliot has written, is "A heap of broken images," "mere withered stumps of time," from which the spirit has fled. The expansion of social organization, of the range of man's reach into the universe of man's control of natural forces—all this has proceeded at the expense of personality. The gain in the expansion of the genus has gone hand in hand with the loss in selfness of the individual. Over-civilization and dehumanization coexist and codevelop. The spread of the greed for life to the masses has destroyed the highest spiritual culture, which is always aristocratic and based upon quality. The age of quantity now reigns supreme. The human mind itself has begun to deteriorate in quality and cultural level. The new men of power are trivial, superficial and pusillanimous, and are destitute of that loftiness of feeling which spells above-the-average ability, which is essentially dependent upon a brooding consciousness of the past and its awful power and reposes on a deep recognition of the difference between the great tragic facts of human existence and the transient dross of our day-to-day activities. Culture has lost its inherent value and there-fore the will to culture has begun to die out. There is no more will to genius and genius has become rarer. Vulgarization and proletariani-zation have invaded the arts and sciences, philosophy and language, religion and ethics, manners and institutions. The few original minds who seek an escape find that the public roads are barred. Despite the movement and commotion of our times ideas, dependent as they are on publicity, move more slowly than they have for a long time. This period of decadence was foreseen by Tocqueville who warned his con-temporaries that they ought not to mistake appearance for reality. "We have witnessed" he wrote, "very rapid changes of opinions in the minds of men; nevertheless it may be that the leading opinions of society will before long be more settled than they have been for several centuries in our history. . . . It is believed by some that modern society will always be changing. I fear that it will ultimately be too invariably fixed in the same institutions, the same prejudices . . . so that mankind will be stopped and circumscribed; that the mind will swing backwards and forwards forever without begetting fresh ideas; that man will waste his strength in senile and purposeless trifling; that, though in continual movement, humanity will no longer advance."[10]

CHAPTER 13

TOWARD A PHILOSOPHY OF HISTORY

In my analysis thus far I have tried to show that the liberal and Marxist concepts of unilinear progress have no basis either in contemporary reality or in history. All civilizations are finite, time-bound and mortal. All social orders are marked by conflict and contradiction and driven by a negativity that is sooner or later bound to destroy them. All things in history move toward both fulfillment and dissolution, toward the fuller embodiment of their essential character and toward decline and fall. Nothing is evergreen, each source of life is eventually exhausted and each concentration of energy eventually dispersed. All life suffers from the deep estrangement and animosity which exists between man's creative processes and their content and products. The cultural products which man creates become the enemy of its creator. Every civilization thus carries within itself, as if by an intrinsic fate, something which is determined to block, burden and distort, to obscure and defeat its innermost purposes. Decay and disintegration, ruin and defeat are as inherently interwoven into the plan of the world as success and progress.

Taking the broadest possible view it is possible to understand all civilizations as being shaped by a "master design" of class relations, ideology and productive forces. It constitutes an assemblage of forms, a coordination of patterns. These include: a system of government and laws; an ideology or a way of thinking; a set of property relations, manual habits and technological skills; a style of art and architecture; and rules for social and personal relations. Taken all together, these styles, ways, attitudes and rules, though rent by conflict and incongruity, by paradox and ambiguity, add up to a more or less coherent design for a society's functioning. We can thus construe a civilization as something that achieves a precarious unity, that works from a start of more or less haphazardness toward greater coherence, and that moves from amorphousness toward definition and from fumbling trials to decisive acts. This process of cultural growth from chaotic, groping beginnings, through growing commitment to particular forms or patterns and growing control of these forms or patterns until they are achieved and their potentialities realized, seems to be basic in the history of civilization. Its unfoldment constitutes what we call the rise of civilizations; its cessation or reversal, their decline or disintegration. Any civilization will thus tend to move in the direction of greater coherence, definitiveness and decisive action as the way toward its culmination; and its peak and apogee can be considered the point beyond which the "master design" no longer shows increase in plastic coordination but begins to fall apart, or to harden into rigidity, or both.

Like every idea, however, this one too should not be applied simplistically or mechanically. Not every civilization has a history of simple rise, maturity and fall. Room must be left for complications of structure and development. Some civilizations destroy themselves when they are young; some are undermined in their maturity; and some continue to live a death-in-life for hundreds of years in their decline. Others may seem to attain a realization of the patterns which they had gradually achieved and shaped; but then instead of either stereotyping or smashing these patterns and thereby dissolving their civilizations they may experience a renaissance and make a fresh start with reconstituted or partly new patterns. We have in such a case a renewed pulse of activity within the same society. Yet this new pulse of activity does not save the civilization from ultimate decline or disintegration.

Every "master design" or cultural style or system thus imposes certain ineluctable boundaries on every civilization. Every notable cultural achievement presupposes adherence to a certain set of patterns; that the patterns to be effective must exclude other possibilities and are limited; that while certain revisions of and deviations from them are possible these can never transcend the broad framework established by these patterns; that with successful development they accordingly become exhuasted; and that a culture can go on to new achievements only if there is a breakdown or abandonment or a revolutionary reformation of patterns. The master design thus forms, develops, matures, decays and either dissolves or atrophies into a dead petrifaction.[1]

Every civilization is therefore ruled by a few general inescapable laws. Though it is very difficult, if not impossible, to predict the exact duration of any civilization or the sequence of its phases, it is yet possible to see civilization unrolling like the consistent plot of a tragedy, inevitable and irreversible. And irreversibility, whether of entropy in physics or of human destiny, carries implications of fate and doom.

In the first place every society is driven by the will to power. Impelled by passion and appetite men seek to impose their will upon the world and upon other men and to fulfill their personal needs. Insecure and anxious, threatened by meaninglessness and absurdity, men seek to overcome these eternal existential agonies by accumulating power. Sprung from chaos and pervasive flux, caught in that blind and involuntary war which is existence, men seek to provide some meaning to their distracted lives by striving to appropriate, dominate, increase and grow stronger. Striving is therefore nothing other than striving for power. All human life is involved in the sin of seeking security at the expense of other life. Men always live at the expense of others and history is as a result always appropriation, overpowering the foreign and the weak and at its very foundation exploitation and injustice. The inability of liberalism and Marxism to understand the demoniacal character of power makes it impossible for these ideologies to comprehend the nature of the human condition and stamps them as shallow and false guides to the enduring problems of history. Driven by the will to power nations, empires and civilizations are subject to decline, ruin and revolution. And this for a number of reasons.

A factor of supreme importance which has throughout history brought about or contributed to the decline of civilizations has been the very character of power itself. The struggle to magnify itself is of power's essence. Being a species of egoism it tends naturally to grow. Every center of force and power is propelled by the will to grow stronger— not self-preservation but the will to appropriate, dominate, increase, grow stronger. States are not merely interested in self-preservation but are centers of inordinate ambitions, lusts and desires. Polities are not essentially tame, cool and calculating collectivities but are motivated by expansive desires and vitalities. Imperialism is hence an inherent component of all inter-state relations. Originating in blind desire and human freedom and vitality imperialism is an expression of the fact that human desire, freedom and vitality have no simple, definable limits. Goaded by the imagination, puffed up with self-love, states desire to expand, to accumulate force, to break limits, to universalize themselves and in these ways to give their existence a significance beyond themselves. Striving unceasingly for power and glory states not only seek to impose their will upon each other but find the sheer intoxication of ruling overriding every other consideration.

Impelled by the blind will to power nations are sooner or later destroyed by their inability to manage or control the power they have so feverishly accumulated. Deluded by power nations can rarely correctly evaluate their own power as against the power of other nations. Nations have fallen because they have tended to believe in the absolute character of their own power. A nation which has been powerful in one period of history is tempted to believe that this superiority is a kind of natural gift that exists irrespective of the power of its rivals and competitors. This tendency to look at the power of one's nation as a kind of absolute, to take it for granted, and not to realize that it is the result of comparison leads to those miscalculations regarding the distribution of military and political power between nations which usually end in disaster. Another typical error which is frequently made in evaluating the power of a nation lies not so much in believing in its absolute character but in believing in its permanency. In this case the nation refuses to see ahead, loses its powers of adaptiveness and flexibility and regards the power which it possesses at a particular period of history as a permanent characteristic which is not subject to change in itself. Idolizing itself or some particular form of military organization or technique it is unable to respond to new changes and challenges in its environment. Obsessed with its own superiority and "chosenness", attributing all the good qualities to itself and depriving all other nations, especially the enemy, of all good qualities, a nationalism which has turned into chauvinism tends to overestimate its own qualities and by underestimating the qualities of other nations so weakens itself as to produce catastrophe. Throughout history nations have fallen because they believed too strongly in their own superiority and because they committed the great error of refusing to look at themselves and at their competitors with that critical faculty and detachment which is required for creative statesmanship.

The most fateful consequence of possessing power lies, however, in its demoniacal character. The ruling groups and collectivities which hold power can never know how to use power with wisdom and prudence for too long. It is in the very nature of power to overextend itself, to expand beyond its natural limits, to become inordinate and oppressive. It greedily and ruthlessly demands objectivation. The will to power is avid to wreak its desire and thus it becomes divided against itself. Striving against itself, seeking its own well-being at the expense of others it constantly sets its teeth in its own flesh. Though power is the impulse to action and growth it is nevertheless ultimately impotent. It is foiled in its blind agitation and devours its own strength in its all-embracing fury. All our large human units, political and social, are tragically transitory. The law of nature at bottom would seem to be that power steadfastly ignores the means of conserving itself; that power destroys itself once it goes beyond its natural limits; that the physical expansion of power is always accompanied by social disintegration; that wars and the preparation for wars sap the strength of societies and that man's vital liberties are smothered and defeated by contrary powers.

The ruling groups that wield power are thus destroyed either by lethargy or stupidity or by outrageous behavior. They are either spoilt by success or they lose their moral and mental balance. Their temporary achievements either induce them to passively "rest on their oars" or provoke unbalanced men into attempting the impossible and by so doing bring catastrophe upon themselves; or filled with folly, among the worst of diseases, they have their judgment corrupted, incur the enmity of their friends or arouse the murderous hostility of their rivals and soon enough total ruin and the loss of all their power follows. Plato has dramatically explained this whole process: "If you neglect the rule of proportion and fit excessively large sails to small ships, or give too much food to a small body, or too high authority to a soul that doesn't measure up to it, the result is always disastrous. Body and soul become puffed up: disease breaks out in the one, and in the other arrogance quickly leads to injustice."[2]

Another law of history which no society has been able to circumvent has been that which determines the rise, growth, decline or fall of ruling elites. All societies are governed by a ruling elite or class of one kind or another and all societies are divided into a ruling minority and a majority that is ruled. All growth is the work of creative personalities and creative minorities. Fired by ambition, and an élan vital, possessing new skills and capacities, these creative ruling minorities impose themselves upon the inert, uncreative mass. Hard working and innovative, filled with self-confidence, flexible and responsive, they organize all those institutions which make it possible for men to live a life in common, to maintain genuine independence, to pursue great projects in common and to compete with other states in the perpetual struggle for power that takes place between them. An elite at the top of its form can lift the society it is governing to new levels of historical existence, can transform the mass into its followers, and can liberate new energies for creative social departures.

The quality of every society is thus determined by the quality of its leadership, that is, of its elite. To lead and to rule require special attributes. It means to decide, to command, to prevail, to advance, to conserve. It involves the creation of a tradition, to bring on others so that the work of the original leader or leadership will be continued with their original pulse and spirit. If this creation of a tradition does not come off, then instead of a coherent ruling stratum we have a congeries of individuals who are helpless when confronted by the unforeseen. If it does, we have a political class, a highly trained, self-replenishing minority with sure and slowly ripened traditions, which attracts every talent into the ruling circle and uses it to the full, and simultaneously keeps itself in harmony with the remainder of the nation that it rules. The art of politics is therefore the art of ruling.

Although every form of rule is shaped by the dialectic of power and the power of the dialectic, by force, cunning, fraud and contradiction, it must, to be effective, be molded by an overriding concern for the society it is ruling. A creative and effective ruling elite will know how to serve the public interest, how to conciliate the diverse and antagonistic groups into which every society is divided into a coherent community, how to rule with both restraint and justice and how to teach a whole manner of life to that community. To rule is to command but also to persuade, to impose one's will but also to arouse respect and trust, to exercise power but also to act wisely and with self-restraint.

In the hierarchy of variables that shapes every society the political variable is the most important. Politics as the "master science" has the supreme task of managing the social conflicts and contradictions that are inherent in every society. Through political leadership societies can be led either to great achievements or toward chaos and disaster. The qualities and skills of the political class, which is a sub-elite within the ruling elite, therefore determines its relations to the ruled majority. The political class is the political manager for the ruling elite. It is the governor of the country. In its role as manager for the ruling class as a whole it has the responsibility for advancing the general welfare. The effective political class has its ear open to the demands of the non-elite groups in the society and attempts to conciliate these groups by giving them legal status and security and well-defined and recognized forums to express their needs and interests. It is able to adjust and adapt to the many and constant changes of its society. It opens its ranks to the most active elements in the society and absorbs those with leadership and governing talents. Through this continuous process of exchange and renewal it keeps its vitality and fitness for the task of ruling and maintains, as well as possible, a certain interaction between the society as a whole and the ruling elite. Practicing a form of dialectical politics, it strives to attain a degree of cooperation between contradictory principles and interests and changes the class that is ruled into a collaborator of the ruling elite. The political class thus becomes the reflector of the society. It holds all the characteristics of that society. If the ruling class is mediocre it cannot produce a great political class. The nature and the capabilities of the political elite mirror the nature and the capabilities of the ruling elite as a whole.

However, all these "ideal" qualities are by their very nature ephemeral and transitory. They are all subject to change and decay. No social or political structure is permanent and no static utopia is possible. All ruling elites sooner or later, and in no fixed or sequential order, begin to lose the superior qualities that raised them to power in the first place. The forces of humanity and reason are ultimately impotent against the forces of beastliness, militancy, corruption and evil. Selfishness, ambition and the lust for power will derange and exhaust them. The charismatic forces that liberated their creative energies will become routinized and the blight of bureaucratic conservatism and stupidity will spread. The latent cruelty and blindness of all competitive life, the pride of absoluteness in the human soul, the radical ignorance of judgment will all overflow the banks of customs and institutions and inundate the society. Irrational passions will break down the weak ramparts of reason. Blinded by passion and ideology the ruling elites will lose contact with social realities and no longer comprehend or control the major social forces at work in the society. Become hidebound, bureaucratic and unadaptable, they will recruit degenerate elements into their ranks and simply lose the will and ability for governing. The ruling elite will cease to serve and lead the society and will substitute its own narrow private privileges and interests for the interests of the community. It will be incapable of renewing itself. The corruption and immorality which are the quintessence of political action will continually inject drops of evil into all its intentions and systematically the evil will spread until it will have contaminated the whole system beyond recovery. The forces of integration will give way to the forces of disintegration, great inequalities of power and wealth will appear, and the majority of people will begin to lose confidence and trust in their rulers. The elite itself will be fractured and disoriented. The bonds of legitimacy will begin to fray. Naked force will replace consensus and attraction. When all these conditions merge, the composition and structure of the elite changes radically—i.e., there is a social revolution —or, if no counter-elite exists which can come to power, the society enters a process of decay and degeneration. Revolution and social decay are not aberrations that can be side-stepped or controlled. Every social and historical formation goes through a process of rise, decay and fall.

Another important factor which disfigures social existence and which ultimately contributes to historical decay is ideology. Every society is shaped by a set of beliefs, myths and symbols which guide and give it a sense of purpose. The beliefs and myths by which every society lives are selected by the dominant group and are acceptable to it. The ideas of the ruling class are the ruling ideas of every age. However, these ideas though rooted in reality, never fully express reality. They always carry with them a baggage of falsehoods and mystifications. The ruling ideology may contain real concepts, scientific insights, yet it must always be inextricably mixed up with rationalizations, apologetics, lies, deceptive representations and self-deception. Every social order shaped by its own specific ideology can therefore only perceive the world through the distorted lenses of its own making, can never totally liberate itself from the bondage of its basic assumptions, can only have a fragmentary and partial conception of reality, and is to a greater or lesser extent immersed in inauthenticity and contradiction.

Contrary to the superstitions of rationalism human reason plays only a small part in human affairs and is subordinate to the blind and unconscious emotions. Most social thought is characterized by illusion, dissimulation, rationalization and mystification. Even the highest form of reason always borders on unreason. Human conduct is not governed by reason but by will, passion, phantoms and material interests. Man's intellect is above all an instrument in the struggle for existence; the function of thought is to serve the life process and the will to power; and all social thought is socially determined and tainted by class and personal interests. Rational, deliberate, conscious belief does not determine what is going to happen to society and men's socially decisive actions spring not from logical but from non-logical roots. Men are influenced in every culture and at every period of history not by rational purposes but by their non-logical impulses of taboos, magic, superstition, personified abstractions, myths, gods, empty verbalisms and vague, ambiguous or meaningless goals.

Ideologies are thus ignorant of the exact nature of their relations with praxis. They are an inverted, mutilated and distorted reflection of reality. Ideologies do not really understand their own conditions and presuppositions, nor the actual consequences they are producing. They are ignorant of the implications of their own theories and they comprehend neither the causes of which they are effects nor the effects which they are actually causing. Involved in practice, serving as instruments in the struggle between classes and nations, they mask the true interests and aspirations of the groups involved. All social thought is enveloped in a fog of deception and self-deception, is rooted in intellectual pride and is the victim of the ignorance of its ignorance. It is deeply sunk in flattery, falsehood, fraud, slander, pretentiousness and disguise. Ideology plays hide and seek on the back of everything.

The role of ideology is particularly dominant in politics. The basic manifestations of politics never appear to be what they actually are. The struggle for power and position, as the underlying objectives of policy, are always explained away and justified in moral, legal or biological terms. The true nature of policy is always disguised by ideological justifications and rationalizations. Vast collective actions are made palatable to their participants by words which have no precise meaning and that are used to persuade, sway and seduce the participants into supporting these actions. The actor on the political stage cannot help but "play an act" and must hide the true nature of his political actions behind the mask of an ideology. Politicians and their servants therefore have an ineradicable proclivity to deceive themselves and others about what they are doing. The ultimate goals of political action—the lust for power—are always concealed behind false fronts and pretexts. It is the very nature of politics to compel the actor on the political scene to use ideologies in order to disguise the immediate goal of his own action. Blinded by ideology, driven by passion, ambition, avarice and pride the ruling elite will sooner or later commit those follies and crimes that will undermine the very basis of its rule.

Every social order, all political, social and philosophical thought, all political action are thus distorted by ideology. The physical sciences are also fettered with preconceptions and the rigidities of paradigmatic thought. The social world is not ruled by reason, the pragmatic or experimental temper or by objective science. Every society creates an ideology, a certain perception of the world, a system of values and beliefs serving to reinforce and rationalize the dominant political, economic and social interests of its society. The ideology it fashions and the system of interests it serves has some basis in empirical reality. It manifests some forms of pragmatic behavior. It can respond to changing conditions and pressures. Yet it cannot attain that degree of flexibility, it cannot be experimental to the degree where it can transcend itself without a revolutionary upheaval. A stiffening process inevitably sets in. Ideology may be supple and adaptable, but the ring around it is closed. It may bend to suit a certain interest but it cannot supersede it. It changes, but at most only imperceptibly and its ideological character is never lost. It walks the same ground, keeps its same place and plays its same ideological role. Whether the ideology is that of capitalism, democracy, liberalism, conservatism, socialism, or any one of the varieties of communism or nationalism or imperialism, each in its own way deletes certain elements of reality from its consciousness and serves as a bar to its perception of reality. The ideologies developed and held by the ruling elites thus never completely embrace the social environment in which they operate. They lag behind social reality. They come into conflict with that social reality. They are all impelled by overweening pride and all become immersed in the illusions, prejudices and mystifications which they themselves had fashioned and which debilitates and ultimately comes to destroy that very social system these had been designed to maintain.

No society can exist without forms, organizations or institutions through which it expresses and realizes itself. However these forms —governments, parties, bureaucracies, armies, corporations, labor unions, universities, etc.,—created by the rivers and rhythms of life assume a character and momentum of their own. Organizations become societies, that is to say, they are not simply places of work but settings in which people live, and sometimes even more important for the quality of their lives than the homes to which they return after work. They provide objectives, formal and informal rules, values, punishments and rewards, styles of personal behavior, identities, a language of their own, and they seek and manage to maintain these characteristics in something like a stable state, even though its members may frequently change. Organizational behavior, built to function on the model of the production process is based on regular, orderly, linear, predictable processes. Each function strives to maintain a constant framework for operation. Organizations want to do predictable jobs under predictable circumstances.[3]

The society of the organization wants to maintain a stable state. Conservatism is thus built into the very nature of all organizations. This effort to maintain a stable state is not only due to inertia and routine but is the result of a policy of active conservatism which all organizations pursue. There is a persistent stress on system maintenance despite the state of oscillation in which organizations always exist. Resistant to change, suspicious of innovation after their initial period of creativity, organizations sooner or later succumb to the "iron law of decadence," that "tendency of all organizations to maintain themselves at the expense of needed change and innovation."[4] They can never maintain that perpetual flexibility and and spontaneity which is required for sustaining growth and innovation.

The conservative nature of organizations and institutions has a baleful effect on the development of all societies. For life is not static. It is always in a state of flux and change. The introduction of new dynamic forces, changes in its internal and external environment, the infinite richness of life, all in due course confront the existing institutional order with the dire challenge to reconstruct the whole existing pattern. In any actually growing society a constant readjustment of the more flagrant anachronisms is actually going on. But because of the "iron law of decadence" every society always tends to keep most parts of the social structure as they are in spite of their increasing incongruity with the new social forces constantly coming into action. All societies come to idolize the ephemeral institutions they have established, become their captives and though they are capable of modifying and reforming some of them in their periods of creativity they soon enough lose their capacities for change and adaptability in their periods of decadence.[5] In contrast with the Promethean stature and exuberant activity of their forefathers in the age of social growth the ruling elites of the declining society shrink into dwarfs or stiffen into arthritics.

Every society consequently suffers from an inherent conflict between life's eternal flux and the objective validity and genuineness of the institutions through which it passes. This contradiction between life and its forms expresses itself in many different areas of social life. In the economic system there is a permanent conflict between the forces of production and the property relations which contain and organize them. All systems of property relations—slavery, feudalism, capitalism, state capitalism or state socialism—either obstruct the development and extension of the new economic forces they have developed or are unable to adjust to the problems they have generated. In time the rigidity of the property system either stifles these new forces or being unable to adapt them leads society to social revolution or catastrophe and decline.

The same contradictions exist in the political sphere. Thus the Greek city-states which were initially responsible for a magnificent outpouring of energies could never transcend the rivalries which the system of sovereign city-states engendered and finally ended in the anarchy and degeneration of the Peloponnesian War. Thus too Rome, though it solved the problem of rival and contending city-states, for a time, through the establishment of a Roman empire, was finally overwhelmed by decline and fall by pursuing a policy of immoderate greatness and by corrupting its own ruling institutions. At the end the Roman empire never had any genuine juridical form, authentic legality or legitimacy. The empire became a shapeless form of government, a form of state without authentic institutions, and its chief of state went back to being—just anybody. The same debilitating disharmony exists between the anachronistic modern nation state which has been one of the most powerful institutions of growth and power and the international environment of multi-national corporations and global technologies, problems and challenges. We build up our power only to see it the better overturned. Every institutional order, of whatever character, carries within itself its own congenital poison and is the cause of its own extermination.

It ought to be more than obvious by now that we have entered one of those decisive turning points of history which separate whole eras from one another. We live in the midst of an epoch comparable to those which saw the passing of the city-state and the collapse of the Roman empire. The capitalist order has entered a period of prolonged crisis. Wildly unstable prices, erratic currencies, scarcities and famines, climbing rates of unemployment, the plight of the cities, failures of economic policy all indicate some of the symptoms of the disease. The shift in economic wealth from the industrialized countries to the under-developed countries through the price increases imposed by the Organi-zation of Petroleum Exporting Countries (OPEC) and other raw material producing countries and without any effective response from the so-called Western world constitutes a phenomenon of portentous significance. It is unquestionably clear than mankind's inordinate consumption of energy, its obliteration of animal, plant and insect species and the disruption of regional balances of natural processes by chemicals and other works of man will, sooner or later, bring about such profound changes in natural systems that it will probably endanger life itself. And when we study the present growth trends in world popu-lation, industrialization, pollution, food production and resource depletion and project them into the future, it is obvious that practically all these trends lead to catastrophe.

The democratic governments of the West are everywhere in decline. They lack the intellectual capacities to master the complexities which have emerged as a result of heedless economic growth and chaotic political development. Authority lacks confidence and the people lack confidence in authority. The demands on democratic government for leadership and management have grown immensely while the capacities of democratic government have everywhere disastrously shrivelled. Government incompetence and corruption is everywhere spreading like a plague. The men and women who attain power are neither willing nor able to change thoughts and values or to play lofty historic roles and are subservient to the unexamined prejudices and preferences of the multitude. Image making replaces policy. Everywhere powerful sectional economic and political interests subvert any coherent view of the public interest. Dominated by powerful economic interests, swayed by mass tastes and standards, torn by exhausting and murderous factional conflicts our democratic states suffer from a breakdown of community, a loss of all sense of civic obligation and co-operation and a universal pursuit of self interest. Nobody seems to know where they are going, because strictly speaking, they have no fixed road, no predetermined trajectory before them. The captains are on the bridge but they cannot find the rudder and the ship of state drifts toward the rocks of breakdown.

The West's position in the world is also in decline. Not only has the power of the United States decreased relative to that of its competitors and adversaries but its whole foreign policy is in disarray. Its humiliating defeat in Southeast Asia, its obsession with military security, its overextended commitments, its failure to understand that the great threat to the West lies not in any danger of military attack but in the political, economic, social and intellectual weaknesses which beset it, all stamp its foreign policy with an indelible imprint of triviality and irrelevance. The Atlantic Alliance is in the process of disintegrating. The national rivalries between its members transcend any common interest that they might have had in the past. The myth of European unity and power finally collapsed not because of Russian antagonism or harassment but as a result of the oil weapon wielded by the Emir of Kuwait and the Sheikh of Abu Dhabi. Europe's decadence springs from a collapse of will, a kind of "European Buddhism" which Nietzsche long ago foresaw as a pernicious form of nihilism. The West is now in full-scale retreat not only because of increasing Communist strength, both within and without, but also because it has been unable to confront the economic blackmail practiced by its erstwhile allies—the King of Saudi-Arabia and the Shah of Iran. The growing self-confidence and arrogance of the world's slum countries, particularly the Arab States, is only surpassed by the confusion, the mediocrity, the divisions, the antagonisms and the self-destructive forces at work in the West. The whole balance of power is shifting against the West and there is no force in the world that can prevent this from continuing to its own ineluctable end.

To understand history we must therefore see it as a mighty drama, as an awe-inspiring tragedy. Driven by the blind will to live, avid of life, greedy to wreak his desires, man is impelled by an irresistible lust for power and gain, by an inescapable impulse toward the fulfillment of his own personal needs. Unbalanced and sick, subject to pain and malfunction, man has to exert energetic and continual force to transform this world which does not coincide with him, which is strange to him, which is not his, so as to achieve some coherence, significance and mastery through the power that he so precariously attains.   Insecure, afraid of death, filled with anxiety, yearning for love and not finding it, man seeks to arrogate a greater power to himself to compensate for the precariousness and vulnerability of his position in the world.   In the light of all this, all human life appears to us as what it is permanently: a dramatic confrontation and struggle of man with the world and not a mere occasional maladjustment which is produced at certain moments.

Driven by necessity and yet capable of freedom and creativity, limited and limitless, weak and strong, blind and far-seeing, an impotent rebel, man is riddled with flaws and contradictions.   History is dialectical as well as dramatic.   On the one hand man produces himself by his own labor, by praxis, starting from nature and from need in order to achieve the satisfaction of his desires.   Everything in society is act, the essence of the human is what it accomplishes.   Man as actor creates history, forms societies, builds states, produces techniques, ideologies, institutions, artistic and cultural works.   On the other hand—or rather, at the same time—he loses himself in his works and objects.   He loses his way among the products of his own labor which turn against him and load him down with all their routines, limitations and contradictions. At one moment he unleashes a succession of acts and events: this is history.   At another moment what he has created takes on a life of its own that limits and subjugates him.   Now his creations bewitch and blind him: this is the great influence of ideology.   Now the things he has produced with his own hands—more accurately the abstract things— tend to turn him into a thing itself, just another commodity, to be bought, sold and discarded.

Though living in a world created by his own labor and knowledge, this world is no longer his but rather stands opposed to his inner needs —a strange world governed by inexorable laws, a "thingified world" in which human life is frustrated.   This is a world marked by a loss of coherence and liberty, by the numerous conflicts that abound in human living, especially in the conflict between man and nature and man and man.   This conflict, which has turned nature into a hostile power that had to be mastered by man and which sets man against man, class against class and nation against nation has led to an antagonism between idea and reality, between thought and the real, between consciousness and existence.   The institutions man founds and the culture he creates develop laws of their own and man has to comply with them.   He is overpowered by the expanding wealth of his economic, political and social surroundings and surrenders to their sway. Men in striving to perpetuate and establish culture perpetuate in the process their own frustrations. The materials that could serve life come to rule over its content and goal and the consciousness of man is made victim to the relationships of material and social production.

Everywhere we see opposition and dissonance in human affairs. The will to live strives against itself, seeks its own well-being at the expense of others and so constantly sets its teeth in its own flesh. The lust for power sets man against man and group against group in unending contention. The two basic instincts of life and death are in a state of perpetual war with each other; civilization opposes and represses the individual and builds tormenting discontents into the very culture that he creates; and man and nature are locked in violent antagonism. The daemonic and corrupt elements within man are in combat with the moral and ethical elements. God and the devil, light and darkness, good and evil, creativity and tradition struggle for dominance in the world. All social arrangements contain within themselves contradictions and negativities which will ultimately destroy them. Unresolvable discord, contradictions and conflicts are inherent in the nature of things. In the great struggle between man's understanding and the riddles of the world and his existence each new answer offers only a new question and each new victory only a new disappointment. There is thus no inevitable progress toward the good evident from year to year or from epoch to epoch but only unresolved conflict, which sees today good and tomorrow evil prevail.

History is then not only dialectical but also tragic. Man's freedom, confidence and imagination, though capable of achieving great feats, always ultimately collide against his natural limitations. Man is capable of wisdom and creativity, but these qualities are equally matched by his follies and crimes. His own inherent natural flaws only serve to bring to ruin his most impressive works. He can be destroyed by a single virtue, if that is overextended, and plunge into insane acts in the cause of a half truth that appears to him to be noble. His very successes can undermine his most glorious enterprises and his most astounding victories are generally only the progenitors of his inevitable defeat.

It is the tragedy of human history that man must be destructive in order to be creative and that his finest moments only lead him to hubris and nemesis. Human life is permanently at war with itself. There is no ultimate solution to the conflict between man's constructive-destructive vitalities and the social and natural restraints which these seek to overcome. The tragic view of human existence must show man in all his strengths and weaknesses. It must acknowledge his freedom and his subjugation, his genius and his finiteness, his heroism and his corruption, his virtue and his evil. All human history shows the defects and excesses of all values, reveals tension, imbalance and contradictions as the essential condition of all civilization and the source of both its rise, growth and fall.

NOTES

NOTES TO CHAPTER 1
1. Georg Wilhelm Friedrich Hegel, *The Philosophy of History*, (New York: Dover, 1956), p. 73.
2. Ibid., p. 21.
3. Arthur Schopenhauer, *The World as Will and Representation*, Vol. 1. (New York: Dover, 1969), p. 196; See also Thomas Mann's Introduction to the *Living Thoughts of Schopenhauer*, (London: Cassell, 1939).
4. Quoted by Patrick Gardiner, *Schopenhauer*, (London: Penguin, 1971), p. 166; See also Max Horkheimer, "Schopenhauer Today," in *The Critical Spirit*, (Boston: Beacon), pp. 55-71.
5. See the Introduction by Richard Taylor, editor, *The Will to Live*, (Garden City: Anchor Books, 1962).
6. Arthur Schopenhauer, *The World as Will and Representation*, Vol. 1, (New York: Dover, 1969), p. 324.
7. Sigmund Freud, *The Interpretation of Dreams*, (London: Hogarth Press, 1953), in *The Complete Psychological Works of Sigmund Freud*, Vol. 5, p. 613.
8. Sigmumd Freud, "My Contact with Joseph Popper-Lynkeus," in the *Collected Papers of Sigmund Freud*, (London: Hogarth Press, 1949-1950), Vol. 5, p. 297.
9. Sigmund Freud, *New Introductory Lectures*, (London: Hogarth Press, 1946), p. 104.
10. Hans Meyerhoff, "Freud and the Ambiguity of Culture," in *Partisan Review*, Winter 1957.
11. Sigmund Freud, *Civilization, War and Death*, (London: Hogarth Press, 1939). p. 51.
12. For a valuable analysis of Freud's cultural importance see Philip Rieff's, *Freud the Mind and the Moralist*, (Garden City: Anchor Books, 1961).
13. George Santayana, *Dominations and Powers*, (New York: Scribners, 1954), p. 41.
14. Reinhold Niebuhr, *The Nature and Destiny of Man*, (New York: Scribners, 1953), One Volume Edition, *Human Nature*, p. 200.
15. See Jean Paul Sartre, *Being and Nothingness*, (New York: Philosophical Library, 1956); *Search for a Method*, (New York: Vintage, 1968); and Roy Pierce's chapter on Sartre in

his *Contemporary French Political Thought*, (London and New York: Oxford University Press, 1966).

16. Martin Heidegger, *An Introduction to Metaphysics*, (Garden City: Anchor Books, 1961). pp. 129-35.

17. Bertrand Russel, *The Scientific Outlook*, (New York: Norton, 1962), p. 14.

NOTES TO CHAPTER 2

1. See Thucydides, *The Peloponnesian War*, (London: Penguin, 1954); Leo Straus, *The City and Man*, (Chicago: Rand McNally, 1964); and David Greene, *Greek Political Theory*, (Chicago: The University of Chicago Press, 1965).

2. Plato, *The Republic*, (New York: The Modern Library), cf. 373-4.

3. See St. Augustine, *The City of God*, (New York: The Modern Library), xi, 28; and the essays by Henry Paolucci and Dino Bigongiari in *The Political Writings of St. Augustine*, edited by Henry Paolucci, (Chicago: Henry Regnery, 1962).

4. Machiavelli, *The Prince and the Discourses*, (New York: The Modern Library), Book I, Chap. 39.

5. Thomas Hobbes, *English Works*, (London; J. Bohn, 1839), Vol. VII, p. 73.

6. Benedict De Spinoza, "A Political Treatise," in the *Works of Spinoza*, (New York: Dover, 1951), p. 289.

7. *The Works of Joseph de Maistre*, Selected, Translated and Introduced by Jack Lively, (New York: Schoken, 1971), p. 199.

8. See J.L. Talmon, *Political Messianism*, (New York, Washington: Praeger, 1960), pp. 295-314.

9. Friedrich Nietzsche, *The Will to Power*, Edited by Walter Kaufmann, (New York: Vintage: 1968), pp. 367-8; See also Karl Jaspers, *Nietzsche*, (Chicago: Henry Regnery, 1965), pp. 287-332.

10. Bertrand Russell, *Power*, (London: Allen & Unwin, 1938), p. 10.

11. Ibid., p. 35.

12. Reinhold Niebuhr, *The Nature and Destiny of Man*, (New York: Scribners, 1953), 1. *Human Nature*, p. 192.

13. Ibid., pp. 190-1.

14. Ibid., p. 194.

15. Reinhold Niebuhr, *The Children of Light and the Children of Darkness*, (New York: Scribners, 1944), pp. 19-22.

16. Reinhold Niebuhr, *Moral Man and Immoral Society*, (New York: Scribners, 1932), pp. 15-19.

17. Hans Morgenthau, "Love and Power" in *Politics in the Twentieth Century*, (Chicago and London: The University of Chicago Press, 1971), p. 190.

18. Ibid., p. 196.

19. Alfred Adler, *The Practice and Theory of Individual Psychology*, (New York: Harcourt, Brace & World, 1929), esp. pp. 7-15.

20. Karen Horney, *Neurosis and Human Growth*, (New York: Norton, 1950), esp. pp. 21-27.

21. Erich Fromm, *Escape from Freedom*, (New York: Rinehart, 1941), pp. 141-2, 164-168.

222. See also his *Anatomy of Human Destructiveness*, (New York, Chicago, San Francisco: Holt, Rhinehart and Winston, 1973), in which he develops the concept of necrophilia as the most malignant form of aggression and human destructiveness.

22. Harold D. Lasswell, *Power and Personality*, (New York: Viking, 1962), p. 39.

23. Quoted by Bertrand de Jouvenel in *On Power*, (Boston: Beacon, 1962), p. 126.

24. Joseph A. Schumpeter, *Imperialism and Social Classes*, (Oxford: Blackwell, 1951), p. 6.

25. Ibid., p. 7. See also Raymond Aron, *Peace and War*, (Garden City: Doubleday, 1966), esp. pp. 71-93.

NOTES TO CHAPTER 3
1. Gaetano Mosca, *The Ruling Class*, (New York, Toronto, London: McGraw-Hill, 1939), p. 50.
2. Ibid., pp. 449-50.
3. Ibid., p. 55.
4. Ibid., pp. 144-5.
5. Ibid., p. 65.
6. Ibid., p. 67.
7. Vilfredo Pareto, *The Mind and Society*, (New York: Harcourt, Brace & Co., 1935), §§2056-7.
8. Ibid., §§2274.
9. Ibid., §§2227.
10. Guido Dorso, "The Political Class and the Ruling Class," in George Armstrong Kelly and Clifford W. Brown, Jr., editors, *Struggles in the State: Sources and Patterns of World Revolution*, (New York, London, Sydney, Toronto: John Wiley, 1970), pp. 74-5.
11. Ibid., p. 75.
12. Ibid., p. 76.
13. Ibid., p. 76.
14. R.G. Collingwood, *The New Leviathan*, (Oxford: Clarendon Press, 1966), pp. 184-5.
15. Ibid., p. 187.
16. Ibid., pp. 190-1.
17. Ibid., p. 17.
18. Ibid., p. 18.
19. C. Wright Mills, *The Power Elite*, (New York and London: Oxford University Press, 1956), p. 4.
20. Ibid., pp. 20 ff.
21. Ibid., p. 7.
22. Ibid., p. 8.
23. Ibid., p. 8.
24. Ibid., p. 9.
25. Ibid., p. 19.
26. Ibid., p. 288.
27. Ibid., p. 289.
28. Ibid., p. 11.
29. Ibid., p. 29.
30. Max Weber, *The Theory of Social and Economic Organization*, (Glencoe: The Free Press, 1964), pp. 358-373.

NOTES TO CHAPTER 4
1. Ernest Jones, "Rationalization in Everyday Life," in *An Outline of Psychoanalysis*, ed. J.S. van Teslaar, (New York: Modern Library), p. 104.
2. Karl Mannheim, *Ideology and Utopia*, (New York: Harcourt Brace & Co., 1936), p. 49.
3. Reinhold Niebuhr, *The Nature and Destiny of Man*, (New York: Scribners, 1953), I. "Human Nature," p. 194.
4. Vilfredo Pareto, *The Mind and Society*, (New York: Harcourt, Brace & Co., 1935), §1401.
5. See John Plamenatz, *Ideology*, (New York, Washington, London: Praeger, 1970), pp. 24, 26, 129.
6. Karl Marx, *Capital*, (London and New York: Everyman's Library), p. 44.
7. Karl Marx, *The German Ideology*, (New York: International Publishers, 1939), p. 39.
8. See also Henri Lefebvre, *The Sociology of Marx*, (New York: Pantheon Books, 1968), pp. 59-88.
9. Thomas S. Kuhn, *The Structure of Scientific Revolutions*, (Chicago & London: The University of Chicago Press, 1962), p. 10.
10. Ibid., p. 150.

NOTES TO CHAPTER 5
1. Niccolo Machiavelli, *The Prince and the Discourses*, (New York: The Modern Library), "The Prince," Chap. XVIII.
2. Ibid., Chap. XVIII.
3. Ibid., Chap. XXV.
4. George Santayana, *Dominations and Powers*, (New York: Scribners, 1954), p. 328.
5. Ibid., p. 328.
6. Ibid., p. 40.
7. Ibid., p. 177.
8. Ibid., p. 191.
9. Ibid., p. 235.
10. Ibid., pp. 246-7.
11. Ibid., p. 297.
12. Ibid., p. 296.
13. Ibid., p. 322.
14. Ibid., p. 435.
15. Ibid., p. 438.
16. Hans J. Morgenthau, *Scientific Man Versus Power Politics*, (Chicago & London: The University of Chicago Press, 1965). p. 189
17. Ibid., p. 189.
18. Ibid., p. 196.
19. Ibid., p. 203.

NOTES TO CHAPTER 6
1. Max Weber, *The Protestant Ethic and the Spirit of Capitalism*, (New York: Scribners, 1958), p. 154.
2. Ibid., p. 17.
3. Gerth and Mills, *From Max Weber: Essays in Sociology*, (New York: Oxford University Press, 1958), p. 196.
4. Cited by J.P. Mayer, *Max Weber and German Politics*, (London: Faber & Faber, 1943), p. 127 ff.
5. Gerth and Mills, op. cit., p. 125.
6. Robert Michels, *Political Parties*, (New York: Dover, 1959), p. 189.
7. Max Weber, op. cit., p. 181.
8. See Hannah Arendt, *The Burden of Our Time*, (London: Secker & Warburg, 1951), especially Chapter 5.
9. See Joseph A. Schumpeter, *Capitalism, Socialism and Democracy*, (London: Allen and Unwin, 1950), pp. 31-32.
10. See E.J. Mishan, "Making the Future Safe for Mankind," *The Public Interest*, Summer 1971; and *Technology and Growth*, (New York, Washington: Praeger, 1969).
11. See S.R. Eyre, "Man the Pest," *New York Review of Books*, November 18, 1971; see also Donnela H. Meadows, et. al., *The Limits to Growth*, (New York: Signet Books, 1972); Paul and Anne Ehrlich, *Population, Resources, Environment*, (San Francisco: W.H. Freeman, 1970); Barry Commoner, *The Closing Circle*, (New York: Knopf, 1971); Robert Heilbroner, "The Human Prospect," *New York Review of Books*, January 24, 1974.
12. See Erich Fromm, *The Sane Society*, (New York and Toronto: Rinehart & Co., 1955).
13. Karl Marx, *Early Writings*. Translated and edited by T.B. Bottomore, (New York, Toronto and London: McGraw-Hill, 1964), p. 192.
14. Clinton Rossiter and James Lare, editors, *The Essential Lippmann*, (New York: Vintage Books, 1965), pp. 162-168.
15. Lord Ritchie-Calder, *Foreign Affairs*, January, 1970
16. Quoted by Shlomo Avineri in "Labor, Alienation, and Social Classes in Hegel's Realphilosophie," *Philosophy and Public Affairs*, Fall, 1971.
17. See Laurence J. Peter and Raymond Hull, *The Peter Principle*, (New York, Toronto and London: Bantam Books, 1970).

18. Julien Freund, *The Sociology of Max Weber*, (New York: Vintage Books, 1969), pp. 25-32.
19. Ibid., p. 24.
20. See Henri Lefebvre, *Everyday Life in the Modern World*, (New York, Evanston, San Francisco, London: Harper Torchbooks, 1971).

NOTES TO CHAPTER 7
1. Henri Lefebvre, *The Sociology of Marx*, (New York: Pantheon Books, 1968), p. 51.
2. Herbert Marcuse, *Reason and Revolution*, (Boston: Beacon Press, 1969), p. 35.
3. Georg Wilhelm Friedrich Hegel, *Science of Logic*, (New York: Macmillan, 1929), Vol. 11, p. 68.
4. Ibid., Vol. 1., p. 45.
5. Robert F. Murphy, *The Dialectics of Social Life*, (New York and London: Basic Books, 1971), p. 97.
6. *The Sociology of Georg Simmel*, Translated, edited and with an introduction by Kurt H. Wolff, (New York: The Free Press, 1950).
7. Georg Simmel, "The Conflict in Modern Culture," in *The Conflict in Modern Culture and Other Essays*, (New York: Teachers College Press, Columbia University, 1968), p. 11.
8. Ibid., p. 12.
9. Ibid., p. 12.
10. See Georg Simmel, "On the Concept and the Tragedy of Culture," op. cit., p. 27.
11. Ibid., p. 30.
12. See Georg Simmel, *The Conflict in Modern Culture and Other Essays*, op. cit., p. 12.
13. Ibid., p. 13.
14. See Georg Simmel, "On the Concept and the Tragedy of Culture," op. cit., p. 43.
15. Ibid., p. 46.
16. See Aristotle, *The Poetics*, translated by S.H. Butcher and with an introduction by Francis Fergusson, (New York: Hill and Wang, 1961); *Hegel on Tragedy*, edited and with an introduction by Anne and Henry Paolucci, (Garden City: Anchor Books, 1962); Arthur Schopenhauer, *The World as Will and Representation*, (New York: Dover, 1969); Friedrich Nietzsche, "The Birth of Tragedy," in *The Philosophy of Nietzsche*, (New York: Modern Library); Walter Kaufmann, *Tragedy and Philosophy*, (Garden City: Anchor Books, 1969).
17. See Ernest Cassirer, "The Tragedy of Culture," in *The Logic of the Humanities*, (New Haven and London: Yale University Press, 1966).

NOTES TO CHAPTER 8
1. Hans J. Morgenthau, "Escape from Power," in *Politics in the Twentieth Century*, (Chicago and London: The University of Chicago Press, 1971), pp. 3-9.
2. René Descartes, *Rules for the Direction of the Mind*, (Chicago: Encyclopedia Britannica, 1952), X-XI; See also a recent cogent discussion of "methodism" by Sheldon S. Wolin, in "Political Theory as a Vocation," *American Political Science Review*, December, 1969.
3. Andrew Hacker, *The End of the American Era*, (New York: Atheneum, 1970), p. 202.
4. Talcott Parsons, *Societies: Evolutionary and Comparative Perspectives*, (Englewood Cliffs: Prentice-Hall, 1966), pp. 5-7.
5. Talcott Parsons, *Sociological Theory and Modern Society*. (New York: Free Press, 1967), p. 297.
6. See Alvin W. Gouldner, *The Coming Crisis of Western Sociology*, (New York: Basic Books, 1970), pp. 252-253.
7. David Easton, *The Political System*, (New York: Alfred A. Knopf, 1967), p. 131.
8. Ibid., p. 8.
9. See David Easton, "The Analysis of Political Systems," *World Politics*, April, 1959.
10. See David Easton's "Equilibrium and the Social System," in Heinz Eulau, et al., editors, *Political Behavior*, (Glencoe: Free Press, 1956).

11. David Easton, "The New Revolution in Political Science," *The American Political Science Review*, December, 1969.

12. Ralf Dahrendorf, *Essays in the Theory of Society*, (Stanford: Stanford University Press, 1968), p. 227.

NOTES TO CHAPTER 9

1. Michel Crozier, *The Stalled Society*, (New York: The Viking Press, 1973), pp. 145-9.

2. Theodore Lowi, *The End of Liberalism*, (New York: Norton, 1969), p. 29.

3. For good examples of the pluralist ideology see David B. Truman, *The Governmental Process*, (New York: Alfred Knopf, 1951); and Robert A. Dahl, *Who Governs?* and Nelson W. Polsby, *Community Power and Political Theory*, (New Haven: Yale University Press, 1961 and 1963).

4. Herbert J. Gans, *The New Egalitarianism*, Saturday Review, May 6, 1972.

5. See Robert L. Heilbroner, *New York Times Magazine*, November 28, 1971.

6. Theodore Lowi, op. cit., p. 289.

7. Theodore Lowi, *The Politics of Disorder*, (New York and London: Basic Books, 1971), p. 32.

8. Alexis de Tocqueville, *Democracy in America*, Philip Bradley, ed. (New York: Alfred Knopf, 1945), Vol. II, p. 261.

9. Ibid., p. 139.

10. John Stuart Mill, "On Liberty", in *The English Philosophers from Bacon to Mill*, edited and with an introduction by Edwin A. Burtt, (New York: The Modern Library, 1939).

11. Glenn Tinder, *The Crisis of the Political Imagination*, (New York: Charles Scribner's Sons, 1964), p. 168.

12. Ibid., p. 155.

NOTES TO CHAPTER 10

1. See Roberto Vacca, *The Coming Dark Age*, Translated from the Italian by Dr. J.S. Whole, (Garden City: Anchor Books, 1974).

2. Ralf Dahrendorf, *Class and Class Conflict in Industrial Society*, (Stanford: Stanford University Press, 1959).

3. Amitai Etzioni, *The Active Society*, (New York: The Free Press, 1968), p. *VII*.

4. Herman Kahn, B. Bruce-Briggs, *Things to Come*, (New York: The Macmillan Co., 1972), p. 11.

5. George Lichtheim, *The New Europe: Today and Tomorrow*, (New York: Praeger, 1963), p. 194.

6. Kenneth Boulding, *The Meaning of the Twentieth Century: The Great Transition*, (New York: Harper Colophon Books, 1965).

7. Marshall McLuhan, *Understanding Media: The Extensions of Man*, (New York: Signet Books, 1966).

8. Jacques Ellul, *The Technological Society*, (New York: Vintage Books, 1964).

9. Harvey Cox, *The Secular City*, (New York: Macmillan, 1966).

10. Romano Guardini, *The End of the Modern World*, (New York: Sheed and Ward, 1956).

11. Daniel Bell, "Technocracy and Politics," *Survey*, Winter 1971, p. 5.

12. Ibid., p. 8; See also, Daniel Bell, "The Post-Industrial Society: The Evolution of an Idea," *Survey*, Spring 1971; "Notes on the Post-Industrial Society" (1), *The Public Interest*, Winter 1967 and Ibid. (2) Spring 1967; and *The Coming of Post-Industrial Society*, (New York: Basic Books, 1973).

13. Zbigniew Brzezinski, "America in the Technetronic Age," *Encounter*, January 1968, p. 16.

14. Ibid., p. 18.

15. Ibid., p. 22.

16. Robert Heilbroner, *The Limits of American Capitalism*, (New York: Harper Torchbooks, 1967), p. 123.
17. Ibid., p. 128.
18. Ibid., p. 130.
19. Ibid., p. 133.
20. Alvin Toffler, *Future Shock*, (New York: Bantam Books, 1971), p. 186.
21. Ibid., p. 45.
22. Ibid., p. 71.
23. Ibid., p. 125.
24. Ibid., p. 161.
25. Ibid., p. 326.
26. Ibid., p. 358.
27. See Victor C. Ferkis, *Technological Man: The Myth and the Reality*, (New York and Toronto: Mentor Books, 1969).
28. See Joan Robinson in *After Keynes*; Papers presented to Section F (Economics) at the 1972 annual meeting of the British Association for the Advancement of Science, edited by Joan Robinson, (New York: Barnes and Noble, 1973).
29. *New York Times*, July 29, 1970.

NOTES TO CHAPTER 11
1. Karl Marx, *Early Writings*, Translated and Edited by T.B. Bottomore, (London: C.A. Watts & Co., 1963), p. 58.
2. Seymour Martin Lipset, *Political Man*, (Garden City: Anchor Books, 1963), pp. 87-115.
3. A.J.P. Taylor, *English History, 1914-1945*, (New York and Oxford: Oxford University Press, 1965), p. 507.
4. Amos Elon, *The Israelis*, (New York: Holt, Rinehart and Winston, 1971), p. 104.
5. Ibid., p. 138.
6. Judd L. Teller, "The Making of the Ideals that Rule Israel", *Commentary*, January, 1954; "Labor Zionism Comes to Power," *Commentary*, February, 1954.
7. *The Jerusalem Post Weekly*, March 13, 1973, p. 11.
8. Eliezer Livneh, "Values and Society in Israel," in *Israel Through the Eyes of its Leaders*. Edited by Israel T. Naamani and David Rudavsky, (Tel Aviv: Meorot, 1971), p. 103.
9. Quoted by Dinah Zohar in "Ben Aharon—Israel's Stormy Labour Leader," *New Middle East*, May 1972.
10. Georges Friedmann, *The End of the Jewish People?*, Translated from the French by Erich Mosbacher, (Garden City: Doubleday & Co., 1967), p. 40.
11. Yehoshua Arielli, "The Price Israel is Paying," *New York Review of Books*, August 31, 1972.
12. See Robert G. Wesson, *The Imperial Order*, (Berkeley: University of California Press, 1967).
13. See Andrei Amalrik, "Will the USSR Survive until 1984?" *Survey*, Autumn 1969.
14. For a more comprehensive analysis of Soviet and Chinese Communism see I. Robert Sinai, *In Search of the Modern World*, (New York: New American Library, 1967).

NOTES TO CHAPTER 12
1. Oswald Spengler, *The Decline of the West*, Abridged Edition by Helmut Werner, (London: George Allen & Unwin, 1961), p. 51.
2. Nicholas Berdayev, *The Meaning of History*, (Cleveland and New York: Meridian Books, 1962), p. 189.
3. *New York Times*, November 19, 1972.
4. Jose Ortega y Gasset, *The Revolt of the Masses*, (New York: Norton, 1957), p. 18.
5. Karl Jaspers, *Man in the Modern Age*, (Garden City: Anchor Books, 1957), p. 56.
6. Quoted by Dwight MacDonald in *Against the American Grain*, (New York: Vintage Books, 1965), p. 5.

7. See Norman Podhoretz, *Making It*, (New York, Toronto, London: Bantam Books, 1969).

8. See Erich Kahler, *The Tower and the Abyss*, (New York: The Viking Press, 1967); and William Barrett, *Time of Need*, (New York, Evanston, San Francisco, London: Harper & Row, 1972).

9. George Steiner, "In Bluebeard's Castle—Some Notes Towards the Redefinition of Culture," *The Listener*, March 18, 1971.

10. Quoted by John Lukacs in *The Passing of the Modern Age*, (New York, Evanston and London: Harper & Row, 1970), p. 112.

NOTES TO CHAPTER 13
1. See A.L. Kroeber, *Configurations of Culture Growth*, (Berkeley and Los Angeles: University of California Press, 1969), pp. 761-848; and *An Anthropologist Looks at History*, (Berkeley and Los Angeles: University of California Press, 1963), pp. 18-27.

2. Plato, *The Laws*, (Penguin Books, 1970), p. 139.

3. Donald A. Schon, *Technology and Change*, (New York: Delta, 1967), pp. 57-66.

4. Theodore Lowi, *The Politics of Disorder*, (New York and London: Basic Books, 1971), p. 5.

5. Arnold J. Toynbee, "The Breakdown of Civilizations" in *A Study of History*, Abridgement of Volumes I-VI by D.C. Somervell, (New York and London: Oxford University Press, 1947), pp. 244-359.

INDEX

225